Teach yourself

Photoshop

The photographic process starts the moment you press the camera's shutter release button, but it doesn't end there. Sometimes the camera makes a mistake, you compose the picture in a rush or an unwanted object needs to be cloned out, and you need the help of an image-editing program to put things right. The camera also captures the world in a very literal way, so that the image you see on your computer screen can look like a rather pale imitation of what you saw in your mind's eye.

This is where you need a really good image-editing program, and Photoshop is the best there is. It's a supremely well-designed application with a clean and simple interface that's welcoming for beginners but offers experts all the power they need. Photoshop can fix those annoying flaws that stand between a good photo and a great one; it can help you restore the drama, beauty and atmosphere you're trying to capture, and it can 'supercharge' reality to produce images that simply take your breath away. We've put together this guide to help you get the very best from Photoshop CC and your own photography. We show you how to organise your images using Bridge or Lightroom, get the best possible quality from your raw files with Adobe Camera Raw, and unleash the full power of Photoshop's selections, masks and layers tools.

FUTURE

Teach yourself

Photoshop

Future PLC Quay House, The Ambury, Bath, BA1 1UA

Editorial
Series Editor **Chris George**
Operations Editor **Steven Raynes**
Art Editor **Chris Hedley**
Compiled by **Charles Ginger & Adam Markiewicz**
Head of Art & Design **Greg Whitaker**
Editorial Director **Jon White**
Managing Director **Grainne McKenna**

Photography
All copyrights and trademarks are recognised and respected

Advertising
Media packs are available on request
Commercial Director **Clare Dove**

International
Head of Print Licensing **Rachel Shaw**
licensing@futurenet.com
www.futurecontenthub.com

Circulation
Head of Newstrade **Tim Mathers**

Production
Head of Production **Mark Constance**
Production Project Manager **Matthew Eglinton**
Advertising Production Manager **Joanne Crosby**
Digital Editions Controller **Jason Hudson**
Production Managers **Keely Miller, Nola Cokely, Vivienne Calvert, Fran Twentyman**

Printed in the UK

Distributed by Marketforce – www.marketforce.co.uk
For enquiries, please email: mfcommunications@futurenet.com

GPSR EU RP (for authorities only)
eucomply OÜ Pärnu mnt 139b-14 11317, Tallinn, Estonia
hello@eucompliancepartner.com, +3375690241

Teach Yourself Photoshop Fourteenth Edition (CTB6447)

FUTURE Connectors. Creators. Experience Makers.

Future plc is a public company quoted on the London Stock Exchange (symbol: FUTR)
www.futureplc.com

Chief Executive Officer **Jon Steinberg**
Non-Executive Chairman **Richard Huntingford**
Chief Financial Officer **Sharjeel Suleman**

Tel +44 (0)1225 442 244

Widely Recycled

ipso. Regulated

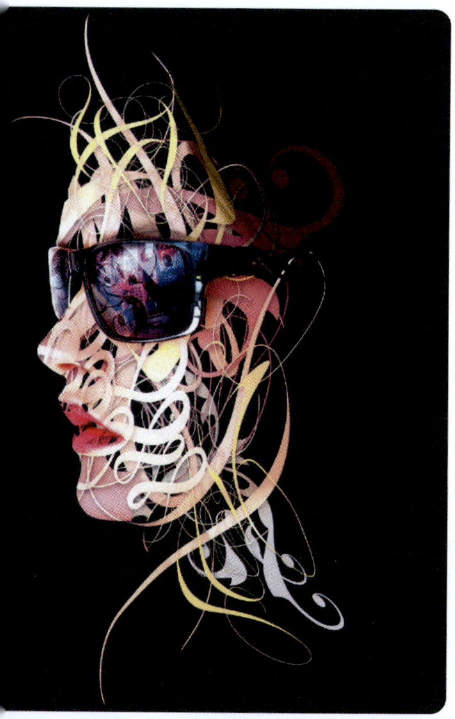

Introducing the Bridge workspace

Before you start work on editing your images, organising and processing them with Photoshop's family of tools is crucial

One of the biggest problems we face as digital photographers is our ever-growing collections of images. We may have thousands of photos scattered across hundreds of folders on our computers. These folders tend to display images according to when they were captured, so we have to rely on our memory of what was shot when as we search for a particular photo. All versions of Photoshop attempt to deal with this asset management problem using similar tools. The Photoshop Elements Organizer allows you to add star ratings and keywords. Lightroom's Library module does a similar job. Photoshop CC and CS use a companion application called Bridge to help you sort the wheat from the chaff. If you access the full version of Photoshop as a download via the Creative Cloud service, you'll need to download Bridge separately.

Bridge is a powerful image browser that enables you to take control over your digital assets before exporting them to Photoshop for editing. On this spread we'll introduce you to the key features of Bridge, and demonstrate how to customise the workspace to display images in a more useful way.

Photoshop Anatomy The Bridge workspace

Get to know the key features of Adobe Bridge

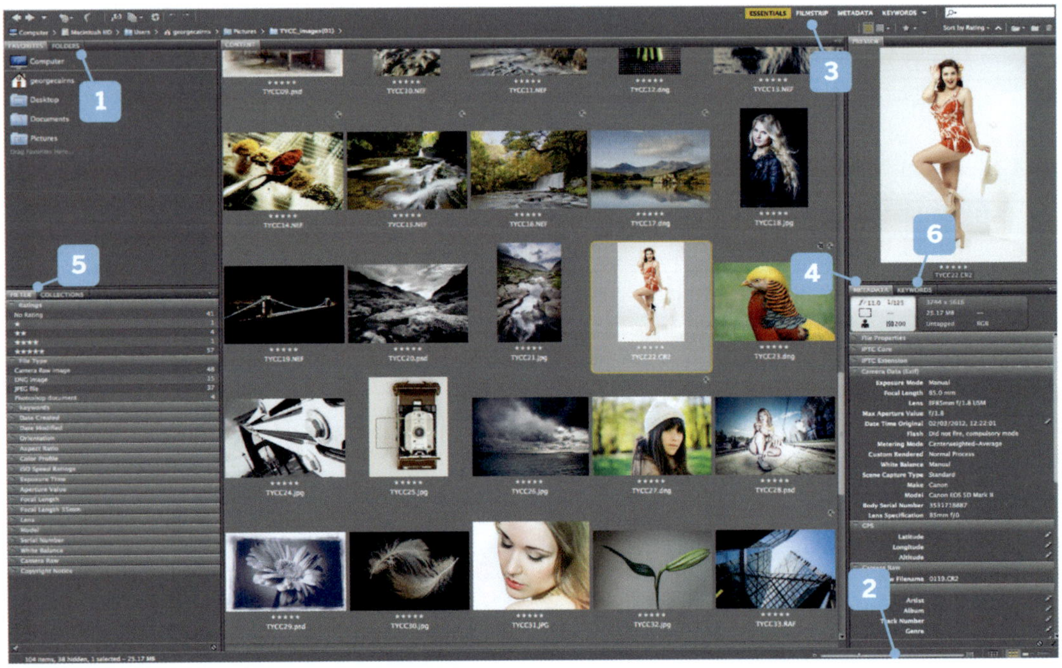

1 FOLDERS

Click the Folders tab to browse to any folder of images stored on your PC. Drag your most commonly used folders into the Favorites panel.

2 THUMBNAILS

Bridge displays your images as thumbnails. You can use the slider at the bottom of the workspace to increase the thumbnail size.

3 WORKSPACES

These links enable you to change the way panels and images are displayed in Bridge. For example, the Filmstrip option gives you larger previews.

4 METADATA

This panel emulates the display on your digital SLR. It reads the metadata stored in the currently active thumbnail so that you can discover what shutter speed, ISO and aperture settings were used to capture the image. It also shows the metering modes.

5 FILTERS

This panel enables you to present files that meet specific criteria, such as those with a specific star rating. You can also filter the files' metadata and discover images that were captured with a particular shutter speed setting, for example.

6 KEYWORDS

This panel enables you to quickly assign descriptive keywords to a photo. You can then use the Filter panel to display photos that contain a specific keyword. You can use keywords to label your photos by a variety of criteria including subject, location and more.

Overview Customising Adobe Bridge

Take a closer look at your pictures using the Filmstrip view

1 FILMSTRIP

By clicking the Filmstrip workspace icon you display the selected thumbnail at a much larger size in the Preview window. Shift-click to select and compare multiple images, as we're doing in this image.

2 LOUPE VIEW

The easiest way to see if an image is in focus is by looking at it at 100% magnification. To do so, click the image to activate the Loupe view. Drag the loupe to examine the image. We can see that the image on the right is blurred.

3 STACKING

To stop similar-looking images from cluttering up the workspace, Shift-click to select them and then choose Stacks>Group As Stack. Click the play icon to see each thumbnail contained in a stack (or drag the scroll bar).

4 EDITED IMAGES

If the colours, sharpness or tones of a raw format photo have already been adjusted in Photoshop, you'll see this icon. You may also spot more specific icons that indicate that an image has been cropped, for example.

5 THUMBNAIL QUALITY

By default you browse a raw file's content by displaying the low-resolution thumbnail that was embedded with the file when it was captured. For a more accurate preview of colours and tones, click here and choose High Quality display. This will demand more processing power, however.

6 SORT BY

To see your files in chronological order (with the oldest ones appearing on the left of the Filmstrip), set this Sort By drop-down menu to Date Created. You can also use this option in the Essential workspace to display the oldest files at the top.

Introducing the Lightroom layout

You can use Lightroom as your photo organisational tool instead of Adobe Bridge, and here's a guide to how it works

Photoshop users now have a choice of image organisational tools. Traditionally, Photoshop has been twinned with Adobe Bridge – Bridge does the organising and Photoshop does the editing. But the introduction of Adobe Photoshop Lightroom has widened the choice. At the time of writing, Lightroom is available both as a standalone program with a regular 'perpetual' licence (Lightroom 6)' or as part of Adobe's subscription-based Photography Plan. The fact is, if you are using Photoshop CC then you almost certainly have access to Lightroom CC as part of your subscription package at no extra cost, and it can prove an extremely useful tool both for managing a large collection of photographs, editing them directly or 'pre-editing' images, including raw files, before passing them over to Photoshop for more detailed work.

Does this make Bridge obsolete? Not at all. Many photographers prefer the simplicity of Bridge and don't need these powerful – and more complex – organisational tools. However, if you start to find Bridge too restrictive and inflexible, swapping to Lightroom could make a big difference.

Lightroom's workflow modules

From import to output, Adobe Lightroom can take care of your entire workflow

4 BOOK

It's possible to design and order printed photo books entirely within Lightroom, which could prove a very useful feature for commercial photographers who want to offer their clients a range of photographic products and services.

5 SLIDESHOW

This is a great way to package up a set of photographs into a multimedia presentation for clients, friends or family. Slideshows can be as simple or as complicated as you want.

6 PRINT

Lightroom offers extensive print layout options for single or multiple images, with built-in templates for common output settings and the ability to create and save your own.

1 LIBRARY

This is where you import your photos into the Lightroom catalogue, organise them into Folders and Collections, add ratings, labels, keywords and more.

2 DEVELOP

This is where you'll find Lightroom's editing tools. They're the same as those in Adobe Camera Raw, but arranged in a smart new interface.

3 MAP

Lightroom can automatically place geotagged images on a map, and you can add location information manually to images that don't have it.

7 WEB

You can also create and publish web galleries directly within Lightroom, which has built-in FTP transfer for uploading straight to your web host.

The Lightroom Library in detail

Lightroom's photo organising tools go far beyond those in Adobe Bridge

1 FOLDERS

Lightroom does not need to move your photos when it imports them – it can simply add them to the library in their existing location. You can see the folders they're stored in using this Folders panel and you can also rename and move photos.

2 COLLECTIONS

These are 'virtual' collections of images, just like the 'albums' in other photo organising programs. When you add a photo to a collection, you're not moving it physically, and a single photo can be in more than one collection.

3 SMART COLLECTIONS

Smart collections are like 'saved searches'. You don't add photos to a smart collection manually; instead, you set up the smart collection with properties you want to search for, such as photos with specific keywords, ratings or shooting information.

4 FILTER BAR

Whether you're looking at photos in a folder a collection or your entire library, you can use this bar to filter them based on ratings, labels, the shooting information saved by the camera, file type (JPEG or raw) and a whole lot more.

5 GRID VIEW

By default you'll view images as thumbnails in this 'grid' view, but you can double-click any photo to view it at full size in 'loupe' view. Click once more and the view zooms in to 100 per cent magnification. It's a really quick way to check photos.

6 METADATA

This sidebar has panels for adding keywords and editing your keyword list, adding copyright information, checking the camera's shooting (EXIF) information and more. You can also carry out quick enhancements with the Quick Develop panel.

Introducing the Camera Raw editor

Learn how to use the workspace that's specifically for processing high-resolution raw images, before moving into Photoshop itself

Once you've organised, rated and key-worded your images in Bridge you can double click them to launch them into Photoshop to edit them. If your files have been captured in a raw format such as CR2 or NEF, they will automatically open in the Adobe Camera Raw editor. JPEG format files will open in the standard Photoshop workspace, although you can send JPEGs into Camera Raw if you prefer using that workspace's tools.

By saving a photo as a JPEG, your camera creates a compressed file that doesn't take up much space on your memory card or your computer's hard drive. However, much of the information about the colour and tone in the image is lost. If you want to restore missing highlight or colour detail to a JPEG, you may end up revealing compression artefacts. A clear summer sky in a JPEG may consist of jagged bands of colour instead of a smooth gradient, for example.

By shooting in raw you capture more information about the colours and tones in a scene. This gives Photoshop more to work with. Here's how to use Camera Raw to reveal more colour and tonal detail...

Overview Camera Raw's tool bar

Discover which tools to use to improve composition and adjust colour and tone

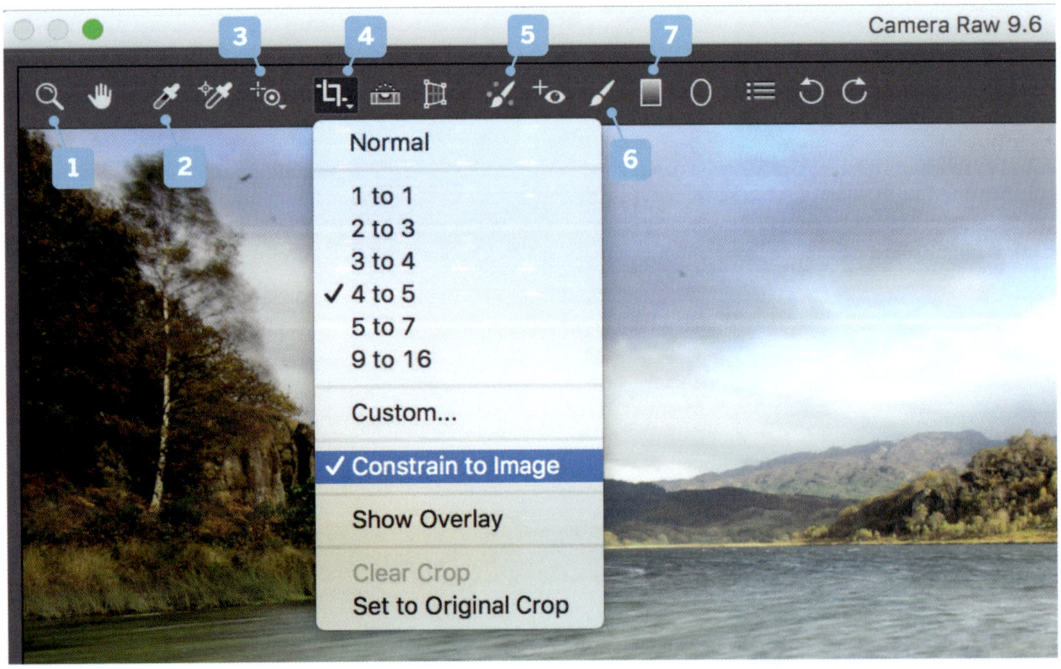

1 ZOOM TOOL

When sharpening a raw image you need to see the individual image pixels. Right click with the Zoom tool and choose 100% from the menu.

2 WHITE BALANCE

This tool enables you to set the white balance by sampling something that should be white. If the pixels are too warm, the tool will cool the colours.

3 TARGETED ADJUSTMENT

This powerful tool enables you to sample an area's colours or tones with a click. You can then drag up to lighten the area, or down to darken it.

4 CROP TOOL

This tool enables you to improve composition by removing the frame edges. The tool is non-destructive, so you can restore missing edge details at any time. The neighbouring Straighten tool enables you to counteract tilted horizons.

5 SPOT REMOVAL

This tool enables you to sample a clear patch of sky, for instance, and use it to hide artefacts such as a sensor spot. It's Camera Raw's version of the Clone Stamp tool.

6 ADJUSTMENT BRUSH

This tool enables you to make selective brush-based adjustments, such as lightening (dodging) or darkening (burning) the tones.

7 GRADUATED FILTER

This tool acts like a graduated neutral density filter on a camera's lens, enabling you to darken bright skies without blowing out a correctly exposed landscape, for instance. Or you could brighten an under-exposed landscape without over-exposing the sky.

Photoshop Anatomy Camera Raw editor

Familiarise yourself with Camera Raw's key features

1 RAW FILE

Our TYCC05.dng raw file has been saved as a digital negative. This native Adobe raw format means that the image will automatically open up in Photoshop's Camera Raw editor. We can then use the suite of tools and tabs to process the image.

2 WORKFLOW (OUTPUT) OPTIONS

Click this link to open the Workflow Options dialog. Here you can choose a colour space (such as the print-friendly Adobe RGB (1998)). You can also increase the Depth to 16 bits per channel to squeeze more information out of the raw file.

3 ZOOM LEVEL

It's often useful to see the image close up when working in Camera Raw, so click this pop-up menu to choose a magnification percentage. You can also click the + or - icons to zoom in or out in increments. Alternatively, press Cmd/Ctrl and the plus or minus keys to zoom in or out.

4 THE BASIC TAB

This tab contains most of Camera Raw's colour- and tone-correcting tools. The adjacent Detail tab enables you to sharpen up your raw images to create a print with more punch. Be careful to use this with a light hand though!

5 BEFORE AND AFTER COMPARISONS

Use these buttons to see before-and-after comparisons of images as you work on them. You can arrange these vertically or horizontally or use a vertical or horizontal split-screen arrangement. It's surprisingly useful.

6 OPEN OR DONE

Once you've finished processing your raw file, click Open Image to take the processed image into the main Photoshop workspace, where you can add text or apply filters, for example. Alternatively, click Done to save all the slider settings, so you can open it later on and continue fine-tuning the look.

Photoshop File Edit Image Layer Type Select Filter 3D View Window Help
Adobe Photoshop CC

Essential tools

Heal, patch and clone, dodge and burn, improve composition and much more with the Tools panel

Introducing the Photoshop workspace

Get to know all of Photoshop's key interface components, and discover how they enable you edit and enhance your photographs

Since its debut in 1990, Photoshop has grown and developed to maintain its role as the world's most popular image-editing application. Indeed, the name Photoshop has become synonymous with the act of digitally processing a photograph (though Adobe doesn't approve of this usage!). Although this book focuses on Photoshop CC and CS, we'll start by placing this most expensive and powerful version in context with the other versions of the Photoshop application so you can understand its strengths.

Adobe has now created a whole slew of free mobile image editing apps for smartphones and tablets, including Photoshop Express, Photoshop Fix and Photoshop Mix. These are designed for quick image manipulation while you're on the move. The next one up is Photoshop Elements for regular desktop and laptop computers. This is a cut-down version of Photoshop that's designed to help amateur photographers organise, edit and share their images. Elements lacks many of the more powerful and creative features found in Photoshop (such as the ability to make HDR composites or use realistic paint brushes), but it has most of the tone- and colour-tweaking tools a photographer might need, as well as many of the creative filters in Photoshop.

Photoshop Lightroom is Adobe's pro image organising and cataloguing tool and it has the same raw editing tools as Photoshop's Camera Raw, but it lacks the ability to edit in layers. Photoshop is still the go-to application in the Adobe photography family for advanced, in-depth image manipulation, allowing you to go beyond simple adjustments to colour, tone and cropping and into a world of creativity.

Photoshop Anatomy The workspace

Get to know the key sections in Photoshop's workspace

1 LAYERS PANEL

By editing in layers you can seamlessly combine different elements together, such as the studio-based model and the exterior street scene in this image. You can also make non-destructive changes to the colours and tones of an image using adjustment layers, as we'll demonstrate later.

2 LAYER MASKS

Layer masks are one of the most powerful tools in Photoshop when it comes to making composites. The black section of the mask makes the corresponding pixels on the attached layer transparent. White pixels create solid areas. You can fine-tune the affect of a mask using a black or white brush.

3 TOOLS PANEL

Here you'll find a host of tools designed to enable you to edit or enhance your images. Selection tools such as the Magic Wand enable you to isolate a subject from the original background. Retouching tools such as the Clone Stamp tool enable you to hide unwanted objects.

4 FLY-OUT PANEL

The Photoshop interface takes up very little space, despite the complexity and depth of its tools. Many options and controls are displayed on these fly-out panels so that they can be left open for as long as they're needed and then collapsed back into a small icon at the side of the screen. This is the Properties panel for the Hue/Saturation adjustment layer.

5 OPTIONS BAR

Once you choose a tool to work with, such as the Brush tool in this example, you'll be able to change the tool's attributes in the Options bar. Here you can change the opacity of the brush tip, its flow, the size, and the way it blends with the colours and tones on other layers using Blend modes. Different tools display different editable options.

6 MENU BAR

These drop-down menus enable you to use commands and access more tools and filters. You can also save your edited files in a variety of formats (such as .jpg for web galleries), share them via Behance (Adobe's online portfolio showcase) or choose to Browse in Bridge. You can even take JPEGs into the Camera Raw editor by using Filter>Camera Raw Filter.

Understanding... THE PHOTOSHOP WORKSPACE

You can access particular panels and commands from the main menu bar, but for a speedier workflow the Photoshop workspace [1] can be customised to suit your particular needs. If you're into photo fixing then choose Window>Workspace> Photography [2]. This opens relevant panels such as the Histogram, so you can analyse the spread of tones in an image to see if it's over- or under-exposed. By choosing Painting [3] you can display the Brush Preset picker and Color Swatch. Feel free to experiment with the different workspaces, because they are a great way to discover new features, and you can always go back to basics with the Essentials [4] option.

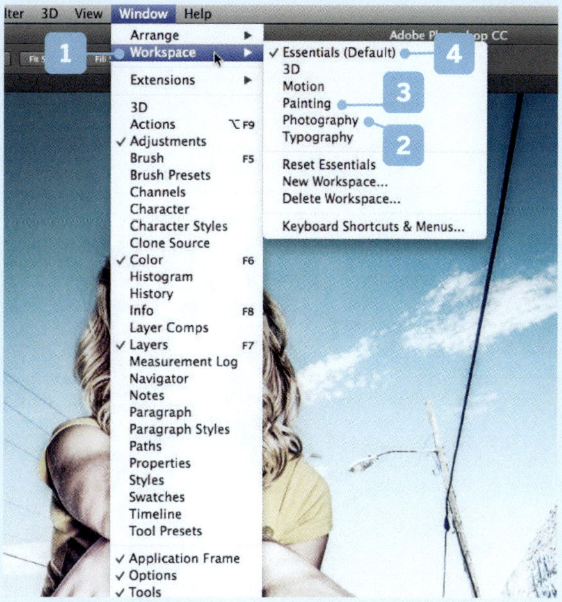

JPEG AND RAW WORKSPACES

As you'll see in this chapter's following pages, Bridge enables you to manage both your compressed JPEG format files and your uncompressed raw format files. To get the most from a raw file's colours and tones, it needs to be processed in the Camera Raw editor. This workspace is effectively a digital darkroom that enables you to develop your images. It has a range of selective colour and tonal adjustment tools, so you can process your pictures to perfection. You can then take the processed raw file into the standard Photoshop workspace to apply creative effects such as filters, text or paint-like brush strokes, for example, using layer masks to restrict your changes to selected areas.

Introducing the Tools panel

Discover how to access Photoshop's comprehensive collection of image-editing utilities in the Tools panel

A traditional darkroom photographer had a suite of tools to call upon when processing images, such as bits of card that enabled selective lightening (dodging) or darkening (burning) of parts of a picture. Other tools included an enlarger that equipped the photographer to produce prints of specific sizes. Photoshop has a vast suite of equivalent darkroom tools to help us process a picture, or to crop them to improve composition, for example. In the darkroom a photographer might use a brush to paint over unwanted objects. We can mimic this challenging retouching task more easily in Photoshop's digital darkroom, thanks to features such as the Clone Stamp tool.

Photoshop has a wide range of image-editing tools packed into panels and buried in menus and sub-menus. The most useful tools are collected in the Tools panel, which you'll find on the left-hand side of the workspace. This panel is docked to the edge as a single vertical column, but you can undock it and make it float closer to hand as a more compact two-column panel. Check out our annotation to get to know the key players in the Tools panel.

At a glance Tools of the trade

Learn how to uncover more tools and discover the key components of the Tools panel

4 ZOOM TOOL

The side-by-side Zoom and Hand tools work in conjunction with each other. They enable you to zoom in and pan around your picture to examine and edit specific areas. Tap Z to summon the Zoom tool or H to switch to the Hand. Double click the Zoom tool to magnify the image by 100%.

5 FOREGROUND COLOUR

The default foreground and background colours in the Tools panel are black and white. Click the black or white swatch to change the colour. Press D to go back to the default colours. These swatches are useful for tasks such as painting on layer masks.

6 SCREEN MODES

Click here to access the screen modes. Full Screen mode hides all the panels so you can focus on a clutter-free image. Minimised panels will slide into view when you move the cursor to the edges of the workspace. Press F to toggle between the screen modes.

1 EXPAND AND FLOAT

Click this little icon to toggle between a long, single column of tools, or a shorter panel containing two columns. You can also undock the panel.

2 COMPARTMENTS

The Tools panel has 20 compartments. To keep the panel at a manageable size, many related tools share a compartment.

3 TOGGLE THE TOOLS

The Tools panel contains 66 tools. Click and hold down the mouse on a compartment to reveal its contents, then click the tool you require.

Photoshop Anatomy The Options bar

Discover how to modify the behaviour of the currently active tool

1 TOOL PRESETS

After selecting a tool you can use the Options bar to edit attributes and modify the way the tool behaves. Click the Tool Preset picker to discover other versions of the selected tool. You can save your own customised presets here too.

2 BRUSH PRESET PICKER

Many tools, like the Eraser, are brush-based. The Brush Preset picker in the Options bar enables you to quickly modify the size and softness of the tool's brush tip to change the way it alters the pixels in the image.

3 BRUSH PANEL

This icon opens the Brush panel. This does a similar job to the Brush Preset picker, but you can change many more tool attributes such as the texture and its scattering properties. The Brush panel has a tab that opens the Brush Preset picker.

4 MODE

You can click the Mode drop-down menu to change the way the brush tip behaves. By default our example tool (the Eraser) is set to Brush, so it can paint with soft edges. You can change it to a sharper Pencil mode, or even a square Block.

5 OPACITY

This option enables you to reduce the intensity of the tool so you can perform more subtle edits. You can set a specific percentage, click the little triangle icon to activate a slider, or simply click and drag left or right on the Opacity label.

6 HISTORY

Some tools have unique options, such as the Eraser's Erase to History box. This enables you to make a global adjustment to the image. You can then tick this box and paint with the Eraser to remove the previous adjustments from specific areas.

The Crop tool

Maximise the potential of your photographs by cropping them to improve their composition

In this Tool School, we look at the Crop tool. This tool has a lot to offer when it comes to making shots look their best. It enables us to remove or crop the edges of a photo to create a new composition or take out unwanted objects at the edges of the frame, much as a traditional photographer would use a guillotine to trim photos after printing them.

When shooting on location, we may not have enough time to think about the best way to compose a scene, especially if we're rushing from A to B. The Crop tool enables us to reframe the photo's subject matter at our leisure.

As well as removing distracting objects, the Crop tool also allows us to correct common mistakes. For example, when shooting with the camera tilted at an angle you'll create an uneven horizon. This can be as annoying as seeing a picture hanging lop-sided on a wall. We'll demonstrate how to use the Crop tool to make the horizon run parallel with the top and bottom of the frame. When preparing a shot for printing, it can be a challenge to get a cropped shot to have the same shape – or aspect ratio – as the other uncropped shots from your camera. This can be irritating if you want to include the photo in a gallery with non-cropped prints. We'll show you how to constrain the Crop tool to make the cropped image have the same shape and proportions as the original. We'll also get the Crop tool to resize a shot so that it prints out with specific width and height dimensions and fits into a standard off-the-shelf picture frame.

The Crop tool is located in a compartment at the top section of the Tools panel, which reflects its status as a frequently used item. It shares this compartment with the less useful Slice tools, which are designed to help web designers chop up a Photoshop document.

Improve composition

Discover how to use the Crop tool's Overlay function to produce well-framed shots

Sometimes we might flick through a series of shots and only a few will stand out as being of any real worth. The odds are that the more aesthetically pleasing shots will conform to the rule of thirds. This is an artistic technique that involves separating the frame into nine equally sized boxes using a grid. By placing certain subjects in these boxes, or getting the grid's intersecting lines to overlap specific objects in the scene, you can create a more pleasing and balanced composition.

For example, you could have a hill in the bottom third of the screen, a tree in the middle third and sky at the top.

The tree could also overlap intersecting horizontal and vertical grid lines at the left of the frame, as in this feature's main image on the previous page. Professional photographers like David Bailey zoom in to frame their shots and crop out the top of their subject's head, producing a tighter and more intimate-looking portrait. We can creatively crop a conventionally framed portrait to make a more eye-catching version with a square frame. We'll show you how to combine a constrained aspect ratio with the Crop tool's rule of thirds overlay grid to create an aesthetically pleasing portrait.

Use the rule of thirds overlay

1 Draw a square

Open a standard portrait. Grab the Crop tool. Hold down Shift to constrain the Crop tool and draw a perfectly square crop box. The areas that will be removed will appear as a grey shield. The areas we'll keep remain 100% visible.

2 Get some balance

In the Options bar, set Crop Guide Overlay to Rule of Thirds. Drag inside the crop window to make the intersecting lines overlap the eyes. Drag outside the crop window to rotate it, correcting the model's head tilt and creating a symmetrical portrait.

3 Creative cropping

Drag the crop window right to remove half of the face. The positions of the remaining features still correspond to the rule of thirds. We have an eye, nose and mouth in the left third, hair in the middle and space at the right. Hit Enter.

Crop to correct

Tidy up problems like uneven horizons with these cropping techniques

As well as improving composition, the Crop tool enables you to overcome common problems. By zooming out to capture this landscape, we caught the edges of the lens hood at the edges of the frame. There's also some vignetting at the top left. When shooting from a moving boat it's harder to get the horizon looking horizontal, and ours tilted downwards towards the right.

To remove these problems, grab the Crop tool from the Tools panel. Select the entire image to start with. Turn on the Rule of Thirds Overlay. Now hold down Shift and this will constrain the cropped shot to match the aspect ratio – the shape and proportions – of the original photo. Drag a corner handle to tighten the crop window and remove the lens hood and vignetted corner. Drag inside the crop window to place the rock in the bottom left corner. Drag outside the crop box to rotate it so that the horizon runs parallel with a horizontal grid line.

If you send your photos off to be printed at a particular size, you may find that they come back cropped, which ruins your careful composition. Check out the guide below to cropping and resizing with precision.

Resize your photos for printing

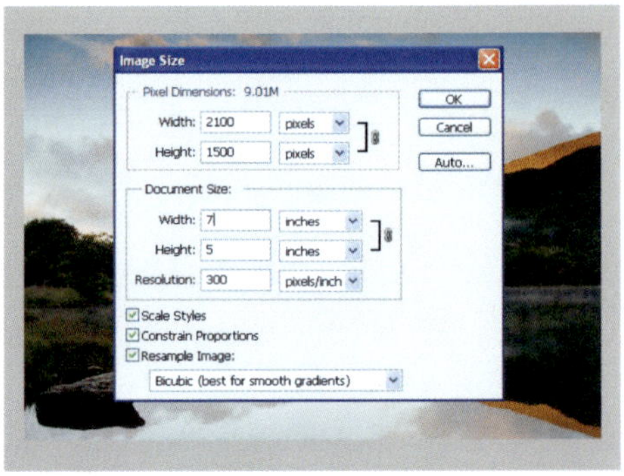

1 Choose a size

Open an image that you've processed and is ready to print. Click the Crop tool icon. Move up to the left of the Options bar and then click the Tool Preset picker's triangular fly-out icon. Select the Crop 5 inch x 7 inch 300 ppi preset.

2 Change the orientation

By default, the preset will create a portrait-oriented crop, but this particular image is in landscape format. Click the Swaps Height and Width icon in the Options bar to correct this. Click and drag to crop the image.

3 Check the size

To complete the crop, hit Enter or click the tick icon on the Options bar. Go to Image>Image Size. Set the units to inches. You'll see that the shot is precisely 7 inches wide by 5 inches high, with a resolution of 300 pixels per inch.

Photoshop Anatomy Crop tool options

Learn how to get the most out of this invaluable tool

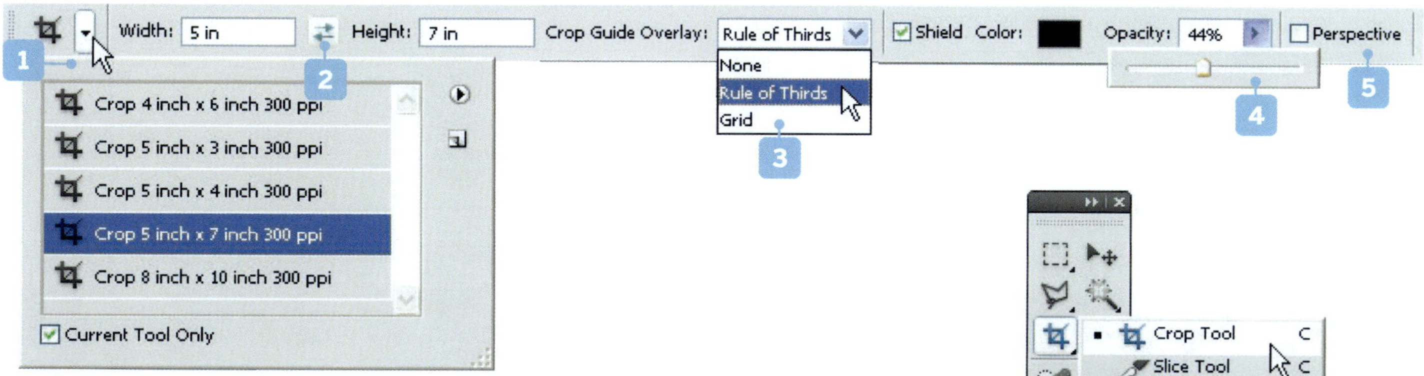

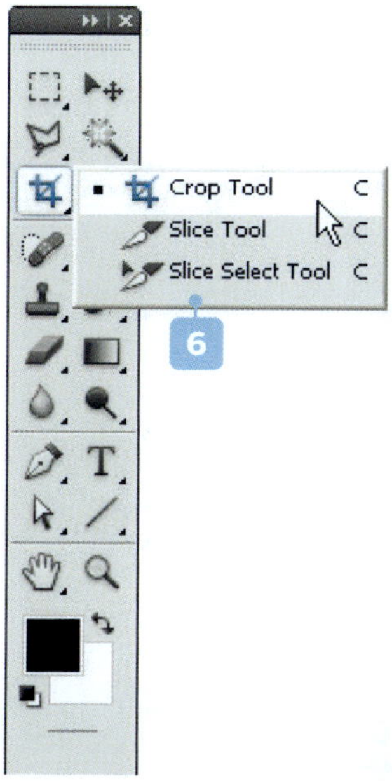

1 TOOL PRESET PICKER

You can use these presets to make the Crop tool resize the cropped image to fit specific dimensions and resolutions.

2 QUICK SWAP

Click this icon to swap a preset's width and height so that you can perform portrait or landscape-oriented crops.

3 OVERLAY

Click here to add a composition-friendly rule of thirds grid to the Crop box, or a more conventional grid.

4 OPACITY AND COLOR

Reduce the opacity setting to make the contents of the shielded areas more visible. You can change the colour of the shield, too.

5 PERSPECTIVE

When cropping photos of architecture, you can use this option to manually straighten converging verticals at the same time.

6 TOOL COMPARTMENT

The Crop tool hangs out in the Tools panel with the less useful Slice tools. Press Shift+C to cycle between them.

Understanding... THE CROP TOOL

After selecting the Crop tool from the Tools panel, click and drag to start drawing a crop box [1]. Use the overlay to add a handy rule of thirds grid [2] to help you create a more aesthetically pleasing composition. By default, cropped areas appear as a dark grey colour, which can make it hard to spot content – especially in monochrome shots. You can make it easier to see cropped areas by changing the shield colour [3] and reducing its opacity. To apply the crop to your photo, hit Enter or click the tick in the Options bar. Alternatively, click another tool in the Tools panel and Photoshop will ask you if you want to complete the crop before it gives you access to the other tool [4].

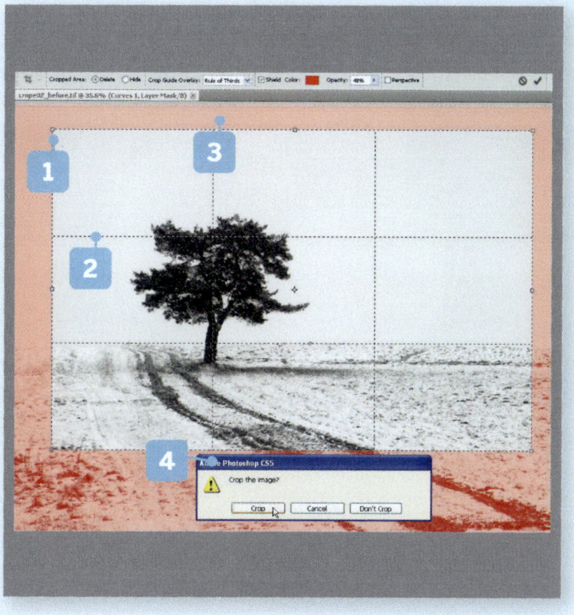

CHANGE THE SHIELD PROPERTIES

The areas outside the crop window are greyed out by a shield, which helps you focus on what will remain once you've cropped it. If you want to hide the preview of the cropped areas entirely, you can change the opacity of the shield overlay to 100%. It will become black and solid. ■

Image and canvas size explained

These are two essential settings which can also be two major causes of confusion! Here's what you need to know

When you're preparing your photos for printing it's easy to get caught up in the confusing array of options for width and height, percentages, pixel dimensions, resolution and resampling. It's just as difficult when you need to resize photos for use online.

The key concept to keep in mind at all times, though, is 'resizing' versus 'resampling'. Resizing is a non-destructive process that simply changes the size at which the pixels will be reproduced. It's completely reversible and doesn't actually change the image itself. This is what you use to create different-sized prints from within Photoshop.

But when you're creating images for online use you need to work directly in pixels. You can't display a 6,000 x 4,000 pixel photo on a web page only 1,024 pixels across! This is where you need to use resampling options to reduce the number of pixels. Resampling is an irreversible 'destructive' process because it permanently changes the pixels in the photo, so you need to make sure you work on a copy, not the original photo. But don't worry – our annotation opposite explains the Image Size dialog in detail.

Canvas Size settings and what they mean

It's right next to Image Size on the Edit menu, but the Canvas Size is not the same thing

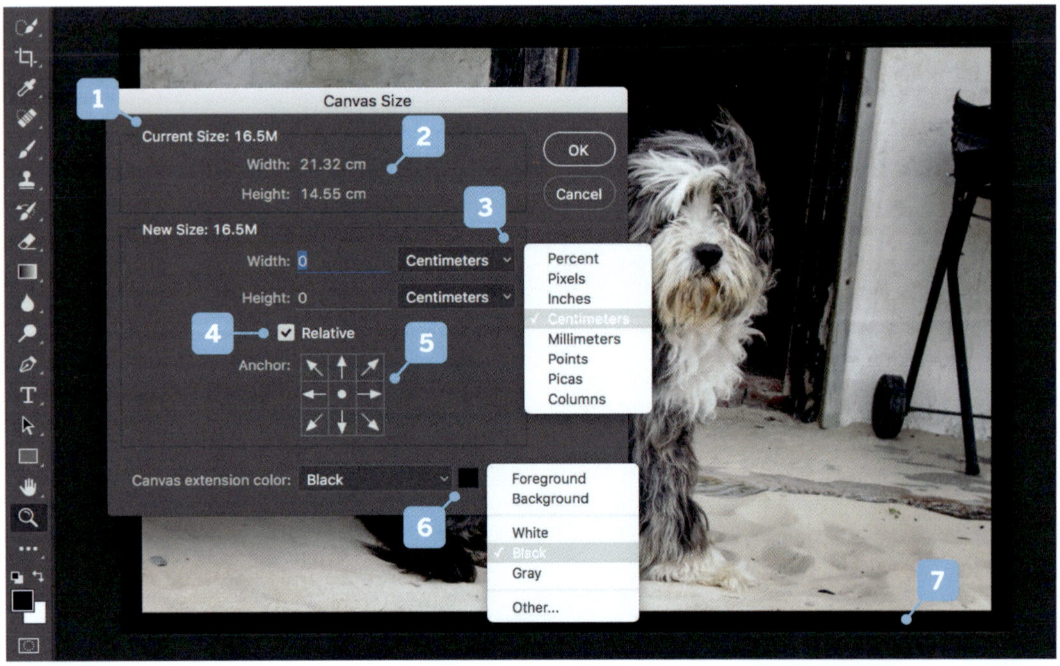

4 RELATIVE SIZES

If you leave this unchecked, the values you type into the Width and Height boxes will set the absolute canvas size. If you check this box, you type in the amounts you want to add to the current size, which is often the easiest option if you're adding a border, for example.

5 ANCHOR GADGET

If you leave the centre box selected the extra canvas area is extended equally around the image, but you can extend the canvas from the left, right, top or bottom or from any of the four corners.

6 CANVAS COLOUR

This is where you choose the colour for the canvas extension. In our example we've chosen black to create a black border around this photograph.

7 EXTENDED CANVAS

The image canvas is the 'pasteboard' the image sits on. Normally it's the same size as the photo itself, but when you increase the canvas size, it becomes visible around the photo. If you want to separate the photo from the canvas, convert the photo to a layer first.

1 CURRENT SIZE

This section shows you your photo's current size, and the units of measurement are the same as those you choose in the New Size section.

2 WIDTH AND HEIGHT

If you increase the canvas size you create empty (background) space around the photo. If you reduce it, you crop off the edges of the picture.

3 SIZE UNITS

You can set the new canvas size in percentage values, pixels, inches and other units – pixels and percentages tend to be the most useful.

How to use the Image Size dialog

Resampling vs resizing: what's the difference and why is it so important?

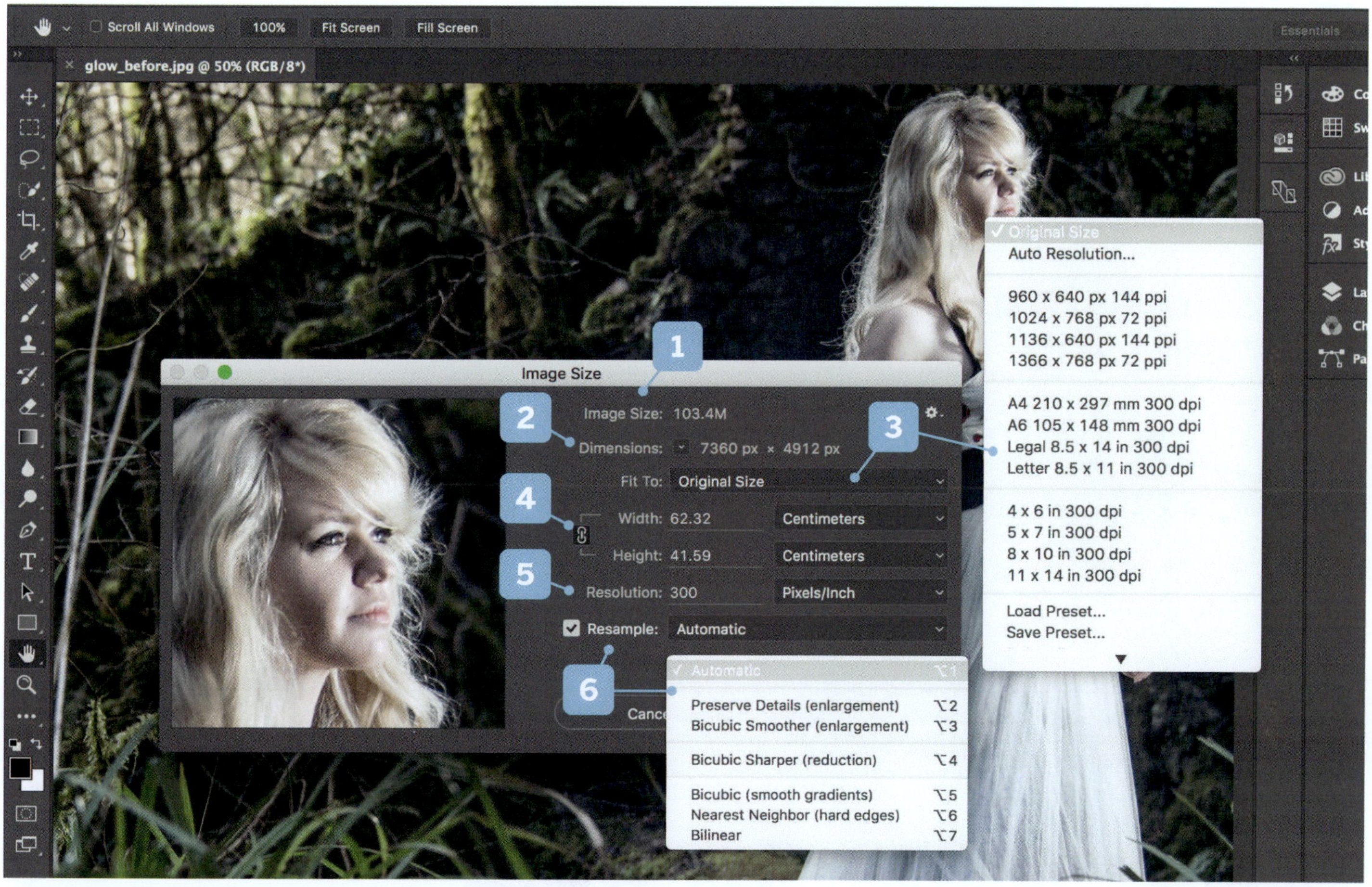

1 IMAGE SIZE (MB)

This is for information only. It tells you the image file size in its uncompressed form, but JPEGs, TIFFs and Photoshop files use compression to reduce the file size. It's useful for checking how much difference resizing the image will make, though.

2 DIMENSIONS

If you leave the Resample box unchecked, this too is for information only. It will display the current image size according to the units of measurement you choose for the Width and Height settings in the section below.

3 FIT TO MENU

This offers preset image sizes for different purposes including on-screen display (the top section), regular office paper sizes (the next section) and common photo print sizes (the section below). These presets will automatically check the Resample box because they need to change the number of pixels.

4 WIDTH AND HEIGHT

You don't have to resample a photo to make it print at different sizes, though. Instead, leave the Resample box unchecked and type in the width or height you want into either of these fields – the chainlink indicates the aspect ratio is locked.

5 RESOLUTION

When the Resample box is unchecked, Photoshop achieves the dimensions you ask for by adjusting the resolution. Don't worry about making your prints 300dpi in Photoshop – that's just an arbitrary measure for good print quality.

6 RESAMPLE CHECKBOX AND MENU

This is the box that should ring alarm bells. When it's checked, Photoshop will permanently change the number of pixels in the photo, so make sure you're working on a copy. The drop-down menu lets you choose different resampling methods according to whether you're increasing or reducing the pixel dimensions.

The power of adjustment layers

With adjustment layers you can stack up as many reversible, non-destructive image adjustments as you like

Once, every adjustment you made to your images in Photoshop was applied directly to the pixels in your photo. There was no going back, at least not without duplicating layers, using the History panel, or reverting to a backup.

But the introduction of adjustment layers changed all that. Adjustment layers merely change the appearance of the layer(s) below without modifying any of the pixels. You can change an adjustment layer's settings long after you've created it and you can stack adjustment layers to produce cumulative editing effects. If you save your images in the Photoshop (.psd) format, the adjustment layers are saved with them and remain fully editable. The only time their effect is made permanent is when you save a copy of your image in another file format.

Adjustment layers are versatile. You can turn them on and off to compare the edited image with the original. You can reduce their opacity to dial down the strength of the adjustment. You can also produce selective colour or tonal adjustments by painting on an adjustment layer's mask, enabling you to fine-tune which areas are being altered.

So while it's still possible to apply levels and curves adjustments, for example, directly to an image layer, why would you? Adjustment layers give you much more control.

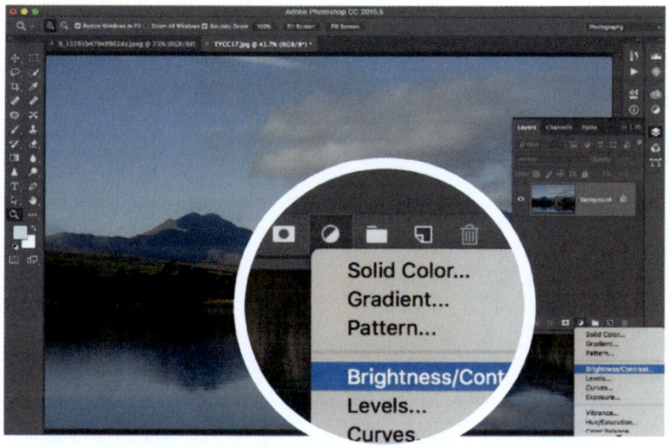

1 Add an adjustment layer

Open TYCC17.jpg. This landscape has rather dull tones and it's a good subject for a whole series of adjustments. If you open the Layers panel you'll see just one 'Background' layer containing the photo. Click the adjustment layer button at the bottom of the panel and chose Brightness/Contrast.

2 Brightness and Contrast

Very quickly we can make our picture look better by increasing the Brightness and reducing the Contrast. By the way, Photoshop's Brightness/Contrast controls used to be pretty crude, but they're much better now. They look simplistic, but they're actually very effective.

3 Adding a Vibrance layer...

You can now see the new adjustment layer added above the Background image in the Layers panel. But fixing the brightness and contrast has made it obvious that this picture has a serious lack of colour saturation, and the solution is to add a Vibrance adjustment layer...

4 And a Photo Filter

You can see the Vibrance adjustment layer's been added at the top of the Layers panel and we've moved its Properties panel over to the left of the screen so that it doesn't get in the way. Increasing the Vibrance and Saturation has helped, but we're going to finish with a Photo Filter...

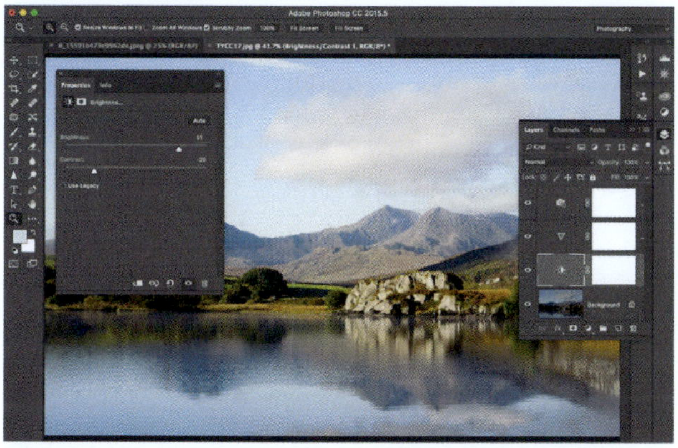

5 Everything can still be changed

This Photo Filter layer has been added at the top of the Layers panel, and it's given our image a subtle, warm look. So now we have three adjustment layers stacked on top of each other, but we can still go back and change the Brightness/Contrast layer, say, to modify the overall effect.

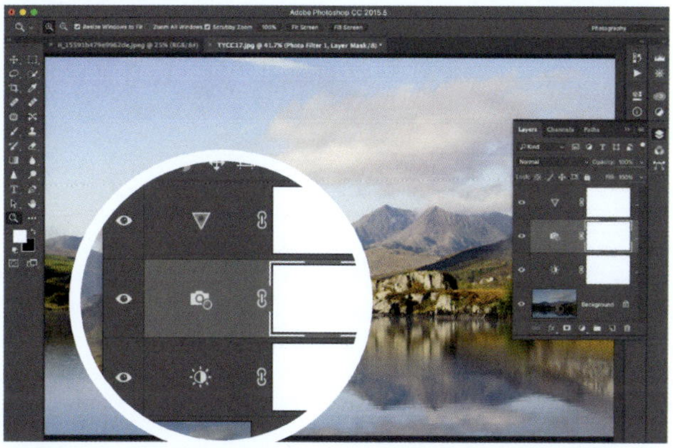

6 The layer order is important

You can drag adjustment layers up and down in the Layers panel to change their order, but be aware that it can change the overall effect. Here, for example, moving the Vibrance layer above the Photo Filter layer means that the Photo Filter's warming effect has been exaggerated.

Basic fixes with a levels layer

Levels adjustments offer a great first step for diagnosing and then fixing issues with your picture's tonal range

Levels adjustments don't look terribly sophisticated when you compare them with what you can do with a curves adjustment layer, but they are a really quick and easy way to optimise your image ahead of any more detailed work. Often, it's only when you've got the levels right that you can properly see what to do next.

The key to this is the histogram display in the levels panel. From this you can tell whether your image has a full range of tones. If not, you can drag the black point and white point sliders underneath to line up the left and right edges of the histogram. Our walkthrough, opposite, shows how this works on a real-life image and some of the hidden depth of levels! By default, levels adjustments are applied equally to the red, green and blue colour channels, but they can also be altered individually – levels are handy for colour corrections, too.

You'll notice that we're creating a levels adjustment layer rather than applying levels directly to the image layer. There are lots of good reasons for doing it this way. One is that your adjustments will be non-destructive – you can go back and change them later. Another is that adjustment layers come with layer masks, so that you can manually mask out areas of your photo which you want left alone. We'll cover layer masks in a later chapter, but for now we'll demonstrate not one but three different approaches to levels adjustments...

1 Use the histogram as a guide

Open TYCC95.jpg if you'd like to follow this process with the image we're working on here. First, create a new levels adjustment layer. You'll see that the left-hand (shadow) end of the histogram doesn't go all the way to a full black, so drag the black point slider to the right to meet it.

2 Be careful with the highlights

Now do the same with the white point slider on the right, dragging it to the left to line up with the right edge of the histogram. This is the usual method for optimising image levels, but this image still lacks contrast even though, technically, it now has a full tonal range.

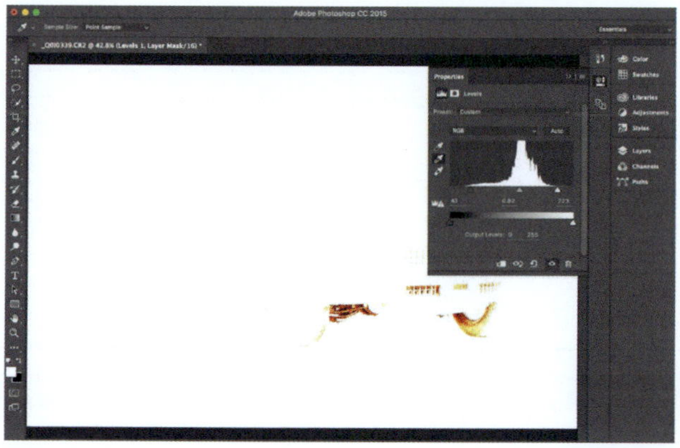

3 Alt-drag the black point slider

The problem is that we're preserving extreme shadow and highlight detail without knowing whether it's important. Instead, hold down the alt key as you drag the black point slider. Now you can see where the image will go to a solid black and which areas you can afford to lose.

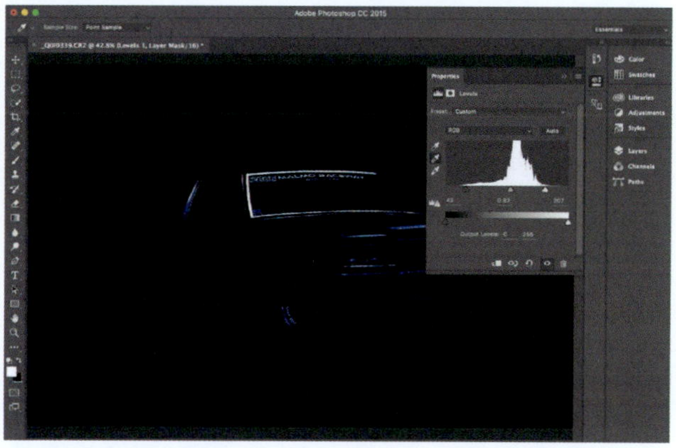

4 Alt-drag the white point slider

You can do the same with the white point slider. Normally, you wouldn't want to clip any highlight detail at all, but we can afford to lose detail in the highly reflective chromework in this car. This different 'alt-dragging' approach is an improvement, but the picture's still a little weak...

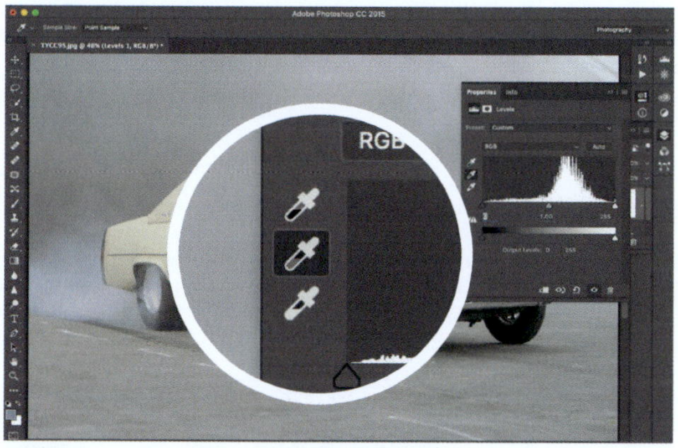

5 Use the eyedroppers

So here's a third approach which doesn't involve the black and white point sliders at all. Instead, you use the black point, white point and middle 'grey point' eyedroppers to click an area you want to be a solid black, a solid white area and a neutral grey tone, like the tarmac near the car.

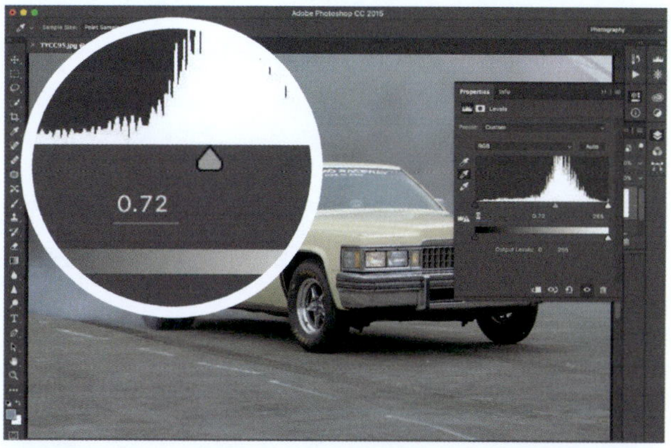

6 Adjust the mid-point (brightness)

The eyedroppers don't just set the upper and lower brightness values, they 'neutralise' the deepest blacks, brightest whites and midtone greys too, adding a colour correction effect. And for a final adjustment we can move the mid-point slider to the right to darken the image a little.

Master Curves in Photoshop

Use Curves, the ultimate tool for tonal control, to add punch and enhance portraits

1 Add punch

Add a Curves Adjustment layer, then drag the top part of the curve upwards to lighten the image. Click the bottom of the curve to add a second anchor point, then drag this point downwards to darken shadows.

2 Tweak the colours

Add a Curves layer, then choose Blue from the drop-down menu. Drag the bottom-left point upwards to add blue to the shadows, and the top-right point down to add yellow to the highlights.

Photoshop Anatomy The Curves controls

Use these Curves controls to bring your images to life

TONE CURVE

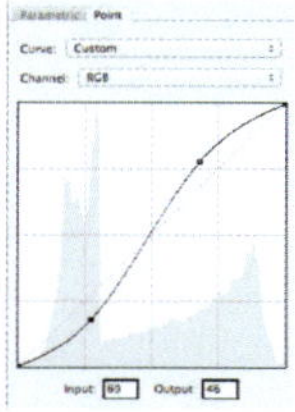

Camera Raw has its own version of the Curves command: called the Tone Curve, it works in much the same way. Raw files are usually a little flat, so will often benefit from increased punch.

1 NEUTRAL GREY EYEDROPPER

Grab the neutral grey eyedropper and click a point in an image you know should be grey; then all the other colours will
re-map around this new grey point.

2 THE CURVE LINE

The diagonal line can be dragged up or down to lighten or darken the image. Each point you click creates an anchor. It's important where you place a point, because this determines which part of the tonal range you wish to change. Towards the left will target shadow tones, and the right will change highlights.

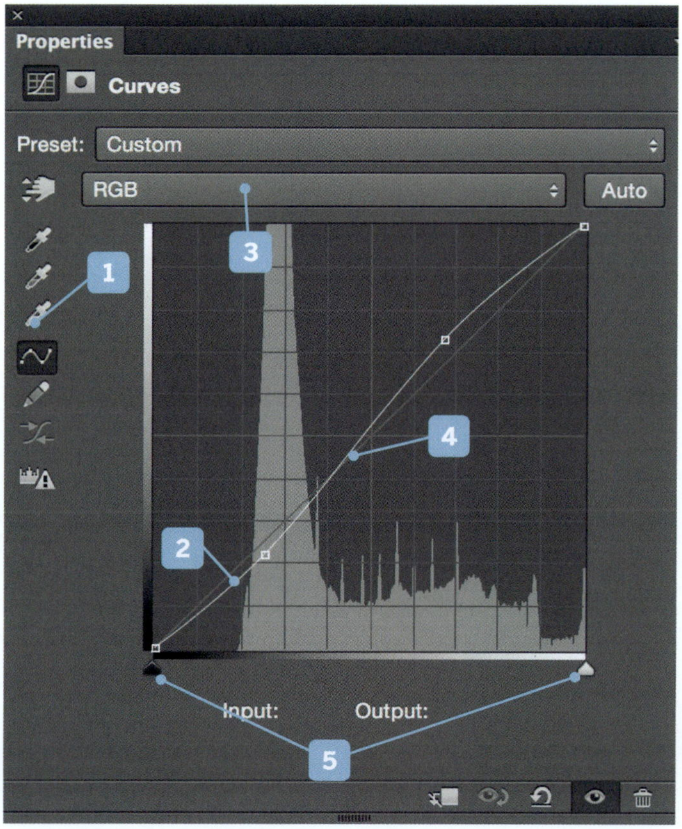

3 COLOUR CHANNELS

An upwards drag on the red line adds red while down adds cyan; up on the blue channel adds blue and down adds yellow; up on the green line adds green and down adds magenta. Try dragging the very top or bottom of the channel lines to add subtle colour shifts to highlights and shadows.

4 S-CURVE

The S-shaped curve is a classic Curves technique for boosting contrast and colour saturation, lending much-needed punch to flat images. The more pronounced the S-shape is, the more the image will pop.

5 WHITE AND BLACK POINTS

Hold Alt and drag the White and Black point sliders, and your display will change to show clipped pixels as you drag. In general, it's best to drag the black point inwards until you see a few black areas appear, and drag the white point inwards until the point just before pixels appear.

Understanding... CURVES ADJUSTMENT LAYERS

Add Curves as an adjustment layer via the Create adjustment layer icon [1]. This gives you lots of layer-based options. You can lower the layer opacity to tone down the effect [2] or change the blending mode [3]. For example, a switch to Luminosity allows you to add contrast without affecting colour saturation. It's also possible to highlight the layer's mask [4] and paint with white or black to apply the Curves edit to specific parts of an image. If you're working in a multi-layered document and you want the Curves layer to affect only the image layer directly below it (rather than all the layers below), Alt-click the line between the two layers to 'clip' the adjustment [5]. ■

Selective Hue/ Saturation tweaks

A Hue/Saturation adjustment layer gives you rather more control over colour rendition than you might think at first

Colour adjustments are central to much of the photo enhancement work we do in Photoshop, and much of the time we simply want more! One way of doing this is with a Vibrance adjustment layer – which actually has two sliders, one for Vibrance and one for Saturation. The saturation slider is a pretty crude tool which increases all colours equally, while Vibrance is more sophisticated and strengthens weaker colours more.

But neither offers any control over individual colours, and for this you need a Hue/Saturation adjustment layer. Now at first sight this doesn't appear to be very helpful because it simply offers global hue, saturation and lightness sliders – and the saturation slider appears to offer no particular advantage over the version in the Vibrance panel.

However, the Hue/Saturation panel has hidden depths. By default, it adjusts your image's 'Master' channel, modifying all colours equally. Often, though, you want to enhance or modify just one or two colours, and by different amounts, and you can do this by opening the drop-down menu and choosing a specific colour range.

This simple trick reveals enormous power! You can change the colour of green leaves or a blue sky or a red coat in moments, and without the need for complicated selections and masks. Our tutorial shows how this process works.

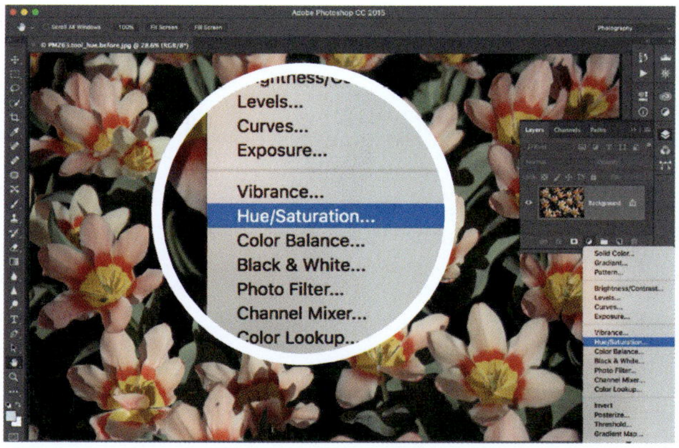

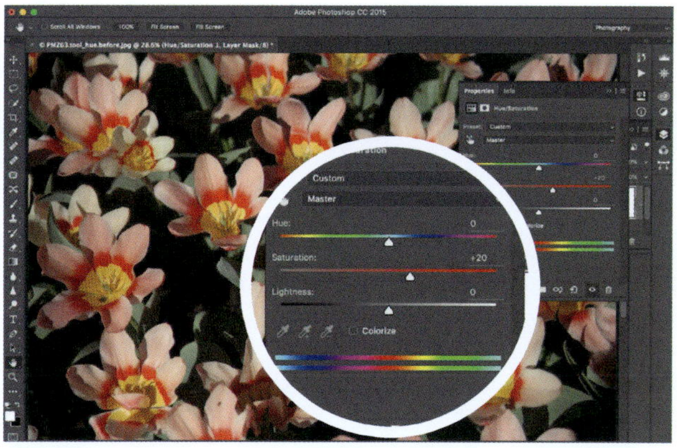

1 Add a Hue/Saturation layer

You can follow this tutorial with the same image as ours by opening TYCC96.jpg from our set of sample images. The first step is to add a Hue/Saturation adjustment layer, and you can do this using the drop-down adjustment layers menu at the bottom of the Layers panel.

2 Increase the saturation

Usually, the only adjustment you apply with a Hue/Saturation layer is the saturation value. Changing the hue shifts the colours wholesale, and there are better ways of changing the colours in Photoshop, and the lightness slider is a very poor way of changing the overall image brightness.

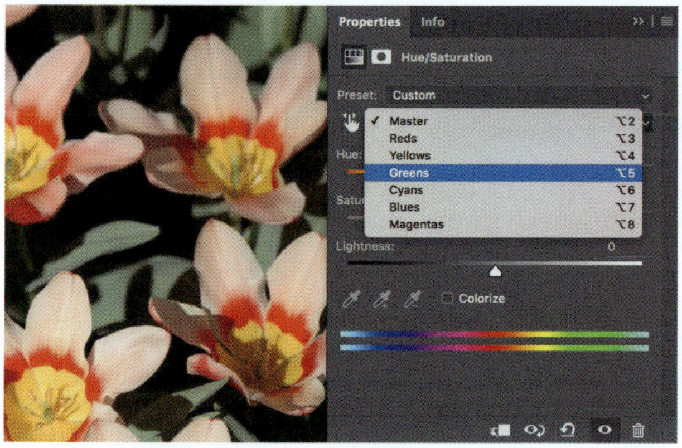

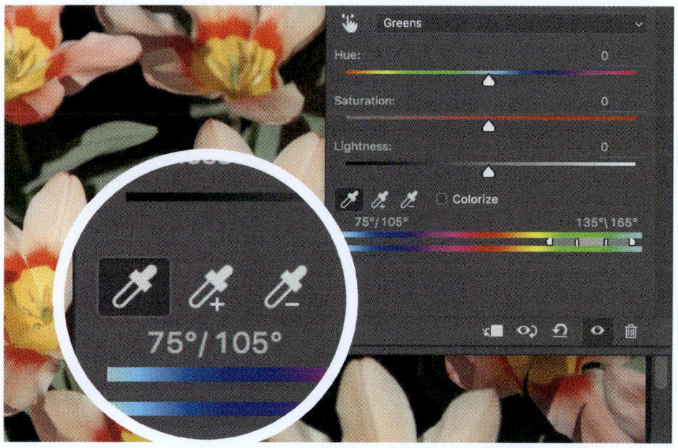

3 Choose the greens

We had to stop at a saturation value of +20 in the previous step because the reds and yellows in the flowers were starting to fill. The green tones are still weak, though – and the answer lies in the drop-down colour range menu. It's set to 'Master' by default, but we need 'Greens'...

4 Fine-tune with the eyedropper

So now any hue/saturation adjustments will only apply to green tones in the picture, but this is a generic colour range and we need to tighten it up a little using the panel's eyedropper tool and then clicking on one of the green leaves. This makes our colour selection more precise.

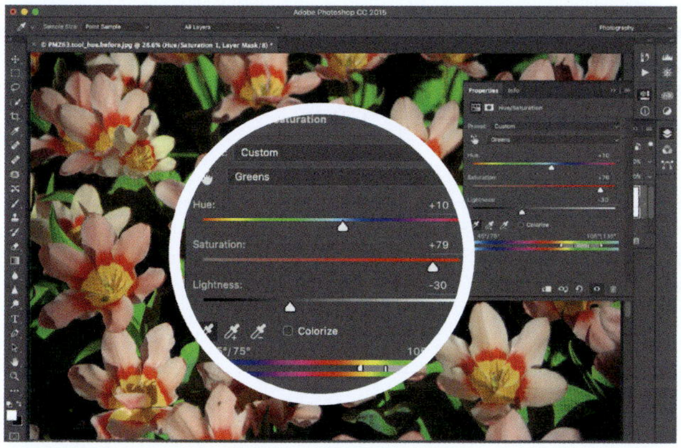

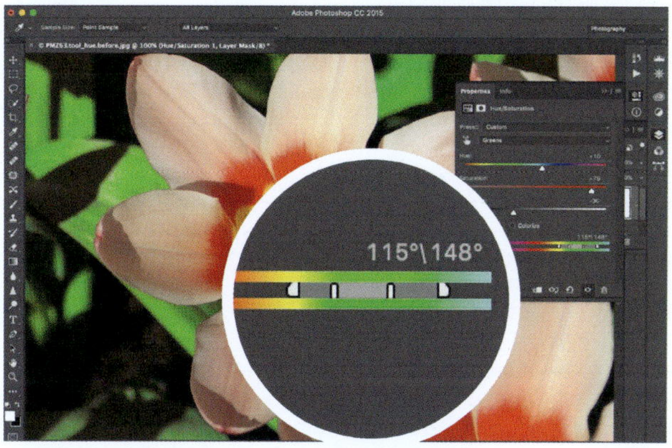

5 Adjust the greens

Now we can really bring out the colour of the leaves but without affecting the flowers. Shifting the hue value to +10 makes the leaves look a little greener and fresher, reducing the lightness to -80 darkens them down a little and pushing the saturation up to +79 makes them more intense.

6 Tweak the colour range

Sometimes the colour selection leaves out parts of the image you meant to include or strays into similar tones that should be left alone. If so, you can drag the bars in the colour selection gadget – the inner bars control the colour range and the outer bars 'feather' this selected range.

Convert colour photos to mono

In black and white photography, colour is crucial – or at least how different colours are converted to grey tones

Black and white photography shows no signs of dying away. In fact, it's become a mainstream creative choice for photographers attempting to capture the world in a dramatic or timeless way. But creating a successful black and white image isn't as simple as just removing the colour information, because the way different colours translate into different shades of grey makes a massive difference to the finished picture.

In the days of film you would control this using different-coloured 'contrast' filters on the lens. These days, you can do it using a Black & White adjustment layer in Photoshop. With this, you can control the relative strengths and hence brightness values of the colours in the photo as they are translated into shades of grey.

In the old days, this would be achieved using Photoshop's Channel Mixer tools, but these only offered adjustments for the red, green and blue channels, whereas Black & White adjustment layers have sliders for six colour: reds, yellows, greens, cyans, blues and magentas.

You'll notice that we're using a 16-bit sample image to get the best quality. This is important when your final image relies heavily on individual colour channels in the photo. Remember – the only way to get a 16-bit image is to shoot raw. This is one time when JPEGs won't do.

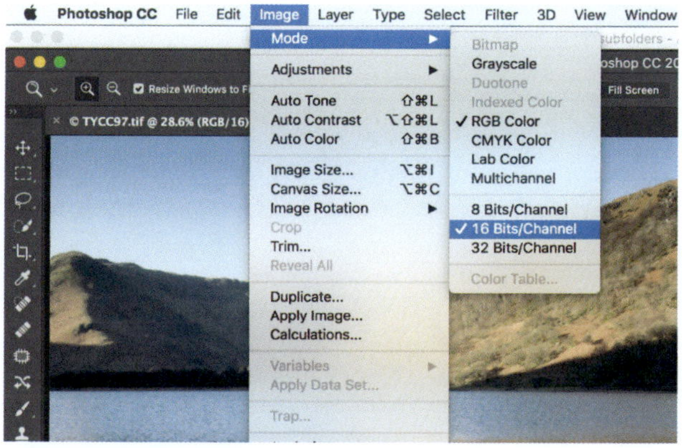

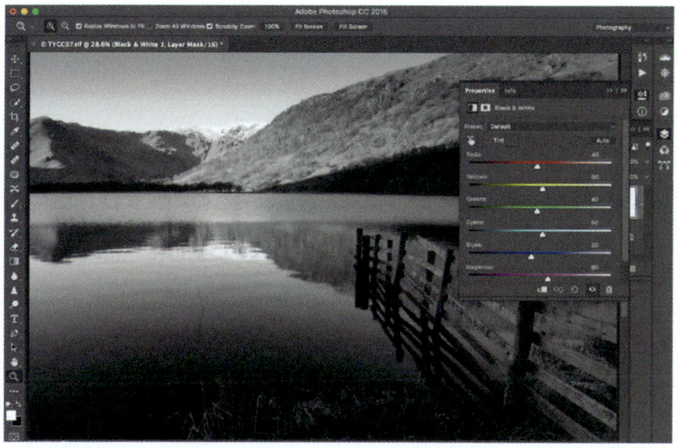

1 Check the bit depth

You can follow this tutorial by opening our TYCC97.tif sample image. We've supplied this as a TIFF file rather than a JPEG because mono conversions like this work much better on 16-bit images. With 8-bit images you quickly get banding effects and other artefacts.

2 Default mono conversion

Now open the adjustment layer drop-down at the bottom of the Layers panel and add a Black & White adjustment layer. At the default settings you'll see that the colour mix isn't exactly even. Some colours (yellow, magenta and cyan) are made stronger and hence lighter than others.

3 Red filter effect

The default colour mix will probably work well with many images, but for landscapes it's definitely worth trying some alternatives from the drop-down Preset menu. The Red Filter effect, for example, makes the blue sky and lake darker and the green hills lighter.

4 Blue filter effect

Compare this with the Blue Filter effect! Because blues are now made lighter, the sky and the water have a brighter tone, while the yellows and greens in the hills (on the opposite side of the colour wheel) are much darker. This shows the importance of colour filtration in black and white.

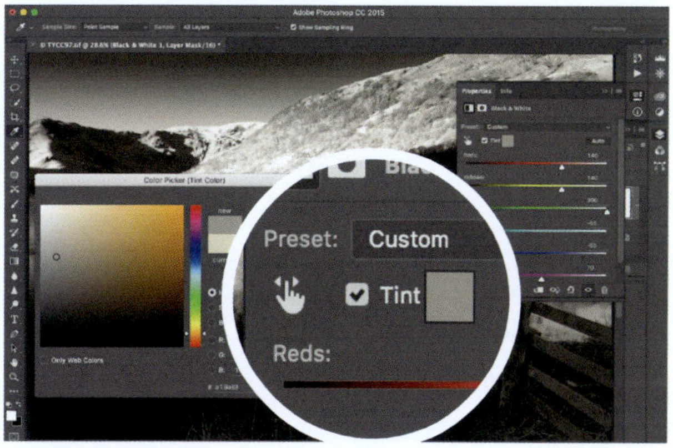

5 Manual adjustments

Once you've found a preset that gets close to the look you want, you can fine-tune the sliders to finish the job. Here, we've increased the contrast and drama in this landscape by making the cyans and blues darker still and slightly lightening the reds and yellows.

6 Adding a tint

Many photographers like the look of 'toned' black and white prints, and you can achieve that effect here by checking the Tint box and then the colour swatch just to the right. This opens the Color Picker, where you choose the tint hue and its strength – subtle tints are almost always better.

Adjustment layer masks in action

Discover how to modify an adjustment layer's mask to modify selected areas only rather than the whole photo

Layer masks are a powerful tool because they enable you to modify selections made by Photoshop's selection tools until they are perfect. By painting white or black strokes on a mask you can show or hide pixels on the image layer the mask is attached to. This enables you to hide an unwanted sky, for example, and show through a more interesting one on another layer underneath.

But layer masks are also invaluable when it comes to common image adjustments – in fact, every adjustment layer you create comes with a ready to use layer mask.

In the case of our starting image here we need to darken the over-exposed sky with a Levels adjustment layer to reveal missing detail and colour. However, this will plunge the correctly exposed foreground rocks into silhouette. We can apply black paint to specific sections of the mask so that it only darkens the sky.

Like image layer masks, an adjustment layer's mask is non-destructive, so you can modify it using a range of tools and techniques until the masking for the adjustment is perfect.

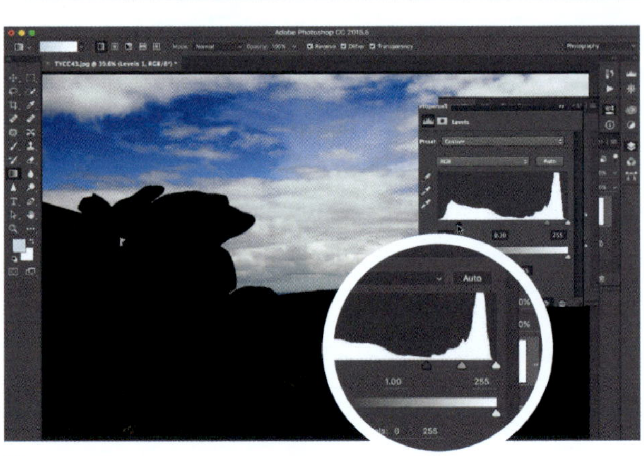

1 Create an adjustment layer

Open the TYCC43.jpg starting image. Due to the contrasting lighting conditions the camera has metered to expose for the rocks, so the sky is over-exposed. To restore sky detail, choose Layer›New Adjustment Layer›Levels. Click OK. A Levels adjustment layer will appear in the Layers panel.

2 Darken the sky

In the adjustment layer panel, we've dragged the black point slider right across to the right to darken the sky. This 'clips' all the darker information in the rocks so that they come out as a near solid black, but that doesn't matter because of what we're going to do next...

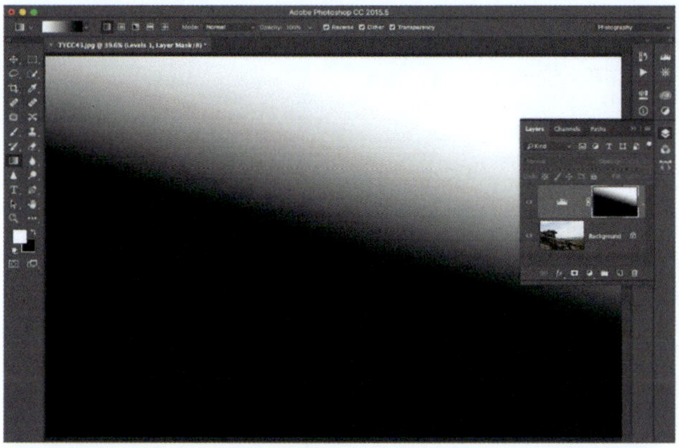

3 Mask the rocks

We need to select the layer mask thumbnail in the Layers panel to edit it – and you can alt/ctrl-click the mask to show it directly. We've added a black-white gradient on a slight diagonal so that the black area 'masks' the rocks from the Levels adjustments we've made.

4 Subtle is best

And here you can see the result. The sky is darkened nicely, and by using the gradient tool we've blended this darkening effect subtly with the rest of the photo – just like using a graduated filter on the camera. Often, a subtly blended mask will look more natural than 'hard' selections.

Photoshop File Edit Image Layer Type Select Filter 3D View Window Help
Adobe Photoshop CC

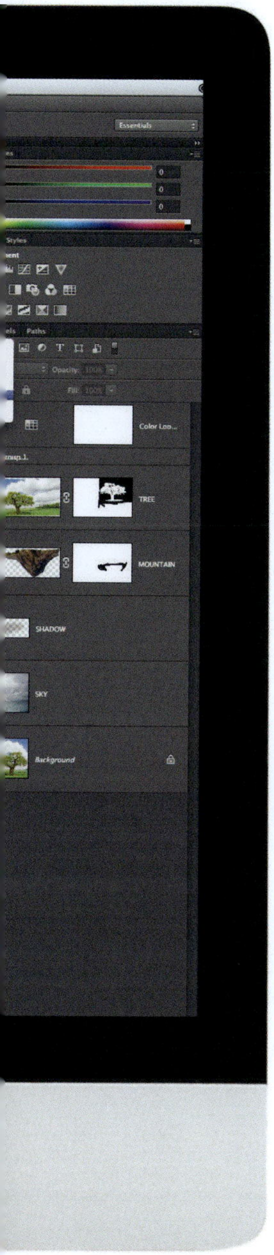

Get creative with layers

Discover how to enhance and transform your pictures using Photoshop's most powerful feature

Introducing the Layers panel

The Layers panel is central to most creative photo projects. Here's how to get to grips with this essential tool

When Photoshop appeared back in 1990, it lacked the ability to edit using layers. You could select and copy pixels from one image and paste them into another to create a montage. However, once you'd pasted an object, you couldn't reposition it later on. The composite image was flat.

It wasn't until the release of Photoshop 3.0 in 1994 that the Layers panel appeared. This revolutionised the way image editors could work. By pasting copied pixels onto a separate layer, you could reposition the layer's content at any time, and fine-tune the layout of your design with ease. You could also edit the colours and tones on individual layers, which provided more freedom and control.

Layers behave like a stack of transparent sheets. You can add content to each of the separate sheets in the stack, and see them from above as a composite image. In our annotated image we have a layered project that contains copied and pasted content from three separate source images. By placing the mountain and tree on individual layers, we can move, scale and transform them to produce an island levitating against an ocean backdrop on the background layer.

Layers can be modified to change the way they mix. Blend modes alter the way colours and tones in multiple layers combine. You can also mix layer content by changing a layer's opacity so that its pixels are translucent.

Photoshop Anatomy The Layers panel

Get to know the key features of the versatile Layers panel

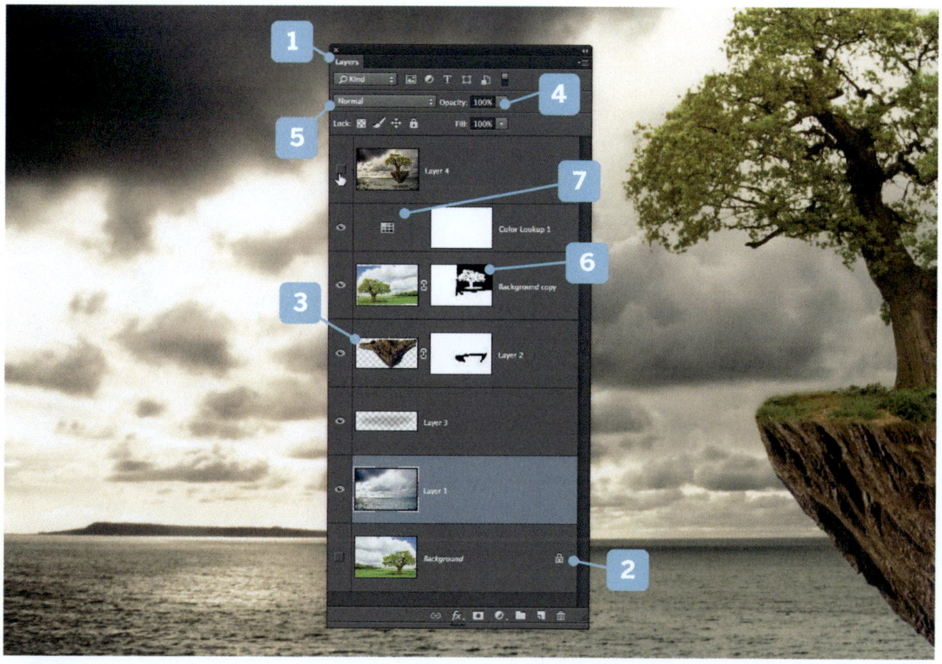

1 FLOATING PANEL

Like our levitating island, the Layers panel can float anywhere in the workspace so that it's closer to hand. Just click its tab and drag it out of the panel dock. You can drag it back to the dock later.

2 LOCKED LAYER

When you first open a photograph you'll see a single locked Background layer. You can double click the layer's thumbnail to unlock it, or select and copy its content onto a separate layer, as we've done here.

3 LAYER TRANSPARENCY

Each layer thumbnail provides a preview of the contents of the associated layer. Here we've copied a mountain and pasted it into this layer. The transparent sections of the layer are indicated by a pattern.

4 OPACITY

Once you've clicked a thumbnail to target the specific layer you want to edit, you can adjust its opacity to make it translucent. We reduced the opacity of Layer 3 to help the painted shadow overlap the ocean.

5 BLEND MODE

By changing Layer 3's Blend mode to Overlay, we were able to make the painted shadow darken the ocean's colours while preserving the lighter tones. This helps the shadow behave in a more realistic way. You'll use the Overlay Blend mode more than most others.

6 LAYER MASKS

By applying black to a layer mask you can hide the corresponding pixels on the attached layer. Here we've hidden some of the edges of the mountain to help it blend more effectively with the tree. White strokes on the mask enable you to reveal hidden content.

7 ADJUSTMENT LAYERS

These useful layer-based tools enable you to change the colours and tones on the layers below. You can click the eye icon on any layer or adjustment layer to turn the layer on or off. We'll look at adjustment layers in more detail in the next tutorial.

Understanding... LAYERS PANEL OPTIONS

To fine-tune the way the Layers panel looks and behaves, click this little fly-out icon [1] at the top right of the panel and choose Panel Options from the pop-up menu. The Layers panel Options window will appear [2]. For much larger and easier-to-recognise thumbnails, click here [3]. Or choose a smaller thumbnail size if you're editing a multi-layered project on a small display. It's usually worth setting Thumbnail Contents to Layer Bounds [4]. This causes the thumbnail to display the layer contents, like a small brush stroke, without showing all of the surrounding transparent pixels, which would make it harder to identify in the layer stack.

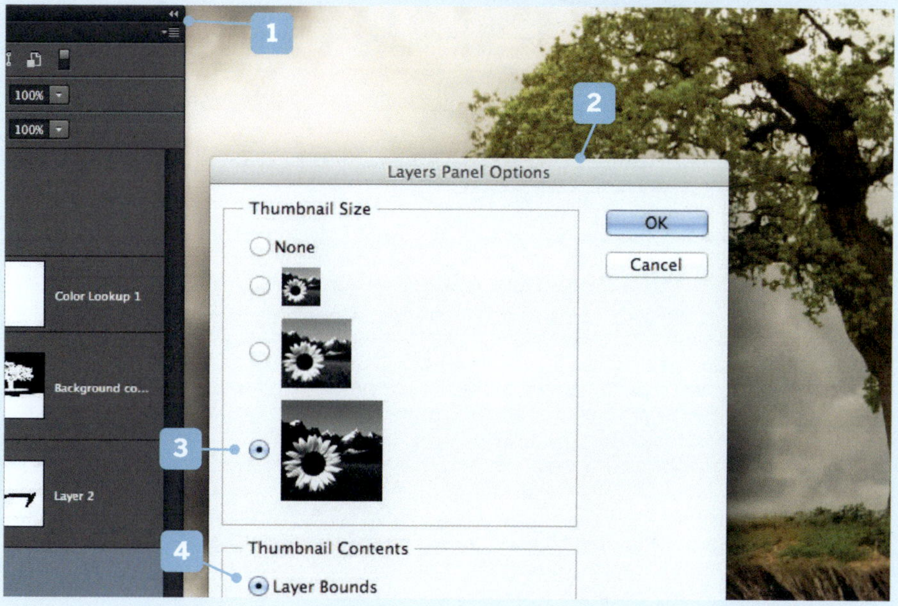

Transform tools

Distort, scale, rotate and even warp layer content with the Transform command's suite of tools

This lesson we look at a set of Photoshop tools that are designed to help you perform a wide range of everyday edits. All the Transform tools work in a similar way – they enable you to reposition some or all of the pixels that make up your image to produce a variety of results. The Transform tools are Photoshop's basic infantry. Each member of the Transform platoon moves a picture's pixels around, but in a variety of ways.

Stationed in the Edit›Transform menu, different Transform commands can be deployed depending on the task in hand. If you're compositing elements from one shot with another then you can use Transform›Scale to shrink a layer's components to fit the new background. You can change the angle of a layer's component using Transform›Rotate.

When you apply a Transform command, a bounding box will appear around the layer's content. Depending on the command, you can drag various control points to scale, rotate or distort the content to suit your creative requirements.

The Perspective tool mirrors the positions of the corner control handles to equally transform horizontal or vertical perspective. This enables you to correct perspectival distortion without rummaging around in the Lens Correction filter. We'll put the Perspective Transform tool through its paces later in this Tool School. The Distort tool lacks the constraints of the Perspective tool, enabling you to drag any of the bounding box's nine control handles to dramatically distort the layer's content.

To help you transform with more precision, you can refer to a collection of boxes in the Options bar. These show a variety of attributes like the Width or Height of the transformation or even the X and Y coordinates of the Transform command's central pivot point.

Take to the skies!

Create an action-packed aerial dogfight by combining a variety of cut-out images

By transforming your source files, you can alter the appearance of reality in really creative ways. By shooting the same two planes a few times, we were able to add them to separate layers and transform their scale, position and angle of rotation to create two warring factions engaged in a fight to the death.

We'll show you how to apply various Transform commands in our step-by-step walkthrough below. However, before you start to transform a plane you'll need to isolate it from its original background. Open an aeroplane photo and double click the Background layer's thumbnail. Grab the Magic Wand tool and set it to a Tolerance of 35. Tick Contiguous. Shift-click to select all bits of sky including those between the wings. Choose Select›Inverse. Click the Add layer mask icon to hide the blue sky. Paint with a black brush on the mask to remove any remaining blue sky pixels. Apply a white brush to the mask to restore any missing blue paintwork on the plane's tail. Right click the layer mask and choose Apply Layer Mask. Press Cmd/Ctrl+J to duplicate the layer. Use Filter›Blur›Motion Blur to add blur to the top layer. Paint on a new layer mask to blend the blurred plane with the original. Then choose Layer›Merge Visible.

Transform the layer content

1 Move transform

Once you've isolated your subject, choose Select›All and then Edit›Copy. Open an aerial background and then Edit›Paste the copied plane into it. Use the Move tool to drag it left and down. Add another aeroplane to the document.

2 Rotate transform

Use the Move tool to move it into position. Tick the Show Transform Controls option. Place the cursor outside the bounding box to activate the Rotate Transform tool. The cursor will change. Drag to rotate the plane −27 degrees. Hit Enter.

3 Scale transform

Click the corner handle to scale the plane. Hold down Shift to constrain the proportions and drag the corner handle to scale the plane by about 62%. Add and transform more aeroplanes using the same techniques.

Perspective transformations

Simple tips to correct perspectival distortion and straighten skewed edges

Most buildings have vertical walls that extend at a 90-degree angle from the ground. However, in some architectural photos the walls appear wider apart at the ground, but tilt inwards towards the top. These converging vertical lines are created by perspectival distortion. As you get closer to a building, you need to tilt your camera to get the top of the structure in shot. This increases perspectival distortion.

To avoid these converging vertical lines you could try shooting your subject from a more distant vantage point, so you no longer need to tilt the camera upwards. This will help the subject's walls to run parallel with the edges of the frame. Fortunately, Photoshop's Perspective Transform command enables you to counteract perspectival distortion.

However, by distorting the shot you can end up creating transparent areas in lower corners.

You can crop out most of these transparent edges or use the Distort command to stretch the edge pixels over them. See the tutorial below.

Vertical verticals

1 Extend the canvas

Open a photo of a building. Before we straighten the converging verticals, we'll need to make some space at the top of the frame. Go to Image›Canvas Size and increase the size of the canvas. Set the Canvas Extension Color to White. Click OK.

2 Correct perspective

Double click the Background layer. Choose Edit›Transform›Perspective. Drag the top left control handle left to straighten the top of the building. Drag the bottom left control handle right until the walls run parallel to the frame edge.

3 Crop and rotate

Crop the transparent areas at the bottom of the corrected image. Drag outside the box to rotate and straighten the wonky horizontal lines. Hit Enter. Finally, use Edit›Transform›Distort to fine-tune the edges of the frame.

Photoshop Anatomy Transform command

Here are the key Transform commands in action on the same rectangular shape

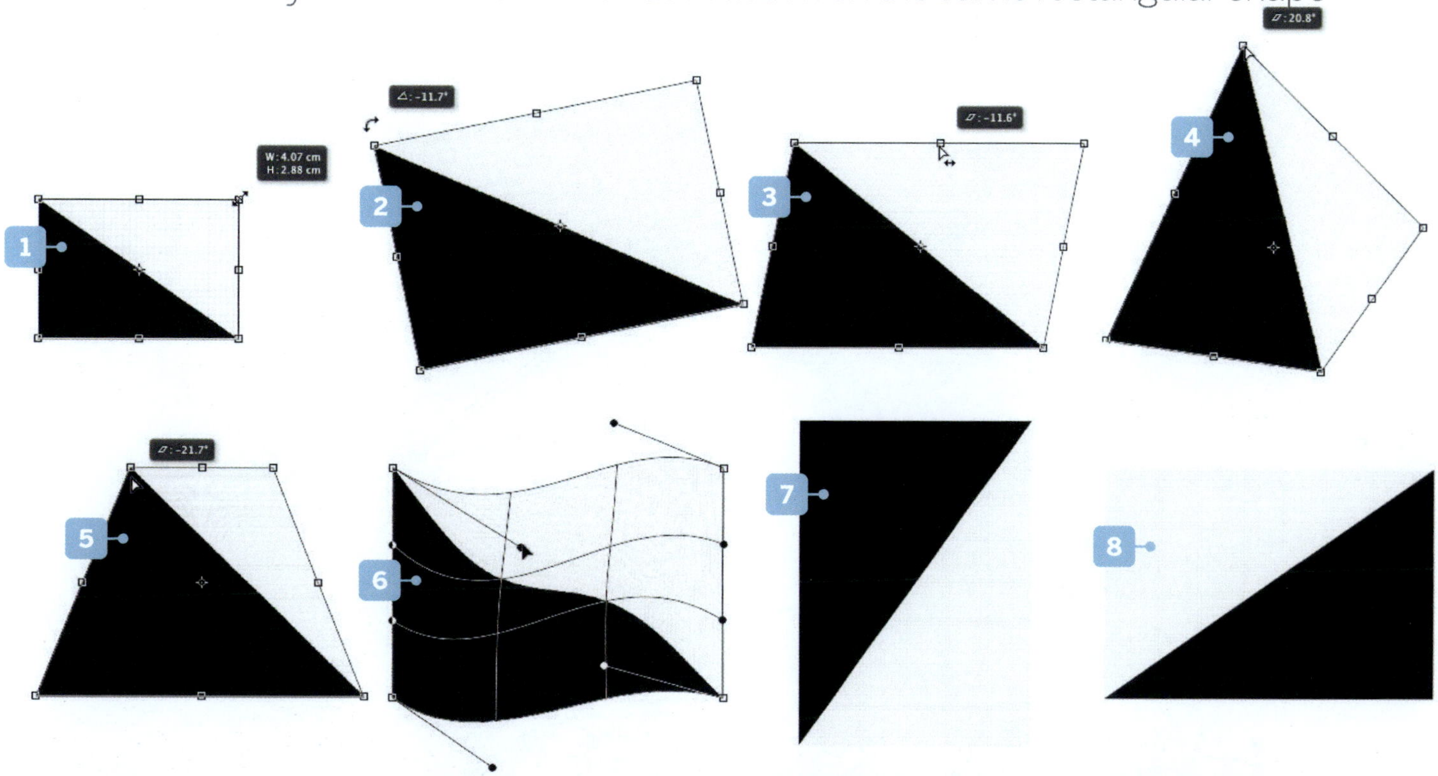

1 SCALE

Choose Edit>Transform>Scale and then drag a corner handle to shrink or enlarge a layer's content.

2 ROTATE

Choose Edit>Transform>Rotate. Drag outside the bounding box to rotate a layer's (or selection's) content.

3 SKEW

Choose Edit>Transform>Skew to activate this option. You can then skew the shape left or right.

4 DISTORT

Choose Select>Transform>Distort and then drag any of the box's control handles to move them independently.

5 PERSPECTIVE

Choose Select>Transform>Perspective. Drag a corner handle and the opposite handle will move by the same value.

6 WARP

Choose Edit>Transform>Warp. Drag the handles to curve the shape and produce organic-looking transformations.

7 ROTATE

There are three fixed value Rotate options. Here we've rotated the shape 90 degrees clockwise.

8 FLIP

The Edit>Transform>Flip command enables you to flip the shape horizontally or vertically.

Understanding...
THE TRANSFORM OPTIONS

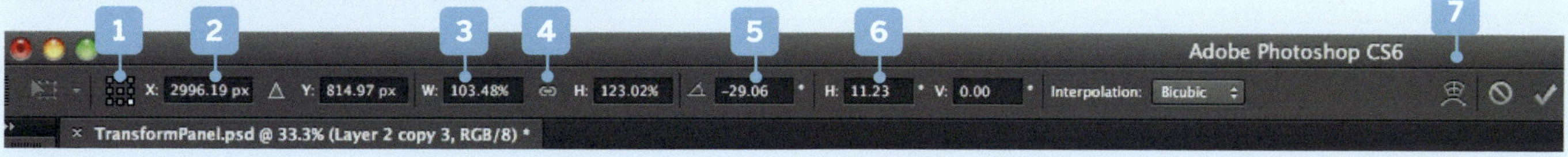

Each transformation occurs around a reference point that acts like a pivot. By default, this reference point is always located at the centre of any shape that you select. You can click the appropriate square here [1] to change the location of the reference point to pivot the shape from any of the corners, the top, bottom or side, instead of the centre. The X and Y fields [2] tell you the horizontal and vertical position of the transformed object's reference point. The W and H fields shown here [3] enable you to scale a shape's width and height with precision.

You can click the chain icon [4] to constrain the transformed shape's aspect ratio. This field [5] enables you to rotate a shape around the reference point by a precise angle. These H and V fields [6] enable you to use numerical values to skew a shape horizontally or vertically. Click here [7] to activate the Warp transform controls, if necessary.

Be creative with blending modes

Discover the special effects you can create in moments by mixing different images together using blending modes

The blending mode drop-down menu that sits near the top-left corner of the Layers panel is a powerful addition to the Photoshop user's toolbox. By changing the blending mode of a layer, you can alter the way that it interacts with the layers beneath it. This enables you to blend layers for creative effect, such as using an abstract texture to age an image. The image above was tinted and aged using a Hard Light blending mode to mix the colours and tones of a rusty metallic texture with a butterfly collage. We also used the Lighten blending mode to add a hint of fog to the canal background. As the following guide shows, there are 27 blending modes in total. We've applied each one to the same butterfly layer to show how it mixes the butterfly layer with the texture layer below. As you can see, there's a wide variety of effects to experiment with, and the results will vary depending on the contents of your layers.

Normal
The default mode shows every pixel on the layer normally, without any blending of the layers. This means that the layers below the butterfly layer have no effect on the butterfly.

Dissolve
Mixes translucent pixels from the top layer with colours and tones on the layers below. The butterfly's feathered edge is translucent, so the effect is most noticeable in these areas.

Darken
Lighter pixels on the top layer are replaced by the colours and tones from the layer below, while darker pixels remain unchanged. The darker rust from the layer below shows through.

Multiply
Multiplies colours in the top layer with those underneath. Colours on the top layer that are lighter (such as the butterfly's white patterns) are replaced with pixels from the lower layer.

Color Burn
This blending mode increases the contrast between the tones on each layer. Light pixels on the top layer make no change to the colours and tones on the layer below.

Linear Burn
Lowers the brightness of the layers underneath to reflect the colours of the top layer. As with Color Burn, lighter pixels on the top layer produce no change to the colours or tones on the layer below.

Darker Color
Examines the colour information and selects either the top layer's colour or the colours on the layer below – whichever is darker – as the resulting colours.

Lighten
Produces the opposite result of Darken. Any colours on the top layer that are lighter than the colours underneath will remain visible, such as the white streaks on the butterfly's wing.

Screen
Works out the inverse of the top layer's colours and multiplies it with those on the layer below. It tends to do the opposite of the Multiply mode and lightens tones.

Color Dodge
Causes lighter tones on the top layer to create more vibrant colours and increase contrast. Darker pixels on the top layer make no difference to the colours and tones on the lower layer.

Linear Dodge (Add)
Produces results similar to those created with the Color Dodge and Screen blending modes, but the brightening is stronger. Dark colours on the top layer make no changes to the colours below.

Lighter Color
This mode studies the total of the three colour channel values for the top layer and the layer below and then chooses the highest values from both layers to create the resulting colour.

Overlay
Provides a subtle way of adding a wash of the lower layer's colour to the top layer while preserving the lower layer's detail. Its handy for painting on brush-based shadow effects.

Soft Light
This blending mode darkens or lightens the colours of the top layer, depending on the colours of the layer underneath. If a pixel on the top layer is lighter than 50% grey, the pixel is lightened.

Hard Light
Multiplies or screens the colours of the top layer, depending on the colours of the layer underneath. If a pixel on the top layer is lighter than 50% grey, the pixel is lightened.

Vivid Light
Lightens or darkens the colours, but with more intensity than Soft or Hard Light. If the top layer is lighter than 50% grey, the image is lightened by decreasing the contrast.

Linear Light
Similar to Vivid Light, but adjusts the brightness rather than the contrast. If the top layer is lighter than 50% grey, the image is lightened by increasing the brightness.

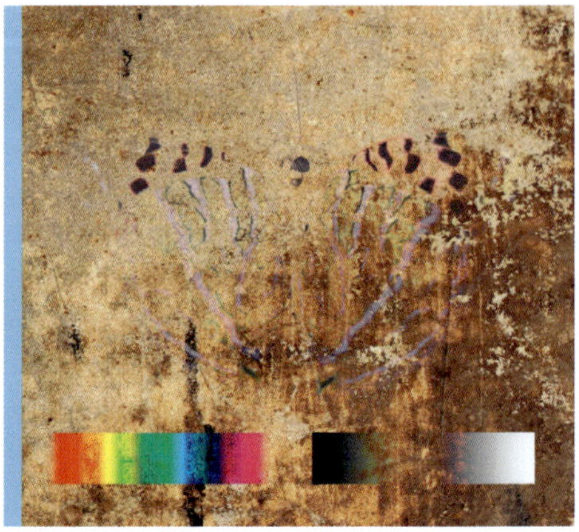

Pin Light
If a pixel on the top layer is lighter than 50% grey, and the pixels on the layer below are darker, then the top pixels are replaced by the ones below.

Hard Mix
Adds the red, green and blue channel values of the top layer to the RGB values of the lower layer. This changes the top layer's pixels to primary additive colours (red, green, or blue).

Difference
Lighter colours on the top layer are inverted, and darker colours are replaced by the pixels below. As you can see from the calibration bar, blending with black makes no change to the layer below.

Exclusion
This blending mode produces a similar result to the Difference mode, but with less contrast. Lighter colours on the top layer are inverted, and darker colours are replaced by the pixels below.

Subtract
Studies the colours in each channel and subtracts the colours in the top layer from the colours underneath. In 8- and 16-bit images, any resulting negative values are clipped to zero.

Divide
This mode examines the colours in each channel and divides the top layer's colours by the colours in the layer below. In the case of our butterfly layer, this creates lots of blown-out highlights.

Hue
Mixes the colours of the top layer with the luminance and saturation of the colours on the layer below. The butterfly's colours remain (although they shift in hue).

Saturation
Mixes the saturation of the top layer's colour with the luminance and hue of the colours on the layer below. In this instance we have a greyscale impression of the butterfly.

Color
This mode produces similar results to the Saturation blending mode, but mixes the hue and saturation of the top layer's colour with the luminance of the colours from the lower layer.

Luminosity
Mixes the luminance of the top layer's colour with the hue and saturation of the colours on the lower layer to produce a variation on the similar Hue, Saturation and Color blending modes.

Organise your layers efficiently

Work faster with your image layers using these easy techniques for keeping the Layers panel organised

When working on creative projects, you can build up a large collection of layers. This can lead to time wasted scrolling through multiple layers in search of specific content, especially if the layers have generic names such as Layer 1, layer 2 and so on. In this tutorial we'll offer you some housekeeping suggestions on how to organise your layers more effectively. We'll also demonstrate how to find layers according to attributes such as their names or assigned colour labels.

Any adjustment layer you add to the Layers panel will alter the colours and tones on all of the layers below it. You may not want to adjust every layer, though, so we'll show you how to restrict an adjustment layer to the layer directly below it, while preserving the colours and tones of other layers in the document. We've provided you with a layered document to work with, so you can put our tips into action to label, group and colour-code the layers as well as clip an adjustment layer to a specific image layer (or layer group).

Once you've created a layered document you may want to apply a creative filter to it. To do this you would normally have to flatten the multiple layers into one and then apply a filter. To get the best of both worlds, click the top layer and then press Cmd/Ctrl+Shift+Alt+E.

1 Name and label

Open Layer tips.psd. This layered document contains several image layers and an adjustment layer. Double click each image layer's label and rename it with a descriptive name such as Shade or Tree. Right click the thumbnail of a layer and choose a colour label.

2 Group the layers

Shift-click the tree and mountain layers to select them both. Go to Layer›Group Layers. This collapses the selected layers into a folder that takes up less space. You can toggle the folder open to reveal its grouped contents. You can drag other layers into a group folder.

3 Find by filter

Despite labelling and grouping layers it can still take a while to find a specific layer. At the top of the Layers panel, set the filter drop-down menu to look for attributes such as Color. Set the adjacent menu to choose a specific colour label. Only layers matching the attribute will be visible.

4 Make a clipping mask

Set the Filter back to Kind to reveal all the layers. Click the adjustment layer at the top. It's altering the colour of all of the layers below. To limit it to the group immediately below it, choose Layer›Create Clipping Mask. Now only the tree and mountain will be adjusted.

Add effects with Layer Styles

Enhance your photos with embossed text using a Layer Style to add simulated depth and lighting effects

Photoshop's Layer Styles enable you to enhance your images with a huge range of creative effects that are fun and easy to use. In this tutorial we'll chisel some text into the stony surface of our starting image courtesy of the Type tool, Blend modes and Layer Styles. You can adapt the technique to create your own custom greetings cards or poster text.

The Horizontal Type tool produces filled vector shapes that you can edit to change the font and characters, just as you would with a word-processing package. This gives you the freedom to tweak your text at any time, even after you've used Layer Styles to make it look like it's carved in stone. We've used the Emboss Layer Style to give the flat 2D text the illusion of depth. The interior of the text has a smoother granite pattern added to it to make the text easier to read. A Blend mode helps to mix the original stone with the granite pattern. You could also change the lighting of the Layer Style so that the shadows and highlights in the 3D text match the lighting in the source image.

In this tutorial we're only scratching the surface of what Layer Styles have to offer in relation to your creative projects, so experiment with other attributes in the Layer Styles panel to see the potential.

1 Type some text

Open TYCC91.jpg. Grab the Horizontal Type tool. Set the Font menu in the Options bar to a bold font such as Source Sans Pro. Set Size to 200. Set the colour to white. Type in some text. A text layer will appear. Press Cmd/Ctrl+T and drag to rotate the text at an angle. Hit Enter.

2 Set the Layer Style

Set the text layer's Blend mode to Darken. The white text will vanish. Click the fx icon at the bottom of the Layers panel to summon the pop-up list. Choose Bevel & Emboss. The Layer Styles window will open. Set the Style drop-down menu to Emboss. Set Technique to Chisel Hard.

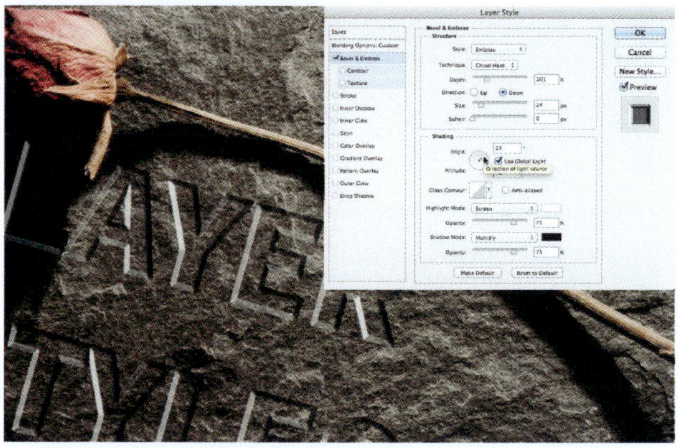

3 Dig deeper

Set the Depth slider to 261%. Click the Down Direction box. Increase the Size to 24 pixels. In the Shading section, set Angle to 23 degrees and Altitude to 48 degrees. This makes the shadows and highlights match the lighting in the source image.

4 Extra effects

Click the Inner Shadow attribute to activate and edit it. Set Distance to 59 and Size to 27. The direction of the lighting will match the settings used in the Bevel & Emboss section. Click Pattern Overlay. Set the Blend mode to Color Burn and opacity to 100. Use the Granite pattern.

Photoshop File Edit Image Layer Type Select Filter 3D View Window Help
Adobe Photoshop CS6
Size: 100
refine_edge_model.jpg @ 50% (RGB/8*)
Layers
Kind
Normal
Lock:
View:
Radius:
Smooth:
Feather:
Contrast:
Shift Edge:
Output
Amount:
Output To:

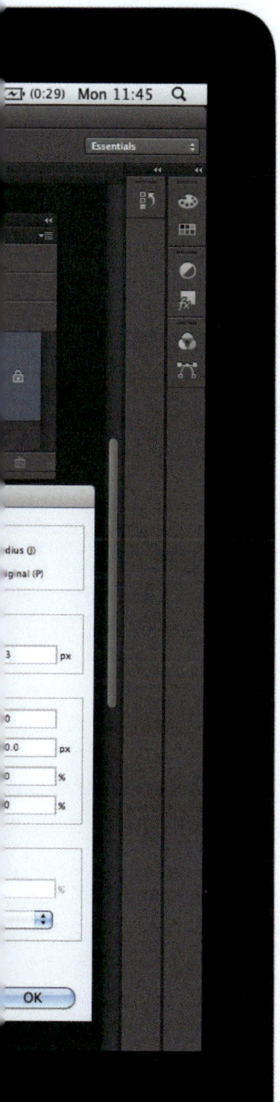

Making selections

Selections are the cornerstone of creative compositing. Learn how to make, modify and perfect them here...

The selection tools

Master the Quick Selection and Magic Wand tools to make detailed extractions from your images

In this Tool School lesson, we take a look at the many applications of the Quick Selection and Magic Wand tools. From replacing dull backgrounds to making faster selective adjustments, these nifty Photoshop devices will help you enhance your images and speed up your selection workflow.

The Quick Selection and the Magic Wand tools select pixels based on colour and tonal similarity, so they share the same Toolbox compartment. However, like any double act they have their own individual strengths. To start making a selection with the Magic Wand tool, you simply click an area to sample it. The tool will then select similar pixels based on the colours and tones that you first clicked.

By brushing the more intelligent Quick Selection tool over your subject, it will create a more complex selection marquee that attempts to include the subject's relevant details. In both cases, you can then use the Add to Selection and Subtract from Selection icons in the Options bar to refine your marquee even more.

The Quick Selection tool is best suited to selecting a single subject – for example, a person standing against a busy backdrop. Once you've made your selection, you can use the Refine Edge option to tweak its edge, turn it into a layer mask, or create an accurate cut-out.

The Magic Wand tool is great for ferreting out every bit of background sky, including those pixels hiding between the branches of a tree. You can modify its Tolerance so it selects a wider or narrower range of pixels with each click. This adjustable sensitivity is very useful. An evenly coloured and toned sky can be selected using a low Tolerance value. A more complex sky that features different colours and tones will need a higher Tolerance setting to select all of it.

Unleash the power of the Magic Wand tool

Select every bit of unwanted background with ease

Some shots – like our Bonsai tree here – have coloured backgrounds that you may want to select and replace. When set up correctly, the Magic Wand tool can tackle these sorts of selection challenges in just a few clicks.

As well as the New Selection option that gives you a basic marquee, there's also Add to Selection and Subtract from Selection. When zoomed in to your image, these incredibly useful tools will fine-tune your marquee, particularly around edges and in detailed areas.

Although small and seemingly insignificant, the Sample All Layers tick box shouldn't be overlooked. This facility ensures that your selection includes similar pixels on multiple layers, and not just the one currently targeted in the Layers panel.

If there are any patches of unwanted background sky hiding among the leaves and branches, then you'll need to clear the Contiguous box. This lets the Magic Wand tool off its leash, so it can track down the sampled colours in every part of the image. The final way to make the tool even more precise is with the Refine Edge button. This opens a new window with multiple options for feathering, smoothing and even shifting the marquee.

Get rid of unwanted backgrounds

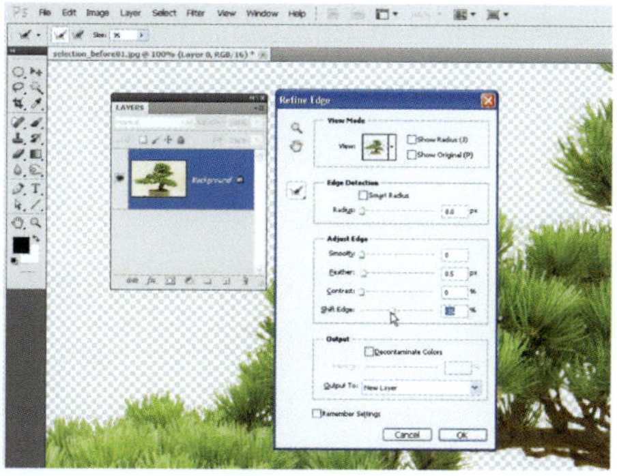

1 Choose your tool

Open an image you want to make a selection in. Grab the Magic Wand from the Tools Panel. Press W to toggle between it and the Quick Selection tool. In this image the background is evenly lit, so you'd leave the Tolerance on 31. Clear Contiguous.

2 Click to sample

Click any patch of background. The selection marquee should appear around all of that colour, even if it's in the branches. Choose Select›Inverse to select the tree. Click Refine Edge. Set the View drop-down menu to On Layers.

3 Delete the selection

The leaves are looking a little sharp and 'cut-out'. To soften things, set Feather to 0.5 pixels. To remove any background sky pixels clinging to the edge of the tree, drag Shift Edge to –16%. Set Output to New layer and click OK.

More advanced selections

Discover how to add fine details to your selections, like wispy hairs and eyelashes

The intelligent Quick Selection tool can work out what subject you're trying to select as you paint over it. If it does get confused, you can call on the help of the Add To and Subtract From icons in the Options bar to fine-tune the selection. Clever though it is, the Quick Selection tool can sometimes find it difficult to locate the edges of your subject. This is especially true if there's minimal contrast between the subject and the background, or if there's any softness to your subject caused by a shallow depth of field. It will also find it a challenge to include delicate edge details like hair and eyelashes – even if they are overlapping a uniformly plain white studio backdrop! For this portrait shot, we ran the Quick Selection tool over the white background and then inverted the selection so the marquee was around the model. However, by zooming in for a closer look at the selection we could clearly see that the marquee didn't include the model's eyelashes or her out-of-focus wispy hairs. So we used the Refine Radius tool to add these details to the selection. We then turned the refined selection into a layer mask so we could fine-tune it by applying brush tips to hide or reveal relevant details.

Including fine details in a selection

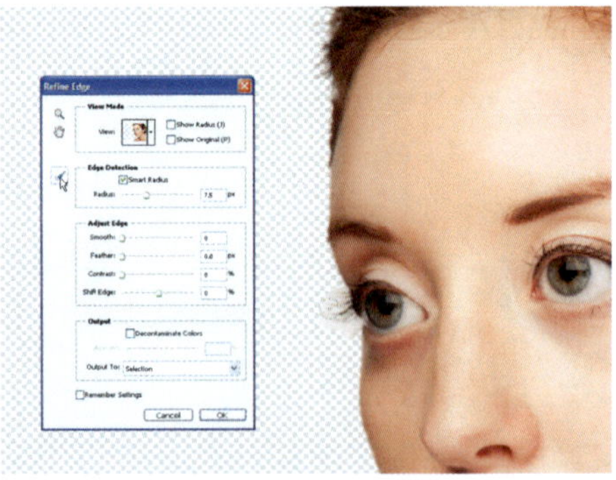

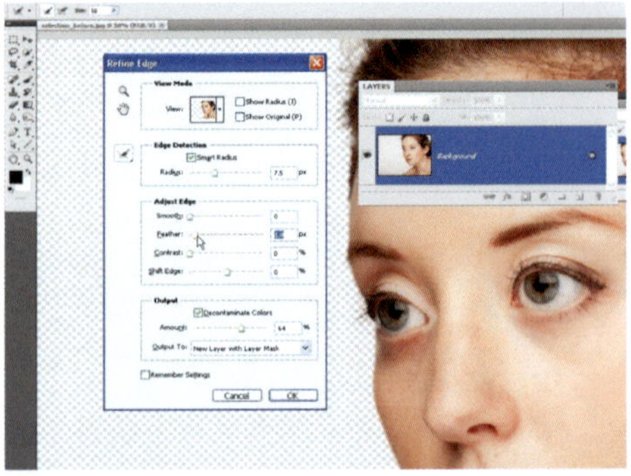

1 Create a selection

Open a portrait shot against a clean background. Use the Quick Selection tool to paint over the background. Tick Subtract from Selection and paint over the hairs. This creates a rough selection that also includes background pixels.

2 The Refine Edge tool

Hit Select›Inverse. Click Refine Edge and set View Mode to On Layers. To restore hairs and hide background pixels, tick Smart Radius. Slide it to 7.5. Tick the Refine Radius tool icon. Set Size to 60. Paint over edge hairs.

3 Fine-tune the selection

Set Contrast to 39. For a smoother selection, set Smooth to 10 and Feather to 1.4. Tick the Decontaminate Colors box and set Amount to 64%. Set Output to New Layer with Layer Mask and click OK.

Photoshop Anatomy Quick Selection options

There's a vast array of options at your disposal to create fast and accurate selections

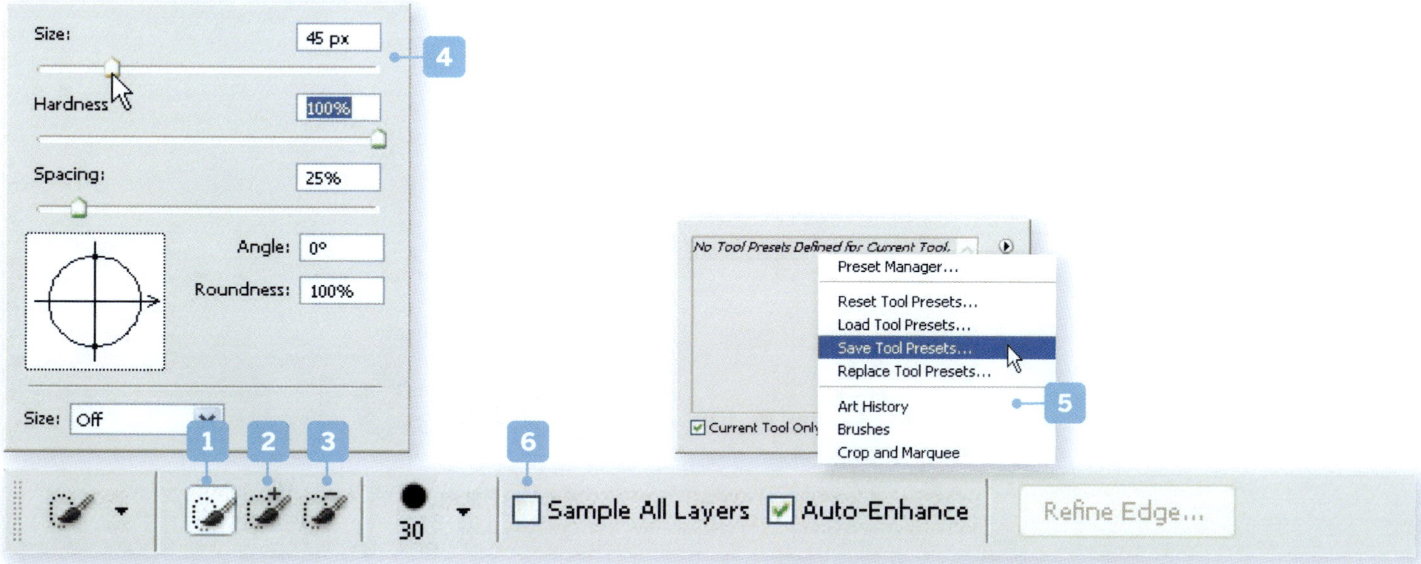

1 NEW SELECTION

Creates a selection marquee independent of any previous selections you may have made. With this highlighted, you can begin brushing over your subject.

2 ADD TO SELECTION

Once you've created your initial selection, the Quick Selection tool will automatically change over to this option that allows you to add further areas.

3 SUBTRACT FROM SELECTION

Enables you to remove unwanted areas from your selection. Select it directly from the Options bar, or hold down Alt to activate it.

4 BRUSH PICKER

Gives you access to options such as Diameter, Hardness, Spacing and Shaping that will customise the brush tip of the Quick Selection tool.

5 TOOL PRESET PICKER

The Quick Selection tool has no presets, but you can save your own for use on other images at a later date. Add tools with characteristics that can be saved.

6 SAMPLE ALL LAYERS

Check the box to sample pixels from all layers in the document; uncheck it to sample pictures only from the currently selected layer.

Understanding... REFINE EDGE

The Refine Edge button will give you a variety of choices for improving the work you've already done with the Quick Selection tool. The options found under the View Mode [1] heading will change how your selection looks in the main window. Edge Detection [2] is a recent introduction to Photoshop, and has several ways to select fine detail, such as fly-away hairs. This is a great way to effectively make a composite of your subjects onto new backgrounds, too. The Adjust Edge [3] options make sure that your marquee has no rough edges or other tell-tale signs that you've created a selection. The Output [4] heading contains several preferences for how to present your final edited selection, such as with a layer mask or as a new document. Click OK to finalise the selection.

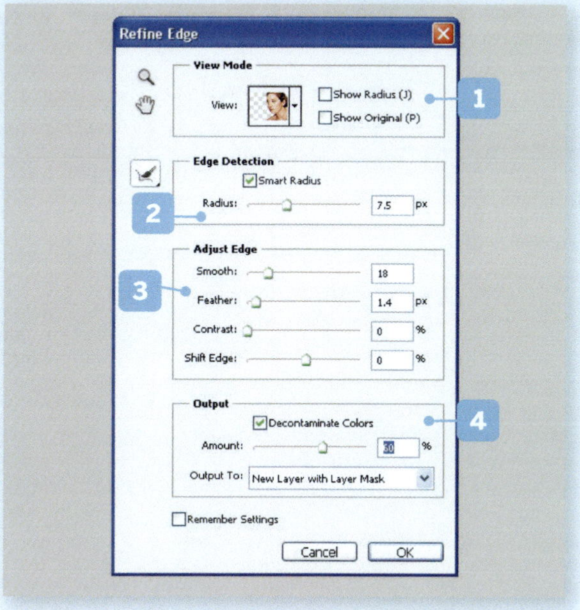

CHANGE THE SENSITIVITY

If the unwanted background areas of your image are fairly even in their colour and tone, then the default Tolerance setting of 32 should be sensitive enough to include every last part of it. However, if the background features a range of similar colours, like in a gradated sky, for instance, then increase the Tolerance value.

If you find that you end up selecting bits of your main subject as well, press Cmd/Ctrl+Z to undo the last selection that you made and choose a lower Tolerance setting. To make a smoother selection, keep the Anti-alias box ticked. ■

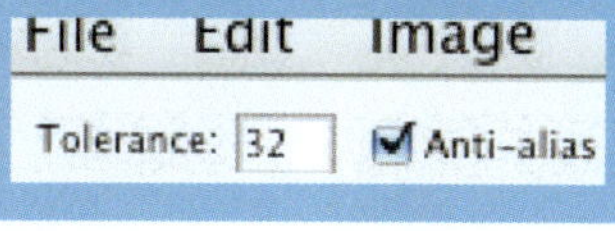

The Eraser tools

Create quick and effective composite images using the underrated powers of the Eraser tools

When faced with the challenge of selecting and replacing an unwanted background we're spoilt for choice thanks to Photoshop's comprehensive collection of tools. If you gave three Photoshop users the task of removing the clutter in our opening image's background you might see three different approaches.

To remove the sky, Photoshop user number one might reach for the Magic Wand to sample the sky pixels and then Shift-click to add other background details to the selection, and use Edit›Cut to remove the selected pixels.

Due to the complexity and variety of some of the background details, Photoshop user number two might decide to select the parrot instead of the background, using the Quick Selection tool. A few swipes of this brush-based tool would select most of the parrot, although some of the bird's feathered edges would elude the initial selection.

If Photoshop user number three moved his cursor over the Eraser compartment it might raise a few eyebrows. It's like using a saw when you need a scalpel, isn't it?

For most of us, the Eraser is probably the last tool we'd think of reaching for when faced with a compositing challenge of any complexity. However, in this Tool School we'll show you why the Eraser tool is capable of much more precise compositing tasks than you'd expect.

The Eraser tool comes in three variants. The standard Eraser enables you to modify options such as size, softness and flow. You use it to permanently remove unwanted pixels. The Background Eraser samples pixel colours and tones, enabling you to paint over the blue sky to remove it. The Magic Eraser tool isn't brush-based like the others. It works in a similar way to the Magic Wand, enabling you to select a range of similar pixels and delete them with a click.

Erase unwanted backgrounds

Get the Eraser tools to gang up so that you can select and delete unwanted backgrounds – or even just parts of them...

When you use any Photoshop tool to create an initial selection marquee it's unlikely to be a perfect selection. You may need to convert it into a layer mask (by choosing Layer›Layer Mask›Hide Selection) and then apply a black brush to the mask to remove any remaining bits.

Alternatively, you'd need to apply white strokes to the mask to restore details. Layer masks are non-destructive, so those hidden details are still available.

You may fear using the Eraser tool and its cousins – the Magic Eraser and the Background Eraser – because they don't create selection marquees that can be fine-tuned with masks, but instead permanently delete pixels.

By getting the three Eraser tool variants to work as a team, we can remove our unwanted background without worrying about fine-tuning selection marquees. Load an image similar to our parrot and go to the Layers panel (Window›Layers), then double click the Background thumbnail to unlock it. Press Cmd/Ctrl+J to duplicate the layer. You can then click the eye icon to hide the Background layer (and use it as a safety net in case you need to start editing from scratch).

How to cut out with the Eraser tools

1 First strike

Grab the Magic Eraser. Set Tolerance to 34 and tick Contiguous. Click to delete the blue sky. Reduce Tolerance to 24 and click to delete the cream and yellow background while preserving the similarly coloured white feathers.

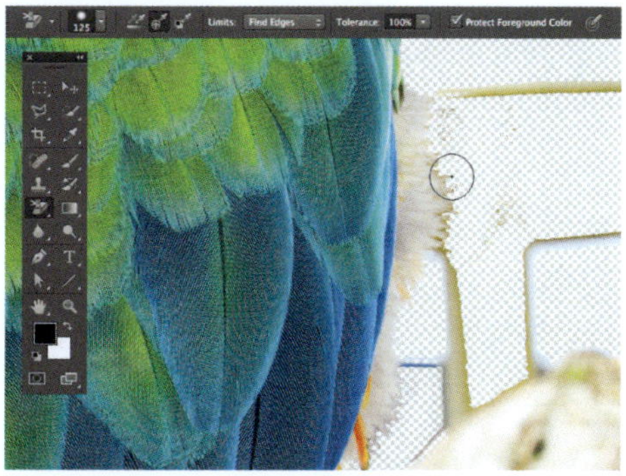

2 Erase the edges

Grab the Background Eraser. In the Brush Preset picker, choose a soft tip with a Size of 125. Tick Sampling: Once. Set Limits to Find Edges. Erase pixels adjacent to the white feathers. To erase less fine edges, set Limits to Discontiguous.

3 Get more control

Grab the Eraser tool. Remove any pixels that aren't adjacent to the bird's fine edges. To erase background pixels near the perch, hold down Shift and click to place a point. Click the cursor on another point and you'll erase in a straight line.

Background and Magic Erasers

Fine-tune the way your Eraser tools behave, and learn some new tricks and techniques

Each Eraser tool has its own strengths and weaknesses. The Eraser tool is a blunt instrument that creates pixel destruction wherever it goes, mopping up surviving pixels that have evaded the more delicate work of the other two Eraser tools.

The Magic Eraser performs a more targeted strike on unwanted background details. Give it the colour and tone of a large swathe of similar pixels and these areas will be erased with a click.

The Background Eraser is the most sophisticated member of the team. It combines the Magic Eraser's ability to recognise sampled colours and tones with the standard Eraser's editable brush-based properties, making it smart and powerful. In this section we'll show you how to get the Magic and Background Eraser tools to perform more effectively.

Each Eraser tool has its own icon. The Magic Eraser's irregularly shaped icon makes it tricky to place it on a precise spot. Because of the icon's shape, you may click to remove some sky but end up clicking the bird's beak by mistake. By pressing Caps Lock you can replace the default icon with a crosshair, enabling you to target pixels with much more precision.

Who's a pretty boy, then?

1 Draw a path

Grab the Pen tool. In the Options bar, set it to Path. Place anchor points around the bird. Once a rough path follows the parrot's outline, place a few points around the sides and top of the frame. Place the last point on the first to complete the path.

2 Sample the bark

Grab the Background Eraser tool. Set Size to 300. Set the sampling option to Continuous. Set Limits to Find Edges. Reduce Tolerance to 20%. Tick Protect Foreground Color. Hold down Alt and click to sample some of the bark.

3 Erase the path

Click the Direct Selection tool. Right click the image and choose Stroke Path. Set the Tool to Background Eraser. Click OK. This Eraser will erase the background pixels. Remove any remaining background with the Eraser tool.

Photoshop Anatomy The Eraser tools

Tweak tones with more precision by modifying the behaviour of these brush-based tools

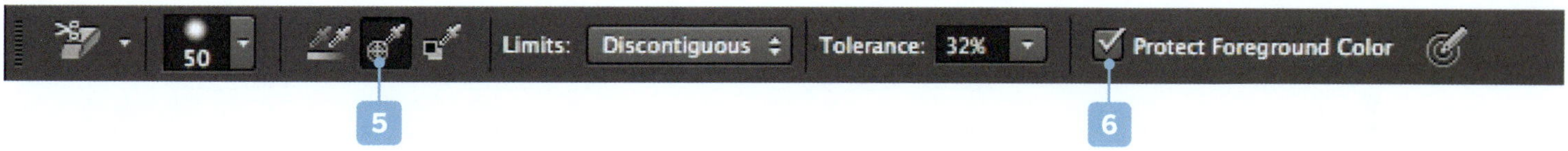

1 BRUSH PRESET PICKER

Click here to modify the hardness and size of the Eraser and Background Eraser tools. The Eraser tool also supports the new Bristle Brush presets.

2 MODE

When using the Eraser tool you can use this drop-down menu to change the Eraser type; from a soft brush to a sharp pencil to a square block.

3 FLOW

A lower percentage produces a weaker stroke, enabling you to build up your erasing in more controllable increments.

4 ERASE TO HISTORY

You can use this option to erase recent strokes with the Eraser tool. Read on below for more details on how to do this.

5 SAMPLING

You can set the Background Eraser to Sampling: Once and it will erase similar pixels, or set it to Continuous to erase a wider range of background details.

6 FORBIDDEN COLORS

This useful option stops the Background Eraser from erasing a particular colour. Alt-click to sample the colour you want to protect.

Understanding... THE HISTORY ERASER

Our parrot's feathers are a challenge to isolate. The Background Eraser may erase some of the feathers as well as the background. You can press Cmd/Ctrl+Z to undo the stroke and restore the feathers, but you may not notice the problem until much later. To restore key detail, you can summon the History Eraser. For this to work, you need to start your project by going to Window> History to open the History Panel [1]. Click the little camera icon to take a snapshot of the unedited image [2]. Use the Eraser tools to edit your image. If you make a mistake, click here to choose a history state [3]. You can then choose the Eraser tool, tick its Erase to History option, and paint over the missing pixels [4].

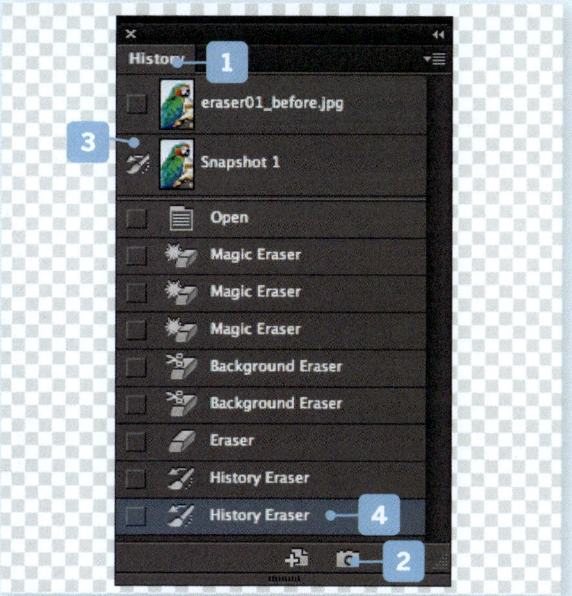

SOFTEN EDGES

The Background Eraser does a great job of deleting sampled background pixels while leaving contrasting foreground subjects untouched. However, when faced with delicate feathery detail that has a similar colour and tone to the background, you may create blocky edges. To smooth these problematic areas out, simply paint over them with the Blur tool to create a soft focus effect. ■

Photoshop's basic selection tools

Create and modify basic selections in your images using Photoshop's simple marquee selection tools

Many of Photoshop's tools and menu commands enable you to change the colours and tones in the entire image. However, in some cases you may need to alter the tones of a particular area without changing the image as a whole. You may also want to isolate a particular element from one photo and add it to another to create a composite image. This is where the selection tools come in handy. There are nine selection tools in the Tools panel, and in this chapter we'll show you how to put them through their paces so that you can find the right tool for any selection challenge.

The selection tools work in different ways, but they all produce a selection marquee – a straight or curved line made up of animated black-and-white dashes, which are often referred to as 'marching ants'. Think of a marquee as a fence that isolates the pixels within it from the rest of the image. You can then copy the selected pixels or change their colour or tone without altering pixels that fall outside the selection marquee.

The most basic selection tools are the Elliptical, Rectangular, Single Row and Single Column marquees. These tools share the same compartment. You can use them to make simple selections. We'll kick off by looking at these basic marquee selection tools and demonstrate ways to modify the shapes they produce so that you can make more complex selections. You'll learn how to add to and subtract from the basic shapes, and how to transform the shapes and soften their edges using the Options bar.

Photoshop Anatomy The marquee tools

Create a basic selection marquee and modify its shape

1 COMPARTMENT

Click this compartment and hold down the mouse button to access the four selection marquee variants. The Row and Column marquee tools produce instant vertical or horizontal lines that you can stroke to create guide lines, for example.

2 ADD OR SUBTRACT

By default the Rectangular and Elliptical marquees produce a primitive shape selection. By clicking these options you can get the tools to add to or subtract from the initial shape that they create, to make more complex selection marquees.

3 FEATHER

By default a selection marquee produces a clean, sharp edge. To create a softer edge to any selection marquee, increase the value in the Feather field. A softer edge enables copied pixels to blend more gently with their new neighbours.

4 STYLE

To create a perfect circle with the Elliptical Marquee tool, set the Style drop-down menu to Fixed ratio. You can also hold down Shift as you draw with the Elliptical Marquee to constrain the shape to a circle. If you choose Fixed Size you can type pixel values into the adjacent boxes.

5 ADD TO

Here we've used the Rectangular Marquee tool to draw two overlapping rectangles. We clicked the Add to selection box in the Options bar to make the rectangles intersect and create a new shape.

6 SUBTRACT FROM

Here we used the Subtract From icon in the Options bar to cut a smaller circular hole in a larger elliptical selection. If you place the cursor in the centre of a circular shape (such as the lens in this image) you can hold down Alt to make the marquee grow outwards from the central point.

Understanding... THE SELECT MENU

Once you've created a selection marquee you can modify the way it behaves using the commands in the Select [1] menu. The Modify commands enable you to expand or contract the selection by a specific pixel value. You can also decide to soften a selection marquee after it's been created by accessing the Feather command [2]. If you drag a selection with the Move tool then you'll move the pixels within the marquee. This handy command [3] enables you to reposition the marquee without relocating its contents. Refine Edge [4] makes light work of selecting tricky subjects such as models with wispy hair. We'll look at this command in detail later in this chapter.

How to use the Lasso tools

Round up a more complex selection of pixels in your photos with the Magnetic and Polygonal Lasso tools

On the previous pages we introduced you to simple selection tools such as the Rectangular and Elliptical marquees. These primitive selection tools are fine for selecting basic shapes, but not much help if you need to select more complex or irregularly shaped objects, such as the jagged mountain in our starting image. The Lasso tools are directly beneath the marquee tools in the Tools panel.

The basic Lasso tool enables you to draw a quick freehand selection marquee, which is good for making quick but rough selections. You have to make a freehand Lasso selection in one operation by clicking the mouse button, then holding it down as you draw. Once you let go of the mouse button the marquee selection is completed.

Some selection challenges require a lasso tool with more control, such as the Polygonal Lasso. To understand how this particular selection tool works, imagine you had some pins, a cork board and a piece of string. You can pin the string onto the board to create shapes. The string (marquee) between each pin (anchor point) will always be a straight line, but with lots of pins you can create curved shapes.

The final Lasso tool is the most powerful – the Magnetic Lasso. This behaves like a more intelligent Polygonal Lasso. The Magnetic Lasso also creates anchor points while making a selection, but as its name suggests, these are placed automatically as you draw freehand around the edge of the object you want to select. Here we'll demonstrate how to use the Magnetic and Polygonal Lasso tools to select a mountain.

1 Open the image

Open TYCC86.jpg. The Mountain has jagged edges, but you can make a quick selection using the Magnetic Lasso. Click the new Selection icon in the Options bar. Set Width to 5 pixels. This stops the tool's anchor points from straying too far from the edge of the mountain.

2 Start drawing

There's plenty of contrast between the edges of the mountain and the sky, so leave Contrast at 10%. Drop Frequency to 36 to reduce the number of anchor points placed by the tool. Place a point at the base of the mountain and start drawing along the edge.

3 Delete wayward anchor points

As you follow the edge, an anchor point may go astray. Move the cursor near the last anchor point and hit Backspace to delete it. Continue to draw your selection. If you hold down the space bar you can temporarily summon the Hand tool and drag to reposition the image.

4 Complete the path

Don't worry about being too accurate because you can modify the selection using other lasso tools. To turn the path and its anchor points into a selection marquee, place the last point on the first. The 'marching ants' will appear.

5 Trim the selection

Grab the Polygonal Lasso tool. Click Subtract from selection in the Options bar. Place points that trim some of the marquee from the sides of the mountain. Place the last point on the first and you'll create a narrower, more triangular-shaped selection marquee.

6 Save the selection

We'll use the mountain as part of a surreal composite in the next chapter, so choose Select>Save Selection. Name the selection 'Mountain Selection'. Tick New Channel. Click OK. We'll reactivate this saved selection in our creative tutorial. Save the file as a Photoshop document.

Intelligent selection tools

Isolate more complex objects using tools that use colour and tone differences in the image to create selections

You can make quick, rough selections by manually drawing a marquee using the Elliptical or Rectangular Marquee tools. Alternatively, you can use manual selection tools such as the Polygonal Lasso tool to select more irregularly shaped subjects such as a jagged mountain. The Tools panel has a third compartment containing the intelligent selection tools. Tools such as the Magic Wand tool enable you to make selections based on similarities in colour and tone, so you can select large areas such as skies with a few clicks. This tool is handy for instantly hunting out bits of sky between tree branches. The Magic Wand tool shares its Tools panel compartment with the Quick Selection tool. Like the Magic Wand tool, the Quick Selection tool recognises changes in colour and tone, making it the perfect choice for selecting contrasting objects.

Like the Magic Wand tool, the Color Range command also selects pixels based on their colours. With the Magic Wand tool you can select the sky and then delete the marquee to leave the tree, but this may also delete leaves and fine branches. The Color range command gives you a useful greyscale preview that enables you to see precisely which areas are part of the selection, as you'll see in our walkthrough.

All these tools make a 'marching ants' style selection marquee that defines the locations of the selected pixels. By experimenting with the selection tools you can work out which tool will be the most appropriate when dealing with a particular selection challenge. In this walkthrough we'll isolate a complex tree from a busy background by combining a range of intelligent selections tools and techniques.

1 Make a selection

Open TYCC87.jpg. One way to make colour-based selections is to choose Select›Color Range. The sky contains a range of blues, so leave the Select menu set to Sampled Colors. Click the eyedropper on a patch of sky. Set the Selection Preview drop-down menu to Grayscale.

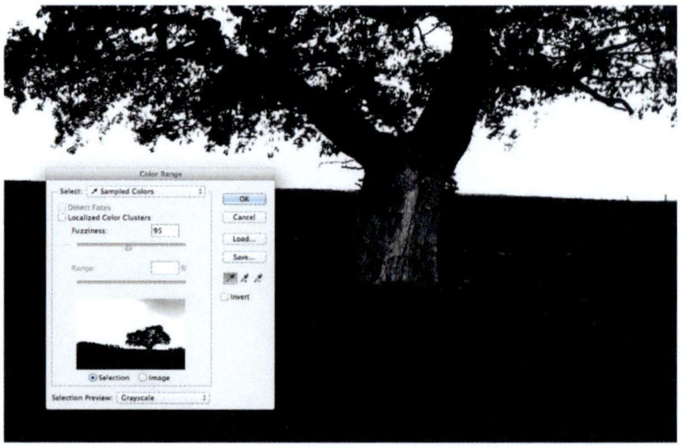

2 Modify the selection

Hold down Shift and click the eyedropper to add more patches of sky to the selection. We want all the sky to look white so that it's selected. To turn the tree and its leaves black, drag the Fuzziness slider to around 95. If necessary, Shift-click to add more patches of sky to the selection.

3 The Quick Selection tool

Click OK. To add the field to the selection, grab the Quick Selection tool from the Tools panel. Click the Add to selection icon in the Options bar. Paint on the field to extend the marquee into it. Click the Subtract from selection icon and paint to undo any mistakes.

4 Delete the selection

In the Layers panel, double click the Background layer's thumbnail to unlock it. Choose Edit›Cut to delete the selected sky and field. This leaves the tree and its complex leaves isolated against a transparent background. Press Cmd/Ctrl+D to remove the marquee.

5 The Magic Wand tool

Now we'll show you an alternative technique so that you can decide which method you prefer. Choose File›Revert to restore the image to its original state. Grab the Magic Wand tool and click the New Selection icon in the Options bar. Set Sample Size to 3 by 3 Average.

6 Adjust the options

Set Tolerance to 52 so that the Magic Wand selects a wide range of colours, given the variety of blues and whites in the sky. Keep the Contiguous box cleared. Click to select a patch of sky, then hold down Shift and click to add more sky and clouds to the selection.

7 Fine-tune the selection

Grab the Quick Selection tool and click the Add to Selection icon in the Options bar. Paint over the field to add it to the marquee. Click the Subtract from Selection icon and paint over the green vegetation at the base of the tree to remove it from the selection, just like we did in step 3. You've now selected the tree using an alternative intelligent selection tool.

8 Make a layer mask

We could delete the sky as we did in step 4, but to give us more editing options we can turn the selection into a non-destructive layer mask. Double click to unlock the background layer. Choose Layer›Layer Mask›Hide Selection. The marquee converts into a black-and-white mask.

BEFORE

Master the Pen tool

Isolate a complex object from a busy background using the mighty Pen tool – it's easier to use than you think!

As we mentioned earlier in the chapter, digital images are made up of millions of tiny square pixels. These building blocks of colour and tone combine to create the illusion of reality. Pixel-based images are called bitmaps.

Photoshop also enables you to produce content from scratch using tools such as the Pen tool. This tool enables you to draw graphic components for design projects (such as an icon or logo, for example). The Pen tool uses mathematics to describe the vector shapes that it produces. A vector shape consists of a series of anchor points. Between these moveable points are curves that you can bend to change the filled vector shape. The vector shape's mathematical nature enables you enlarge a shape without any drop in quality, whereas a bitmap photo can look a bit fuzzy if you enlarge the image.

The Tools panel also has a collection of other vector-based tools such as the Rectangle and Polygonal tool, which provide primitive shapes that you can modify to enhance your graphic designs. The Custom Shape tool provides you with a number of preset shapes that you can use to complement your design projects.

As well as creating colour-filled shapes for designers, the Pen tool can also be used to create paths to help photographers edit images. Pen-produced paths can be converted into selection marquees.

In our walkthrough we'll demonstrate how to modify the Pen tool's curves and anchor points to select the curved contours of the sports car in our starting image. You'll then be able to use the selection to protect the car while you clone out distracting background objects that overlap its edges.

1 Open the image

Go to File›Open and browse to TYCC61.jpg. Click Open. The JPEG file will open in the standard Photoshop editor. There are a few distracting elements in the background that we couldn't avoid capturing, but we can remove them with the Clone Stamp tool to create a cleaner scene. However, to avoid cloning over the car we need to isolate it. Click and hold the mouse down over the Pen tool's compartment and select the Pen tool.

2 Choose paths, not shapes

To make sure the Pen tool draws a path and not a filled vector shape, go to the Options bar and choose Path from the drop-down menu. Untick the Auto Add/Delete box. Press Cmd/Ctrl and the + key to zoom in. Click to place the Pen tool's first anchor point where the rear wheel intersects the chassis. Click to place a second anchor point near the first. A straight line (or path) will join the two points together.

3 Curve the path

As you place a third anchor point, click the mouse button and drag at the same time. This summons two bezier curve handles that enable you to create a curved path between the two anchor points. Don't worry if the curved path doesn't follow the edge of the car perfectly because you can fine-tune it later. Click to place a fourth anchor point and drag the curve handle to keep the path curving around the edges of the car.

4 Tight or loose

To draw a path around the sharper angles of the car's bumper, place a few points closer together. Once you get to the longer sweeping curves at the top of the car, click to place points further apart and drag to make the path follow these curved contours. The more confident you get with the Pen tool, the wider apart the anchor points can be. The bezier curve handles enable you to select complex curved shapes more quickly.

5 Close the path

Keep clicking to place more anchor points around the edges of the car. Try to be more precise when placing points along the top and sides of the car, but feel free to place more rough-and-ready points where the lower section of the car overlaps the grass because we won't need to clone out details in these parts of the image. To complete the path, place the last anchor point on the first one you started the path with.

6 Tidy up the path

At this stage, the path won't be perfect. To refine it, click and hold down the mouse button on the compartment below the Pen tool. Choose the Direct Selection tool. You can now drag any of the path's anchor points to fine-tune their positions. Drag the bezier control handles of an anchor point to adjust the adjacent curved path so that it follows the contours of the car more effectively.

7 Turn the path into a selection

To select fiddly edges you may need to use the Add Anchor Point tool and click to insert more anchor points into the path. You can then use the Direct Selection tool to tweak the positions and bezier curve handles of the new points. Once the path follows the top and sides of the car, click the Pen tool icon. Go to the Options bar and click the Make Selection button. Set Feather Radius to 1.0. Click OK. A selection marquee will appear.

8 Clone out the background

Choose Select›Inverse to select the sky instead of the car. Grab the Clone Stamp tool. Choose a soft round tip from the Brush Preset picker with a Size of 200. Alt-click a patch of sky to sample it. Paint around the top and sides of the car to extend the sky over the unwanted people. The path-shaped selection will protect the car's edges from being cloned. Sample and paint grass to create a clean horizon.

Quick Mask edits

Fine-tune a selection marquee quickly and intuitively by using a brush in the Quick Mask editing mode

After making an initial selection with one of Photoshop's marquee tools, you may need to tweak the shape of the marquee to select your subject more effectively. You can use the Add to or Subtract from icons in the Options bar to change the way the active selection tool behaves. Alternatively, you can adjust existing selections by using the Select menu's Modify commands to expand or contract the selection around the edges of the subject.

The Select›Modify commands are useful when fine-tuning the selection overall, such as giving it a feathered edge, but for more control you can try editing it in Quick Mask mode. A Quick Mask replaces the selection marquee with red colour. By manually painting with a black or white brush on the mask you can add to or subtract from the selected areas until the selection has been improved. The temporary Quick Mask mode is a close cousin to the permanent layer mask. It's a great way to check that your selections are complete.

1 Make a selection

Open TYCC88.jpg. Grab the Magic Wand tool. The model's dress is a similar colour to the backdrop, so reduce Tolerance to 23 and click Contiguous to make the tool only select areas that are connected to the sample section. Shift-click to add all the background to the selection.

2 Activate Quick Mask

To remove parts of the dress from the selection, press Q to turn the marquee into a Quick Mask. Unselected areas appear as red patches. Grab the Brush tool. Choose a hard round brush tip from the Brush Preset picker. Set the foreground colour to black by pressing D for default.

3 Edit the Quick Mask

Paint over any areas of the dress that should be excluded from the selection. These areas will turn red as you paint. To remove the edges of the dress from the selection, hold down Shift and click to place points. The Brush tool will draw a straight line between each point.

4 Modify the marquee

Press X to switch the foreground colour to white. Now you can paint to add bits of backdrop to the selection (such as the area near her elbow). The red patches will disappear, indicating a selected area. Press Q to exit Quick Mask mode and see the modified selection marquee.

Refine Edge

Get perfect selections every time, no matter how complicated the subject, with the powerful Refine Edge tool

Many photo-fixing tasks involve making selections. You may need to select a specific part of an image, such as a bland sky, and replace it with something more interesting, or tone down an over-exposed sky without altering the correctly exposed landscape. Alternatively, you might want to cut out a model from an image, so that you can composite her into a new background image. The Tools panel contains several selection tools, from the handy but basic marquee tools to the intelligent Quick Selection tool. The selections these tools create are demarcated by a border of animated dashes. However, it's unlikely that the edges of a selection you make will be perfect, and the Refine Edge dialogue enables you to fine-tune its shape, width, position and softness.

When you make a selection using tools such as the Rectangular Marquee or Magic Wand, you'll notice that the Refine Edge button becomes active in the Options bar. The button will also appear if you make a selection using menu-based commands such as Color Range. As a rule, if a tool creates a selection marquee you'll be able to fine-tune it with Refine Edge. You can also call up the Refine Edge dialogue by choosing Select›Refine Edge, and you can use it to fine-tune the edges of a layer mask.

Before the Refine Edge tool was introduced, to fine-tune a selection marquee you had to go to the Select›Modify menu and apply refinements one at a time. The most useful of these were Smooth, Expand, Contract, and Feather. Refine Edge presents all these options in an easy-to-use window, enabling you to apply them interactively and preview the results. There's also a Radius slider, for adjusting the width of the edge over which refinements are applied. Refine Edge has many more tricks up its sleeve, as you'll discover...

Replace a background

Use Refine Edge to blend a subject into a new background

When you're shooting public events, you have little control over your subjects' movements. In this image, the naturally posed soldier looks good in profile, but the partially obscured vehicle and figure in the background are distracting. We could have repositioned ourselves to cut out the background clutter, but the main subject might have moved by then. Thanks to selection tools and layers, we can isolate the soldier from the background, and improve the composition by dropping in something more interesting from another photo taken at the same event.

When you select a person or object, they can look obviously 'cut out' because they have a hard edge, and by feathering the edge of a selection you can make a subject blend in more naturally and effectively with the new background, to create a more convincing composite. We'll show you how to soften an initial selection using Refine Edge, and how to ensure that no tell-tale pixels from the original background are left clinging to the outline.

Kick off by opening a picture containing a figure. Choose the Quick Selection tool, tick Auto-Enhance, and brush over the figure to select him. You can now fine-tune the selection by following the steps below...

Create a seamless composite

1 Soften the edges

After selecting the figure, click Refine Edge in the Options bar. Choose the On Black preview, so that you can see the traces of background pixels. Set Smooth to 11 and Feather to 2.5 to soften the edges, and set Shift Edge to –15%.

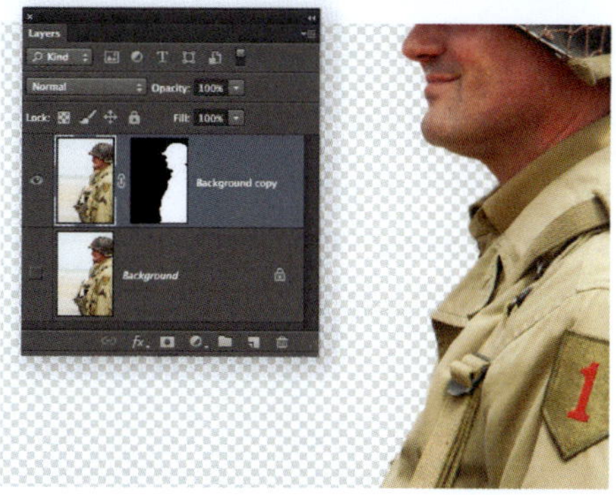

2 Decontaminate

Tick Decontaminate Colors, and set Amount to 45%: this shifts colours of the background still clinging to the subject's edge closer to those of the subject, so they're less noticeable. Set Output to New Layer with Layer Mask. Click OK.

3 Add a new background

Open a new background image. Go to Select›All, then Edit›Copy. Target the main document, go to Edit›Paste, and move the layer below the subject. Choose Filter›Blur›Gaussian and set an appropriate Radius to make the images match.

Challenging selections

Select complex edge detail, such as fine hair, using Refine Edge's Radius options

Some subjects have a mix of edge detail, with both sharp, well-defined areas and softer, fine details. Take our studio-shot model, for example: the outline of her arm and shoulder is nice and sharp, while her flyaway hair is much more complex and fine. We can select the studio backdrop easily enough using the Magic Wand tool, but if we use Refine Edge to Feather or Expand the selection to include more hair detail, we run the risk of adding unwanted background pixels to the well-defined edges.

The Radius slider in Refine Edge enables you to adjust the width of the edge over which refinements are applied, but in older versions of Photoshop you could only adjust the Radius of the entire outline. In CS5, a Smart Radius option was added, and when you enable this the edge radius will be adjusted automatically to take account of the detail in different areas, so it'll be narrower where edges are sharp, and wider where edge detail is less well-defined. For even greater precision, you can manually target problematic areas using the Refine Radius tool, which enables you to adjust the radius in localised areas with a brush. See the tutorial below...

Selecting complex edges

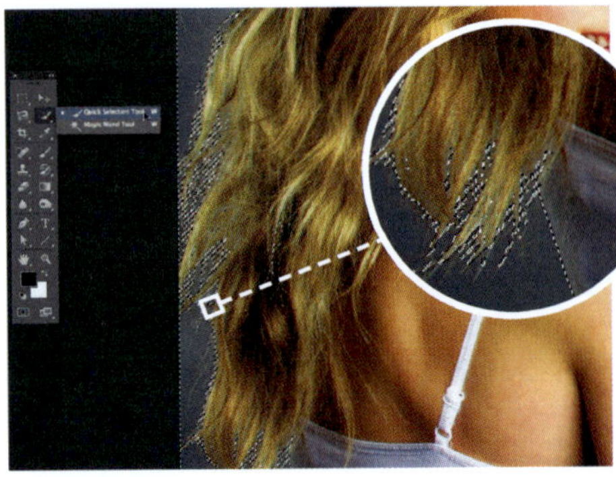

1 Make a selection

Choose the Magic Wand tool, set Tolerance to 20 and clear Contiguous. Click the backdrop to select it. Next, take the Quick Selection tool and click the Subtract from selection button. Brush over the background to remove it from the selection.

2 Refine Radius

Click Refine Edge, and set View to On Black. The selected hair will look sharp and jagged. Tick the Smart Radius box, and set Radius to 3 pixels. Click the Refine Radius icon. Set the brush Size to 100, and brush around the edges of the hair.

3 Clean up the colours

To hide the remaining hints of backdrop, tick Decontaminate Colors and set Amount to 60%. Set Output to New Layer with Layer Mask, and click OK. You can now paste in a new backdrop, and you'll see that the hair has been preserved.

Photoshop Anatomy Refine Edge options

Get even more from Refine Edge with our close-up look at its editable options

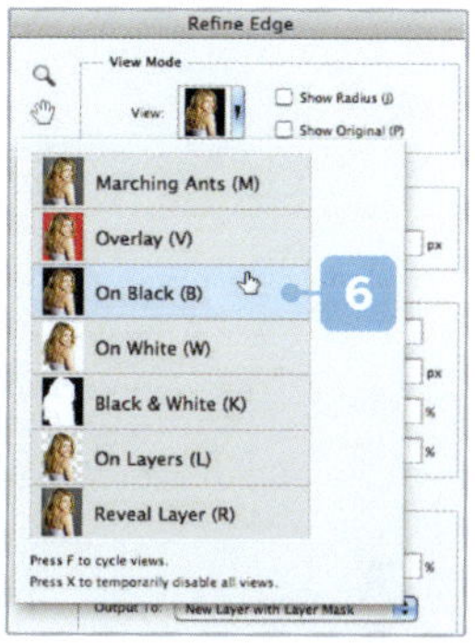

1 SMOOTH

When you select an object, its edges may include jagged or blocky clumps of background pixels. Use this slider to smooth out the edges.

2 FEATHER

Increase the Feather value to soften the edges of the selection. This will help a selected subject blend more effectively with its new surroundings.

3 CONTRAST

Increases the contrast between partially selected pixels, like increasing the contrast between light grey and dark grey areas of a layer mask.

4 SHIFT EDGE

This slider enables you to strike a balance between revealing edge details and hiding fringes of unwanted background pixels.

5 LAYER MASK

If you output your refined selection as a New Layer with Layer Mask you can continue fine-tuning it by applying white or black brushes to the mask.

6 POINT OF VIEW

Choose the View option that best enables you to see the edge pixels, for example On Black if you're trying to select blonde hair.

Understanding... EDGE DETECTION

Many selection subjects, especially people, have outlines that comprise both hard and soft edges. The Edge Detection section [1] of the Refine Edge dialogue enables you to select varied edges more effectively. If your subject's edges vary in softness, tick Smart Radius [2]. This automatically increases the width of the edge over which refinements are applied where required. Click and hold the brush icon [3] to access the Refine Radius tool. This enables you to brush over areas to increase the edge width. If the tool reveals unwanted background pixels, use the Erase Refinements tool [4] to make the edge narrower again. Click Show Radius [5] to display the radius. ■

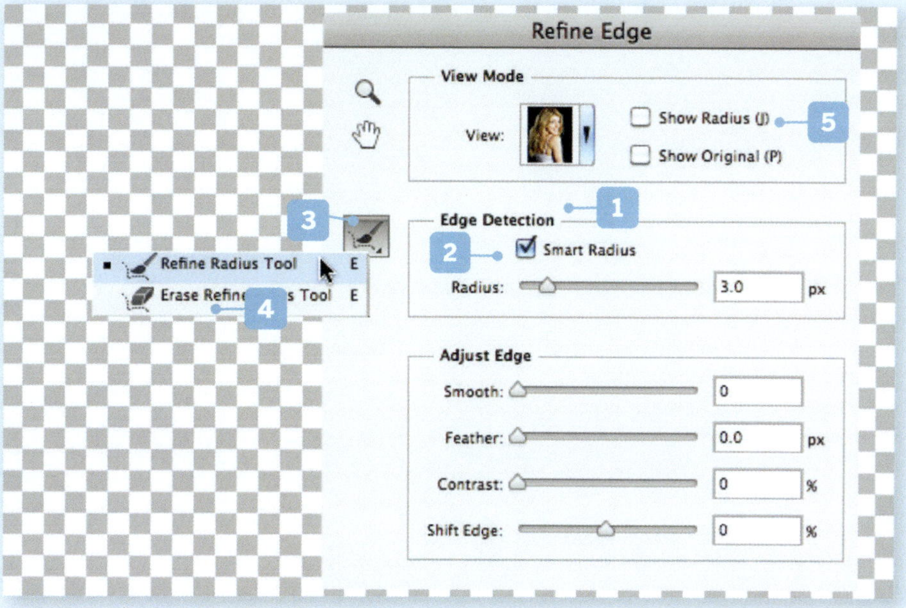

Photoshop File Edit Image Layer Type Select Filter 3D View Window Help
Adobe Photoshop CC 2014
X: 5125.50 px Y: 4961.00 px W: 100.00% H: 100.00% 4.11 H: 0.00 V: 0.00 Interpolation: Bicubic
flying01.dng @ 25% (RGB/16)
flying02.dng @ 31.6% (Layer 1, Layer Mask/16) *
walkthrough.psd @ 36% (Layer 6, RGB/16) *
Layers
Kind
Normal
Lock:

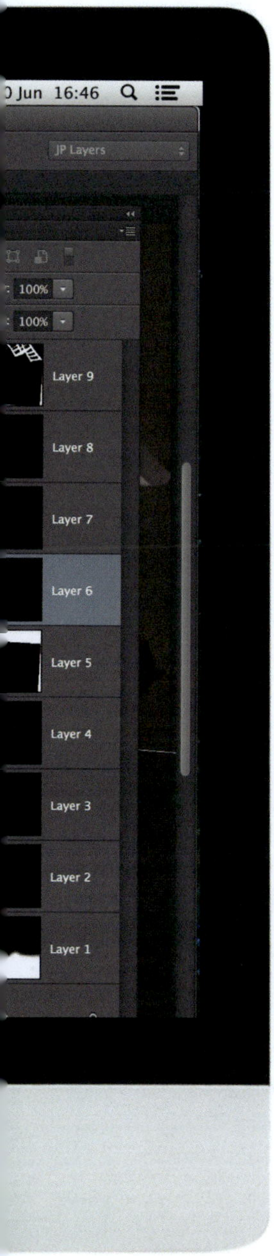

Masks and montages

Discover how to take more control over your selections and adjustment layers using layer masks

Introducing layer masks

Combine selected parts of images non-destructively using layer masks, so you're free to refine the selections at any time

Photoshop has plenty of tools that enable you to select parts of images based on properties such as colour or tone. In the case of our starting image, we have a basic sky that can easily be selected with a few clicks using the Magic Wand tool. After selecting the unwanted sky we could double click the background layer to unlock it and then choose Edit›Cut to remove the sky. We could then replace the original sky with something more interesting, such as a dramatic cloudscape. After cutting out the sky they will be permanently deleted from the image layer. If it turns out that you've also selected and deleted the edges of a building, then you won't be able to recover those deleted details. However, by converting a selection into a layer mask you can hide unwanted areas on the attached image layer without permanently deleting them. This enables you to restore missing details from your image layer.

Layer masks turn a selection into a black-and-white image. The white part of the mask makes the corresponding pixels on the attached image layer 100% solid. The black sections of the mask make the associated pixels 100% transparent. You can then paint with black or white on the mask to change which pixels are visible and which are hidden, which enables you to refine the results of any selection tool until they are perfect. Unlike the Edit›Cut command, layer masks are non-destructive. This makes them the key tool in making more effective selections and producing convincing composite images.

Photoshop Anatomy Layer masks in action

Hide or show details on an image layer in a non-destructive way

1 SELECTION TOOL

To select the sky in the starting image, grab the Magic Wand tool from the Tools panel. By holding down Shift you can click and select most of the sky's similar-looking pixels as a 'marching ants' marquee.

2 HIDE SELECTION

After selecting most of the sky you can hide the unwanted pixels by choosing Layer>Layer Mask>Hide Selection. This attaches a black-and-white layer mask to the original Background image layer that hides the selection.

3 TRANSPARENCY

Once you turn a selection into a layer mask, the masked (or hidden) pixels are replaced by a chequerboard transparency pattern. You can then drop another image layer into the background to replace the sky in these transparent areas.

4 LAYER MASK

After converting a selection into a layer mask, the black parts of the mask hide the corresponding pixels on the attached image layer. In this case the sky is being hidden. The white parts of the mask make the unselected buildings on the image layer solid.

5 MODIFY THE MASK

In this example the Magic Wand has failed to select all the sky, so some blue pixels remain after the mask has been created. By painting with a black brush on the layer mask you can hide the remaining unwanted pixels.

6 REVEAL DETAIL

If you want to restore any pixels hidden by the selection tool's initial layer mask, set the Brush tool to white and paint. Hidden details will be revealed. Press X to toggle between a white and black brush to show or hide the pixels until you're happy with the mask.

Understanding...
MASK OPTIONS

If you right click a layer mask, a pop-up menu will appear. Here you can disable the layer mask to see the layer's original pixels. A red X will appear when the mask has been disabled [1]. You can turn the mask back on using the Enable Layer Mask command [2]. If you choose to apply the layer mask [3] it will disappear and replace the masked black pixels with transparent ones. In effect, you would be deleting the unwanted image elements permanently. You can also use the powerful Refine Edge command to soften the mask or expand its area of influence [4]. We'll cover this tool later.

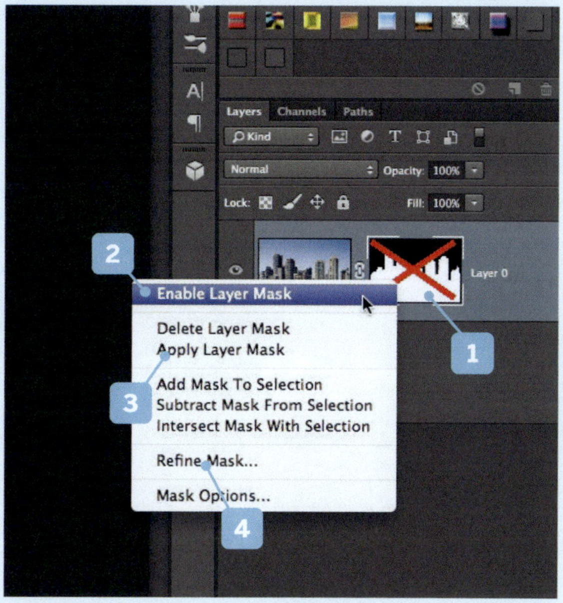

PAINT LAYER MASKS FASTER

You're not limited to simply painting on a mask with a black or white brush to hide or show pixels. You can quickly hide or reveal larger areas by making selections with other tools. In our annotated screen grab above we used the Brush tool to paint black on the mask to hide the remaining traces of sky. Alternatively, we could have used the Rectangular marquee tool to select the sky at the top. We could then click the layer mask to target it and choose the Edit>Fill command to add black to the selection. This would hide the remaining sky more quickly than painting over it. It also ensures that you don't miss the corners, which is easy to do when using a brush, especially if the opacity is set to less than 100%.

Make better layer masks

Create more effective composites and selective adjustments by adjusting the properties of your layer masks

Photoshop CC has a 'Select and Mask' option that enables you to refine and improve existing layer masks with rough or pixelated edges. In fact, it offers tools that you might be familiar with from the Refine Mask option in previous versions.

To show you how this works, we've created a layered image montage combining this travel shot with a new and more interesting sky on the layer below – to try this out yourself, load up the TYCC102.psd sample file.

This Select and Mask dialog can be used to modify an existing selection, or to make a new one from scratch. In our example image here, we're using the Quick Selection tool to select the blank blue sky in the top layer (it's quicker than trying to select the more complex foreground) to create our layer mask. It works well enough along the hard edges of the building, but not quite so well around the irregular outlines of the trees on the right-hand side.

With the Select and Mask dialog, though, we can not only preview the new layer mask, but also modify it as we work.

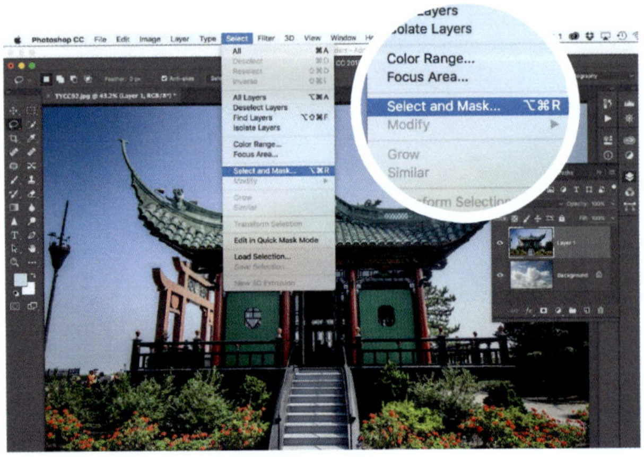

1 Select and Mask

We've opened our sample image and you can see the two layers in the Layers panel on the right side of the screen. We need to mask out the blue sky in the top layer so that the new and more interesting sky underneath shows through. The Select and Mask command is on the Select menu...

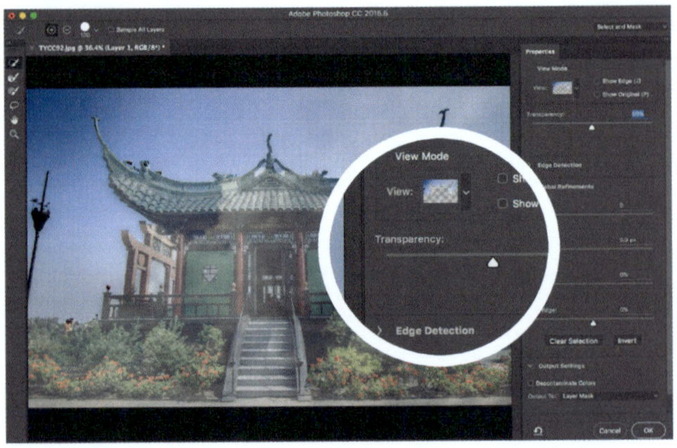

2 Use the Transparency setting

You can use the Transparency setting near the top of the Properties panel to show both layers at once. This can help you see which areas you need to be masking. We're using the Quick Selection tool to select the sky – we can then invert this selection to select the building instead.

3 Check the edges

Once the sky selection is complete, we click the Invert button in the Properties panel to switch the selection to the building. The edges around the roof and walls look fine, but the selection hasn't worked well in amongst the branches of the trees alongside – we need to fix that.

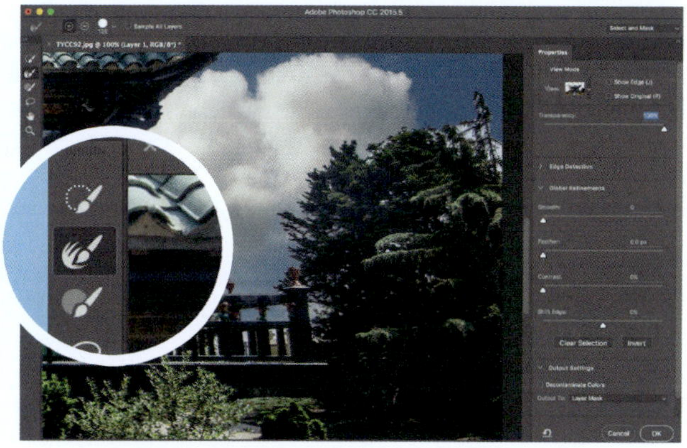

4 Refine Edge Brush tool

To do this, select the Refine Edge Brush tool from the small toolbar on the left of the window. Now just brush over the problem areas to refine the selection. If the selection still looks unnatural, try dragging the Shift Edge slider to the left to reduce fringing.

Make a surreal portrait

Discover how to shoot and combine a series of frames to create a seamless mid-air self-portrait inspired by Dali

For this tutorial we set out to shoot a mid-air self-portrait inspired by an image of Salvador Dali, taken by one of the greatest portrait photographers, Phillippe Halsman. Halsman captured Dali mid-air among flying cats, canvas, chairs and a plume of water. 28 attempts were needed before the combination of flying objects looked right, with everything having to be cleared and reset after each attempt. Here, rather than doing it all at once, we'll show you how to capture several levitating objects separately, then combine the frames in Photoshop using simple masking and selection skills. To shoot images for this effect, use a tripod and keep the focal length, focus point and exposure consistent. We used a remote trigger to fire the shutter. For lighting, we set the speedlight to act as a slave, then synced the camera to a studio flash. After shooting the portrait, we captured other objects in mid-air, flagging the light to match the mid-air shot.

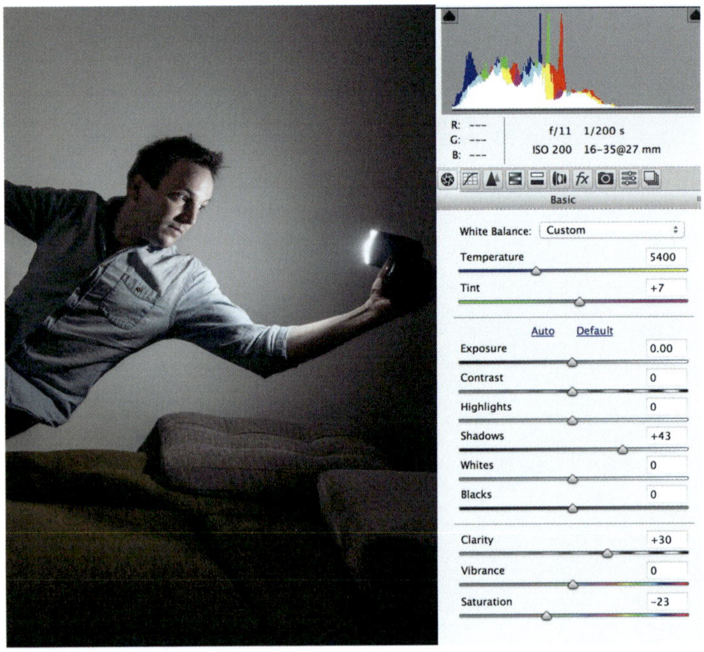

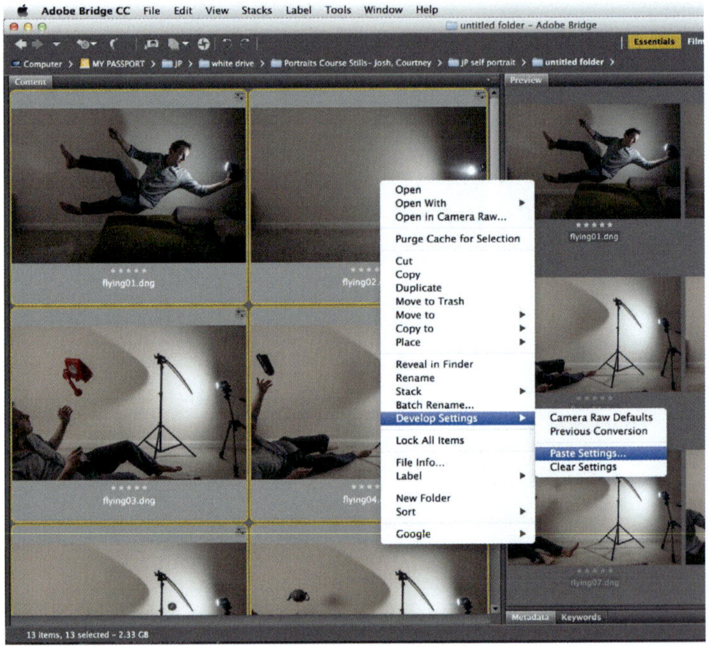

1 Adjust in Raw

Once you've captured all the objects, you're ready to combine them in Photoshop. Begin by opening Adobe Bridge, then navigate to the flying object files. Double click the image of the falling person to open it in Camera Raw. Set Temperature 5400, Tint +7, Shadows +43, Clarity +30, and Saturation -23. Click Done to save your settings.

2 Paste settings

Back in Bridge, right click the same image and choose Develop Settings›Copy Settings. Next, hold down Cmd/Ctrl and click to select all the other files that you're going to use for the composite. Right click over them and choose Develop Settings›Paste Settings to give all the images the same adjustments you made to the first image.

3 Copy the layer

Highlight the flying01 and 02 images in Adobe Bridge, then hold down Shift and double click them to open them directly into Photoshop. Grab the Move tool, check Auto Select Layer and Show Transform Controls. Hold down Shift and drag the falling man up to the tab of the other image, then down in to copy it over and align.

4 Mask cushions

Click the Add layer mask icon at the bottom of the Layers panel, then grab the Brush tool and set the active colour to black using the swatch in the Tools panel. Using a soft-edged brush, paint over the sofa cushions scattered on the floor in the bottom left corner of the image to hide them, revealing the empty background scene on the layer below.

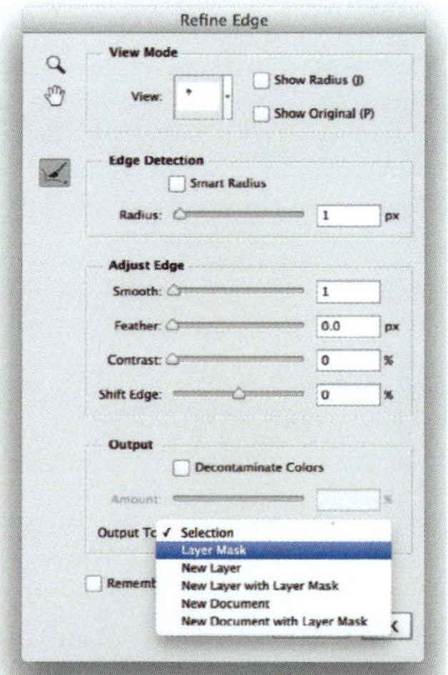

5 Refine the edges

Open one of the mid-air objects into Photoshop, then grab the Quick Selection tool from the Tools panel. Paint over the object to select it (hold down Alt to subtract from the selection if it goes wrong). Click Refine Edge and set Radius 1px, Smooth 1px, and use the other sliders to improve the selection. Choose Output to: Layer Mask and click OK.

6 Add objects

Grab the Move tool and use it to drag the object into the main image. Position it wherever you like. If you need to rotate or resize it, hit Cmd/Ctrl+T, then use the bounding box (hold Shift while resizing to constrain the proportions). Be mindful, however, of the way the light hits the objects, and try to keep it consistent with the main image.

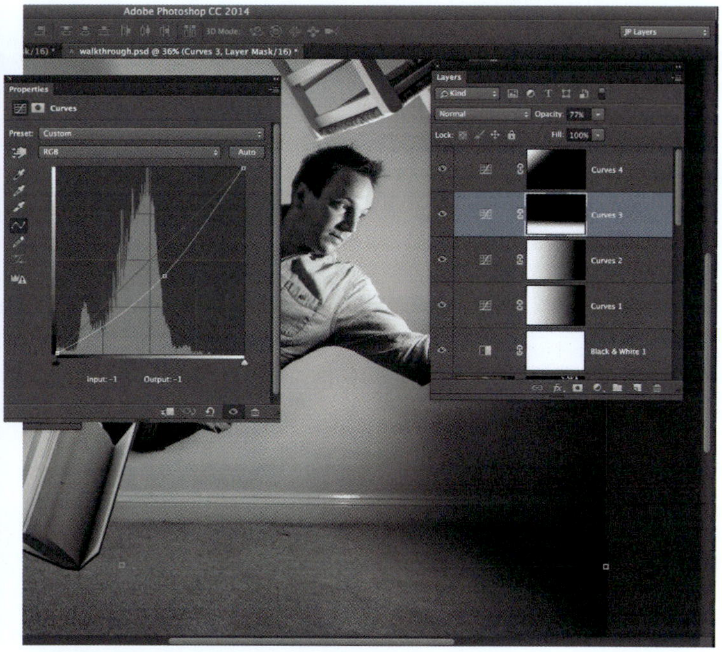

7 Convert to monochrome

Add more objects in the same way. Once you're happy with the arrangement of the objects, highlight the top layer, then click the Create adjustment layer icon and choose Black and White. Adjust the colour sliders to fine-tune the brightness of the individual colours to get the look you're after, or click Auto for Photoshop to do it for you.

8 Darken the image

Click the Create adjustment layer icon and choose Curves. Drag down the curve line to darken the image, then grab the Gradient tool. Press D to reset the colours, then choose the Foreground to Background gradient preset. Drag up from the bottom to darken it. Use separate curves layers to darken the top left corner and lighten the left side.

Paint with filters

Learn how to transform any photo into a work of brush-based art with a simple combination of filters and layer masks

In this tutorial we'll show you how to transform your photos into paintings, complete with brush strokes and watercolour borders. We'll begin by using a neat trick with Photoshop CC's Camera Raw filter to smooth out the detail of the original image (if you have an earlier version, open the image in Camera Raw via Bridge to apply the settings in step one). Then we'll apply a combination of filters on several duplicates of the original layer to give our portrait a painterly look, using blending modes to combine each effect. Once done, we'll add a layer mask and use the Wet Media brush set to create brush strokes. It's quick, easy, and it works even if you can't paint! Open paint_before in Photoshop. Go to the Layers panel (Window›Layers) and press Cmd/Ctrl+J to duplicate the background layer. Rename the layer Camera Raw filter. Go to Filter›Camera Raw, then click the Detail Panel on the right-hand side. Set Noise Luminance to 100, and Detail to 35. Now proceed to step one.

1 Make copies

Click OK to exit Camera Raw. Back in Photoshop, press Cmd/Ctrl+J three more times to make three duplicates. Name the first one Cutout, the one above Median, and the top one Glowing Edges. Click the eye icons to hide the top two layers and highlight the Cutout layer. Naming the layers makes it easier to see what you've done later.

2 The cutout filter

Go to Filter›Filter Gallery. Click Artistic and choose Cutout. Press Cmd/Ctrl+0 to zoom out to see the entire image in the preview window. Set Edge Simplicity to 4, and Fidelity to 2, then experiment with the Levels slider. Click OK to apply, then click the blending mode menu at the top of the Layers panel and choose Luminosity.

3 The Median filter

Highlight and reveal the Median layer by clicking the eye symbol, then go to Filter›Noise›Median. Set the Radius to about 12 pixels. Change the blending mode to Soft Light. Set Cutout to 22% opacity and Median to 50% opacity. Highlight and reveal the Glowing Edges layer.

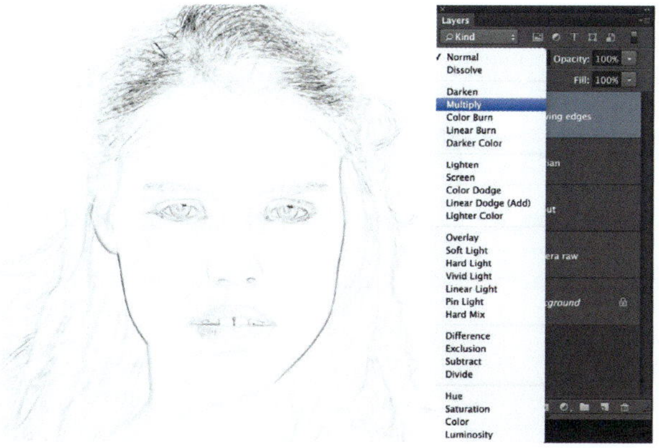

4 Glowing edges

Go to Filter›Filter Gallery. Choose Stylise›Glowing Edges and set Width to 3, Brightness to 7, and Smooth to 5. Next press Cmd/Ctrl+I to invert the tones, then Cmd/Ctrl+Shift+U to desaturate the entire image. Finally, change the blending mode to Multiply in the Layers panel.

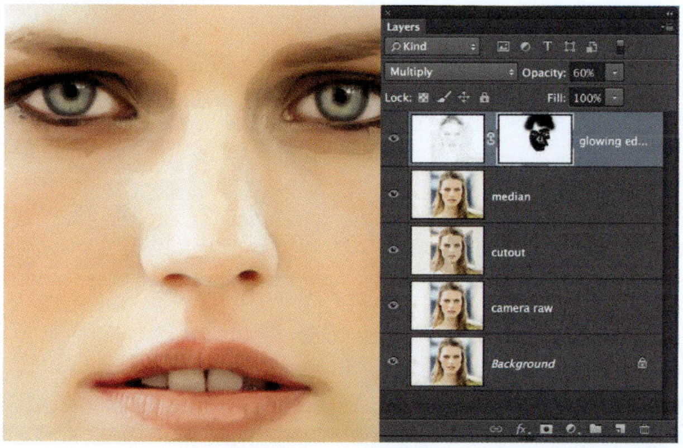

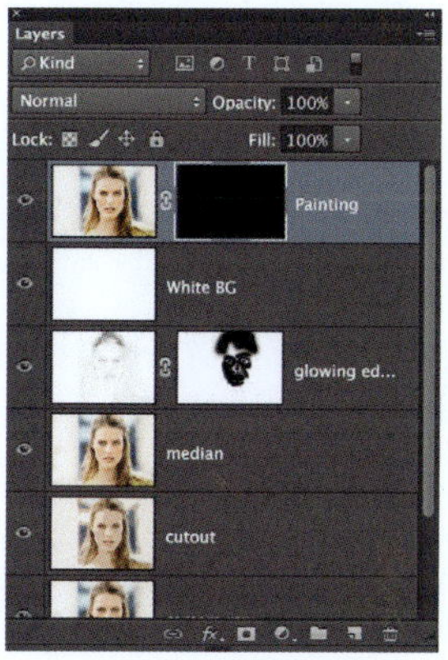

5 Hide messy edges

Click the Add layer mask icon, then grab the Brush tool and set the colour to black. Paint on the mask to hide the sketch effect over the hair and in any places where it looks a little messy. Press Cmd/Ctrl+Shift+Alt+E to merge a copy of all the layers. Name it Painting.

6 Hide the layer

Hold down Cmd/Ctrl and click the New layer icon to add a layer below the selected layer. Go to Edit›Fill, choose Use: White and click OK. Name the layer White BG. Highlight the Painting layer, then hold down Alt and click the Add layer mask icon to add a full black mask.

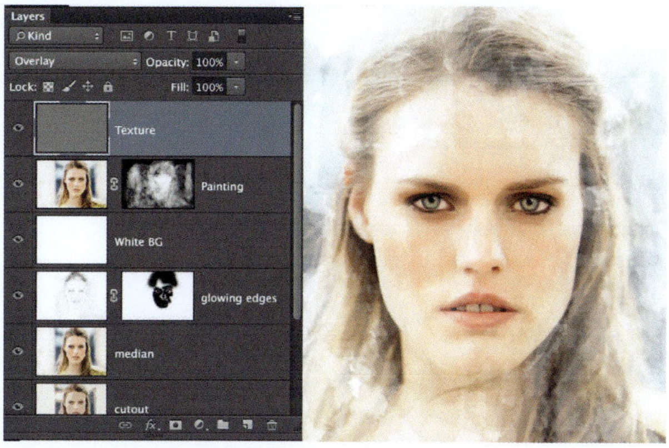

7 Brush to reveal

Grab the Brush tool and set the colour to white by pressing D, then X. Open the Brush Preset Picker, then click the cog to open the flyout menu. Load the Wet Media brushes. Choose the Oil Medium Brush Wet Edges brush tip and hit 4 for 40% brush opacity, then begin painting to reveal the image. Keep painting to build up the effect.

8 Add texture

To randomise the brush strokes, open up the Brush panel and change the Shape Dynamics Size and Angle jitters. Finish by adding texture: Alt-click the New layer icon and choose Mode: Overlay and check the Fill option. Go to Filter›Filter Gallery, choose Texture›Texturizer, set Texture to Canvas, Scaling to 130, then click OK.

Photoshop File Edit Image Layer Type Select Filter 3D View Window Help
Adobe Photoshop CC

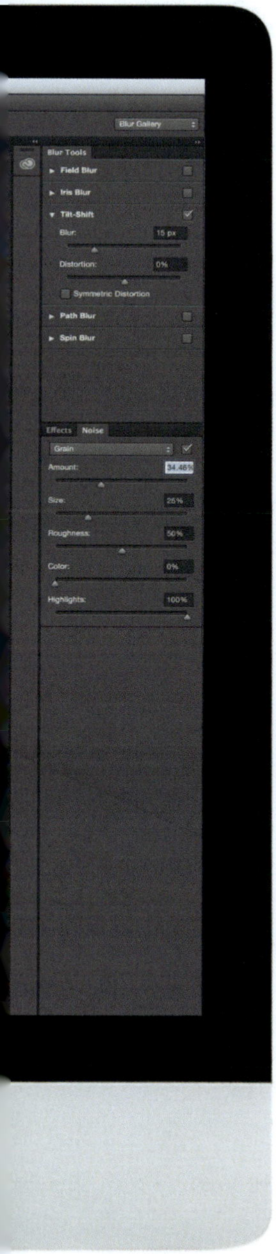

Photoshop filters

Transform your photos quickly and easily using one of Photoshop's many powerful processing filters

Apply editable filter effects

Once filters are applied to layers, their effects can be edited later if you first convert the image layer to a Smart Object. Here's how...

In previous tutorials we demonstrated how to adjust colours and tones by using adjustment layers. These layers sit above the original image layer, so you can fine-tune their sliders at any time. Adjustment layers enable you to edit in a non-destructive way, because the picture's original colours and tones are always available on a separate layer.

For more non-destructive editing options you can convert an image file into a Smart Object. This smart version of the file remembers its original properties, such as the colour and tone. You can then make changes using menu commands that aren't available as adjustment layers, such as Photoshop's huge range of filters, safe in the knowledge that the file's original look can be recovered at any time, even after you close and then reopen the document.

Smart Objects enable you to apply non-destructive filters to an image to create a wide range of artistic looks. This is much more useful than applying a filter directly onto an image layer, because you'd be stuck with the results it produces. Once a filter becomes smart, you can access and tweak it at any time to refine its effect on the image. Here's how to make an image smart so that you can enjoy the creative freedom provided by Smart Filters.

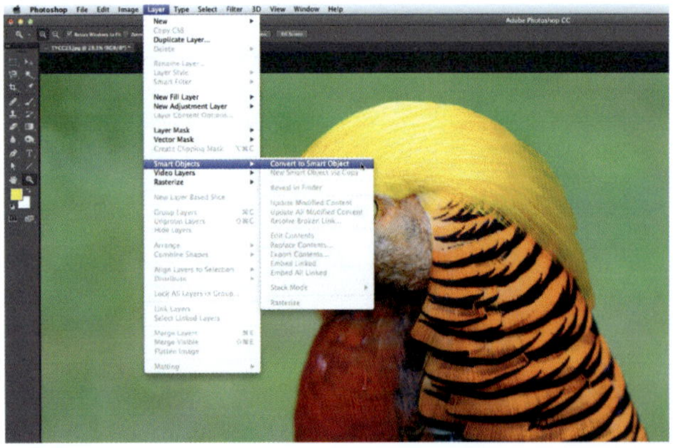

1 Convert to a Smart Object

Open our TYCC23.jpg starting image. Go to Layer›Smart Objects›Convert to Smart Object. In the Layers panel you'll notice a Smart Object icon appears at the bottom right of the image thumbnail. Behind the scenes, Photoshop has created a PSB document that stores the original image.

2 Apply a filter

Go to Filter›Filter Gallery. Toggle open the Brush Strokes folder and click the Angled Strokes thumbnail. Set Direction Balance to 66, Stroke Length to 21 and Sharpness to 3. Click OK. In the Layers panel, you'll now see a Smart Filter layer that contains a Filter Gallery option.

3 Apply a second filter

In the Layers panel, double click the Filter Gallery effect name to relaunch it. You can fine-tune the Angled Stroke filter to refine the look. Click the New Effect Layer icon. Click the Accented Edges thumbnail. Set Edge Width to 4 and Edge Brightness to 6. Click OK to apply.

4 Save a layered document

Go to Filter›Oil Paint. Set Stylization and Cleanliness to 10, Scale to 4 and Bristle Detail to 0. Click OK. You can access and tweak the Oil Paint or Filter Gallery effects by doubling clicking their labels at any time. Choose File›Save and set Format to Photoshop to preserve the Smart Filters.

Add creative effects to your photos

Learn how to apply different artistic filters to your photographs, and modify their properties to produce unique looks

For the majority of this book we've looked at how to use Photoshop to enhance images by correcting problems with colour, exposure, and so on. In this chapter we'll have a bit more fun by applying a host of creative effects to photos. Thanks to Photoshop's filters you can stylise the colours and tones in an image to produce a wide range of creative looks, from pencil sketches to oil paintings. To help you find suitable creative effects, the Filter menu groups filters in folders such as Artistic and Brush Strokes. When choosing any filter, you'll launch the Filter Gallery. This window gives you preview thumbnails of how the filtered image might look, as well as providing editable attributes that will change the results produced by the chosen filter. This tutorial will introduce you to the key features of the Filter Gallery and showcase the effects they create. Filters can dramatically alter an image's appearance, so it makes sense to use the Convert for Smart Filters command that we looked at in the introduction to this chapter. You can then experiment with different filters and fine-tune their effects more easily.

Photoshop Anatomy The Filter Gallery

Familiarise yourself with the Filter Gallery's key features

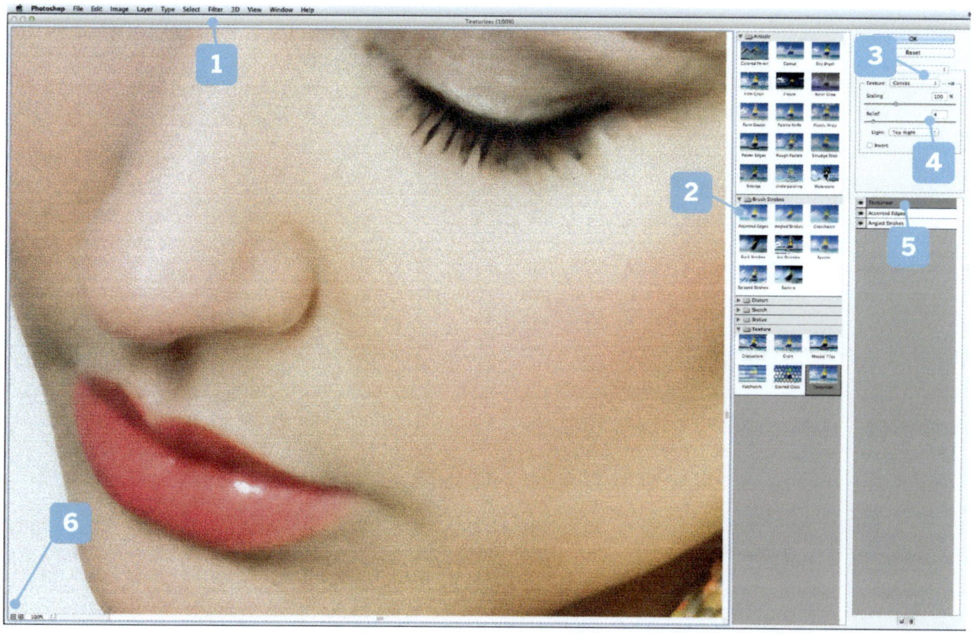

1 FILTER MENU

This menu command gives you access to standalone artistic filters such as Oil Paint, as well as enabling you to launch the Filter Gallery and its collection of 47 art effect filters.

2 FOLDERS

You can browse different types of filter by toggling opened themed folders such as Brush Strokes. Here you'll see thumbnails that preview the type of look produced by a particular filter.

3 FILTER LIST

You can replace a currently selected filter with something new by clicking this drop-down menu. You'll then see filters listed alphabetically, from Angled Strokes to Watercolor.

4 EDITABLE ATTRIBUTES

Once you select a filter by clicking its thumbnail, any editable properties such as the Stroke Length of a brush will appear in this section. Altering these is the key to producing more convincing art effects.

5 FILTER LAYERS

You can create more convincing artistic looks by combining multiple filters. Drag a filter up or down in the layer stack to change the art effect. Click the eye icon to turn it on or off.

6 ZOOM IN

It can be difficult to see the filter effect when looking at the entire image. Click here to zoom in for a closer and clearer look at the filtered image. You can then adjust the sliders more effectively.

Understanding... THE FILTER MENU

As well as enabling you to access the Filter Gallery, the Filter menu also includes additional collections of filters you can use to enhance your photos. For example, the Pixelate [1] collection enables you to mimic impressionistic art techniques such as Pointillism [2], which was popularised by Seurat. The most recently applied filter [3] can be reapplied by pressing Cmd/Ctrl+F. This keyboard shortcut enables you to build up a filter's look in more manageable increments. The powerful Oil Paint filter [4] has more editable attributes than many of the other filters, so it gets a menu command of its own.

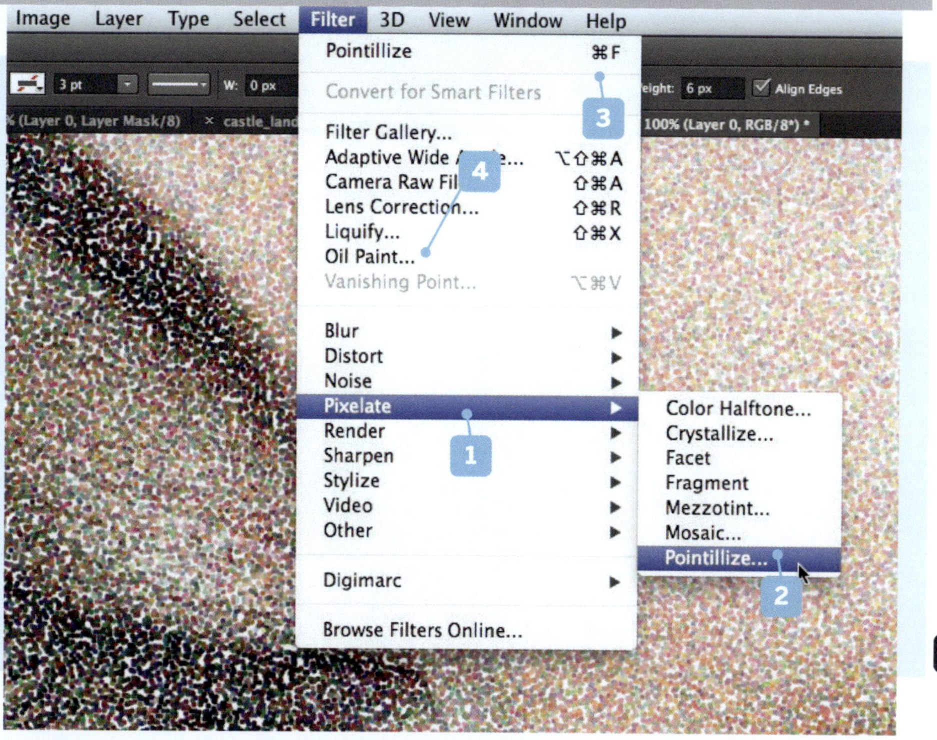

Accented Edges
Adds a light or dark edge around contrasting areas to produce a hand-drawn effect.

Angled Strokes
Use the Direction Balance slider to paint strokes in one direction or produce a cross-hatch effect.

Bas Relief
Create a metallic embossed effect by changing the drop-down menu's Light direction.

Chalk & Charcoal
Adjust the balance between Chalk and Charcoal to create a scratchy mixed-media effect.

Charcoal
Vary stroke thickness and use light and dark balance sliders to create a charcoal effect.

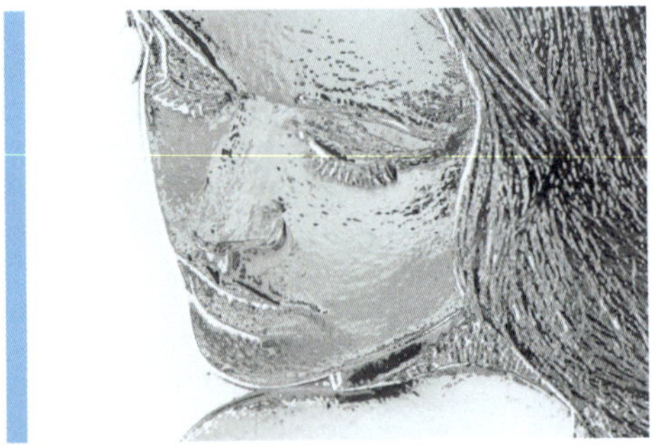

Chrome
Produce etched tin-foil style effects with this simple two-slider filter.

Colored Pencil
Bash out a hand-drawn pencil sketch in a few seconds with this filter.

Conte Crayon
This more complex filter enables you to add textured paper effects to the mix.

Craquelure
Adds eroded canvas artefacts to enhance your filtered photo paintings.

Crosshatch
Creates overlapping diagonal strokes of varying lengths, sharpness and intensity.

Cutout
Recreates the stencilled look produced by the screen-printing process.

Dark Strokes
Create clipped and stylised dark shadows with this moody and striking filter.

Diffuse Glow
This portrait-enhancing filter flatters complexion and creates a high-key look.

Dry Brush
Quickly add scratchy paint strokes that echo a traditional painting technique.

Film Grain
Use this filter's sliders to add grain to shadows, highlights or a mix of both.

Fresco
Mimics the effect of painting directly onto a textured wall with editable properties.

Glass
This fun filter enables you to distort your image through a range of glassy surfaces.

Glowing Edges
This filter adds a glow similar to that produced by a neon light to contrasting features.

Grain
Add different grain types to your images, such as horizontal, clumped or contrasty.

Graphic Pen
Creates contrasting areas by adding pen strokes that are densely clustered or wide apart.

Halftone Pattern
Mimics the pop-art look produced by the comic and newspaper printing process.

Ink Outlines
Outlines contrasting forms using three sliders to change the stroke length.

Mosaic Tiles
Builds up a version of your image by overlaying a collection of resizeable interlocking tiles.

Neon Glow
Provides a colour picker so you can add specific glow colours to a photo.

Note Paper
This filter adds raised edges and grain to a greyscale version of the source image.

Ocean Ripple
Like its Glass filter cousin, this distorting filter breaks up the image using patterns.

Paint Daubs
Creates a hand-painted effect. Works well in conjunction with other filters.

Palette Knife
Mimics the effect of applying rough smears of paint with a knife instead of a brush.

Patchwork
Creates the illusion that the image is built up of thousands of raised square tiles.

Photocopy
Mimics the effects created by copying a colour image using a mono photocopier.

Plaster
Sliders enable you to make the key details in the image rise up above a smooth surface.

Plastic Wrap
This bizarre filter adds specular highlights to the image to mimic plastic wrap.

Poster Edges
Creates a posterised look by simplifying the palette. A popular look in the 1990s.

Reticulation
Converts your image to a high-contrast monochrome, and adds grain.

Rough Pastels
Gives an image the look of a pastel drawing, with many editable attributes.

Smudge Stick
Makes a simpler and perhaps less successful pastel effect than Rough Pastels.

Spatter
This converts the pixels of an image into airbrush-style specks of paint.

Sponge
This one simplifies an image and overlays an editable texture onto it.

Sprayed Strokes
Creates a very rough 'painted' rendition of an image. Probably one to avoid.

Stained Glass
This filter might be more useful for mimicking a mosaic rather than stained glass.

Stamp
Produces an effective monochromatic lithograph-style print by tweaking two sliders.

Sumi-e
Produces a simplified and stylised look similar to the one made by the Dark Strokes filter.

Texturizer
Combine this useful filter with a host of others to add a canvas-style texture.

Torn Edges
Another way to create a simplified high-contrast black-and-white version of the source image.

Underpainting
Creates a painterly image with added texture, with controls similar to the Texturizer filter.

Waterpaper
Weaves a paper fibre texture into a filtered image's simplified colours and tones.

Watercolor
A popular filter that reproduces the watercolour effect. Best used alongside other filters.

Oil Paint
Creates a very convincing oil-paint effect. Not part of the Filter Gallery.

Use the Camera Raw filter tools

You can use Camera Raw's powerful adjustment tools on images you've already opened up in Photoshop

In earlier sections we've taken a good look at the handy processing tools in Camera Raw. These tools are designed to work with uncompressed raw files, but they're so useful you often wish they were available in Photoshop itself. Well they are!

The Filter menu in later versions of Photoshop has a new Camera Raw Filter option that launches the currently open image into the raw editor workspace.

By editing a JPEG in Camera Raw you have a cleaner image-editing environment for routine enhancements such as Shadows, Highlights and Clarity, which can be more effective and faster than regular Photoshop adjustment layers. You can also apply sophisticated Curve, hue, saturation and lightness adjustments to modify contrast and individual colours. If you've spent any time at all in Adobe Camera Raw you'll quickly find the tools you need in the 'filter' version.

It's not quite the same as working on a raw file, of course, since the image data has already been converted, so you don't have access to the full tonal and colour information in the original raw file any more – but this is still a great editing environment for everyday enhancements.

What's more, if you convert the image layer to a Smart Object first, the adjustments you make will be non-destructive – you can re-edit the settings later.

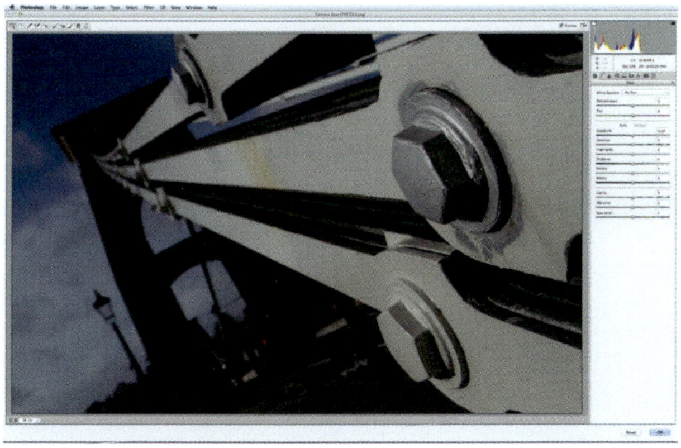

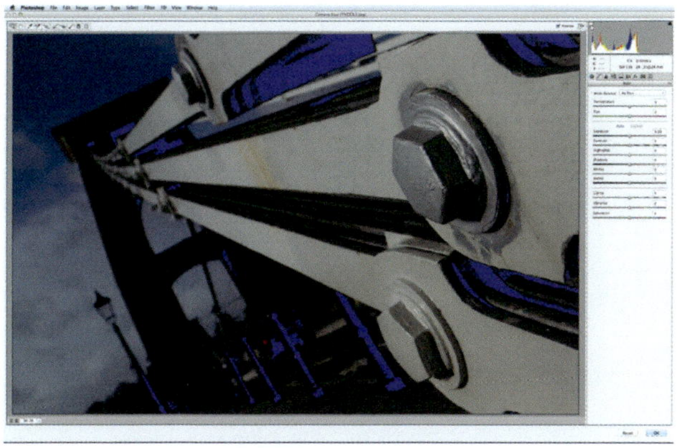

1 Open the image

Go to File›Open and browse to TYCC63.jpg. Click Open. This image is a regular JPEG file, so it will open in the standard Photoshop editing workspace. To tweak this under-exposed and desaturated image with the Camera Raw tools, choose Filter›Camera Raw Filter.

2 Examine the histogram

We can see from the histogram that the image lacks strong highlights, so it's under-exposed. By clicking the Shadow Clipping warning icon, we can see that many of the shadows are clipped. These blue patches indicate areas that will print without any detail.

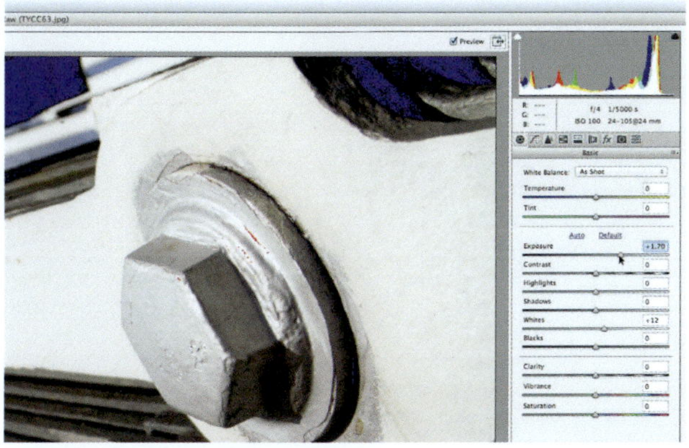

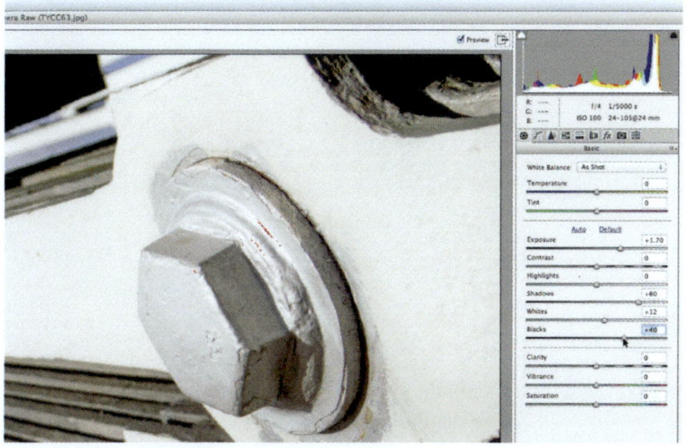

3 Increase Exposure

To remap the under-exposed midtones and highlights to a brighter value, drag the Exposure slider to +1.70. The graph will slide towards the right, indicating the presence of brighter pixels. Push Whites to +12 until a little highlight clipping appears as patches of red.

4 Lighten the shadows

Selectively lighten the shadows by dragging the Shadows slider up to +60. Reduce the presence of clipped shadows a little more by dragging Blacks to +40. Press U to remove the remaining shadow clipping warning patches. We now have a better exposed JPEG.

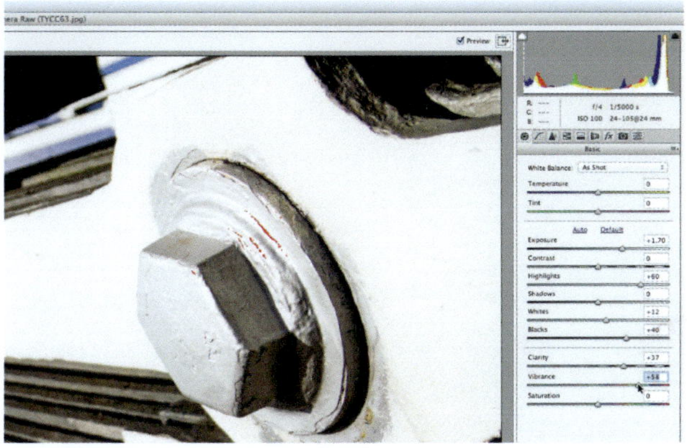

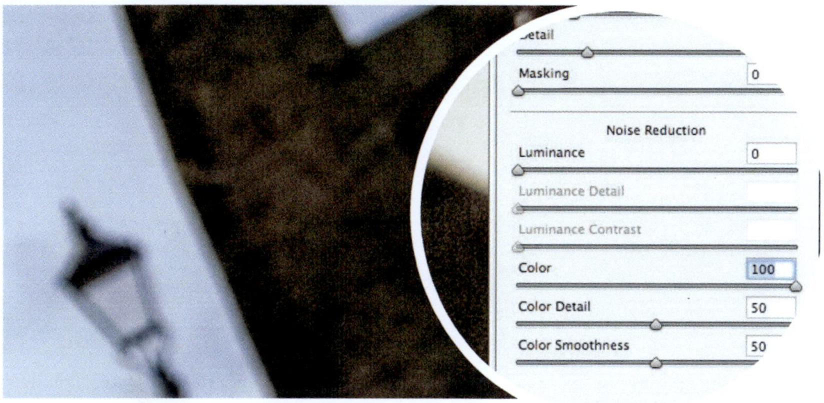

5 Increase the midtone contrast

To give some of the fine textures on the weathered metal more impact, increase the midtone contrast by dragging Clarity to +37. This technique is much harder to reproduce in the standard Photoshop workspace. Create a more vibrant blue sky by dragging the Vibrance slider to +58.

6 Remove colour noise

Lightening the shadows of a JPEG creates artefacts and undesirable colour noise. Click the Detail panel. In the Noise Reduction section, drag Color to 100. This removes the colour noise. Click OK to commit the changes and return the edited file to the standard Photoshop workspace.

Improve images with controlled blur

Discover how to improve your photographs by adding creative and selective blur effects using the Blur Gallery

When you capture an image on a digital SLR you can add in-camera blur effects to enhance your images. By using a wide aperture setting such as f/2 you create a shallow depth of field, for instance. This makes the focal point, such as the face in a portrait, look nice and sharp, while blurring out the distracting background elements.

If you have a tilt-shift lens you can take even more control over where blur appears in your images. This specialist lens enables you to create a narrow band of focus sandwiched between two blurred sections. This narrow band of focus mimics the effect you get when shooting a small subject close up, which makes life-size scenes look like scale models. Producing good selective-focus or tilt-shift effects in camera can be tricky, so we'll demonstrate how to create these effects using Photoshop's Blur Gallery. This gives you more control over the strength and location of blur in any image, which helps you avoid the hit-and-miss approach of capturing blur in camera. The Blur Gallery's Field Blur filter adds a natural-looking lens blur to the entire image. Here's how...

Overview Create a background blur

Use the Blur Gallery's Iris Blur filter to reduce the impact of background distractions

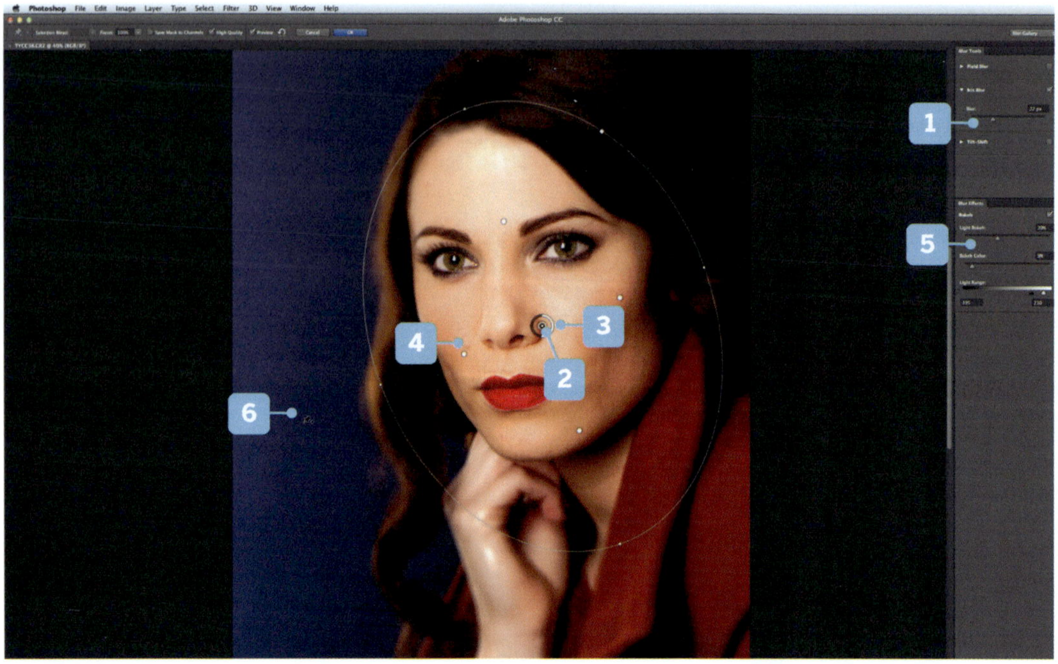

4 FALL OFF

You can feather the area between the sharp and blurred pixels by dragging any one of these four control points. This enables you to control how gradual or steep the blend is between the focused and blurred pixels.

5 LIGHT BOKEH

Lens-produced bokeh may feature artefacts such as clipped (or blooming) highlights. Recreate these effects by dragging this slider right. The Light Range slider shrinks or enlarges the range of tones with blown-out highlights, such as on the hand in this shot.

6 MORE PINS

Click to place additional Iris Blur pins. This enables you to take more control over the strength and location of the bokeh in any part of the image.

1 IRIS BLUR

Go to the Filter menu and choose Blur. The top section of the Blur menu features the Blur Gallery – Field Blur, Iris Blur and Tilt-Shift. Choose Iris Blur.

2 POSITION PIN

A control pin will be placed at the centre of the image. Drag the pin to position it over the area that you want to keep sharp.

3 BLUR AMOUNT

You can increase or decrease the amount of blur by dragging this dial. Areas outside the ellipse will become softer or sharper.

Photoshop Anatomy Tilt-Shift blur filter

Give ordinary snapshots the look of photos of scale models

1 TILT-SHIFT

If you're already working in the Blur Gallery, click here to activate the Tilt-Shift option, and then toggle it open to access the editable properties. Or choose Filter>Blur>Tilt-Shift from the main menu bar.

2 POSITION PIN

As with the Iris Blur, you can drag a pin to fine-tune the position of the sharp and blurred pixels in your filtered image. You can also drag the pin's dial to increase or decrease the Blur amount.

3 ROTATE

You can rotate a real tilt-shift lens to create a diagonal line of focus that suits your subject matter's composition. Recreate this effect by dragging the rotate icon that appears when you rest the cursor near a control point.

4 BLUR BORDER

Drag this dotted line to create a narrower or wider transition between the blurred and focused parts of the image. You can adjust the top and bottom transition lines independently.

5 FOCUS

The centre of any blur filter's ellipse in the Blur Gallery is 100% in focus. You can make the blur effect seep into the sharper areas of the image by reducing the value of this slider.

6 NOISE

The Noise tab enables you to add image noise that might have been blurred by the effects of the filter so that the resulting image will have noise on top of the blur – just like you'd get with in-camera blur.

How to use plug-in filters

The filters built in to Photoshop are just the start – there's a world of plug-in filters that work perfectly with Photoshop

Powerful as Photoshop is, there are some jobs it just can't do – or which would be too difficult and time-consuming to figure out. Adobe happily acknowledges that there are specialist tools out there which can do particular jobs better or faster than Photoshop can, which is why it's built in support for plug-ins. These are essentially mini-applications which you can invoke from within Photoshop and which return a new version of the picture to Photoshop when they're done.

There's a booming market in plug-ins, and for this tutorial we're using the Google Nik Collection, which has recently been made completely free and can be downloaded from **www.google.com/nikcollection**. If you've never tried plug-ins before, prepare to be amazed...

The Google Nik Collection, like other plug-in software, comes with an installer that automatically places the plug-in files where Photoshop can find them – but make sure no Adobe applications are running when you install the software or you'll get an error message. Most major plug-in collections these days also work with Lightroom, by the way.

It is possible to make filtered images re-adjustable by first converting the picture to a Smart Object. For this walkthrough, though, we've kept things simple.

BEFORE

1 How to launch installed plug-ins

Let's start off with our sample image, TYCC98.jpg – you can of course try this out with your own shots. If your plug-in filters have installed correctly they'll appear towards the bottom of the Filter menu. We're using the Google Nik Collection, which offers a further sub-menu.

2 Choose your filter settings

For this walkthrough we're using the Google Analog Efex Pro 2 plug-in, which offers a vast array of film, darkroom and image manipulation effects. This is one of its Multi-lens presets, which splits the photo up into cells and recombines them a new arrangement. We'll click OK...

3 Back in Photoshop

Once the plug-in has finished processing the image its window closes and you're back in Photoshop. You can see that the effect has been added as a new layer, whereas Photoshop's in-built filters act directly on the Background layer. We can save the image as it is or go just a step further…

4 Blend modes and opacity

The fact that the filtered image is on a new layer enables us to combine it with the original in a variety of ways. Here, we've set the blending mode to Linear Light and the layer opacity to 50% to create an abstract blend of the original image and the filtered version.

Photoshop File Edit Image Layer Type Select Filter 3D View Window Help
Shake Reduction (TYCC64_edited.tif @ 66.7%)
Place mouse over control for help.

Common photo fixes

There are some image adjustments you'll make to almost every photo. Discover what they are and how to apply them

Sharpen up your images

Discover how to make your images appear crisp and sharp, even those blighted by camera-shake blur

It can be a challenge to get your images looking sharp. Many digital cameras have a built-in filter that blurs the image in an attempt to avoid producing moiré patterns. This low-pass (or anti-aliasing) filter can also soften important details and create a photo that lacks impact. What looks sharp on the camera's LCD screen may turn out to be soft. A slow shutter speed may also induce blur, which is more difficult to fix.

Photoshop has sharpening tools that are designed to tease out detail in a soft-looking shot. This post-production sharpening works by increasing the contrast around the edges of details in the image, giving them more impact. However, when you sharpen an image using filters you risk exaggerating picture noise in smooth areas, such as in the background of our starting image. You can also introduce artefacts such as blown-out highlights.

In our first annotation we'll point out the key techniques involved in using the Smart Sharpen filter to reveal fine details in a soft photo. We'll then demonstrate how the Shake Reduction command can counteract motion blur caused by camera shake.

Overview The Smart Sharpen filter

Give details more impact and keep sharpening artefacts at bay

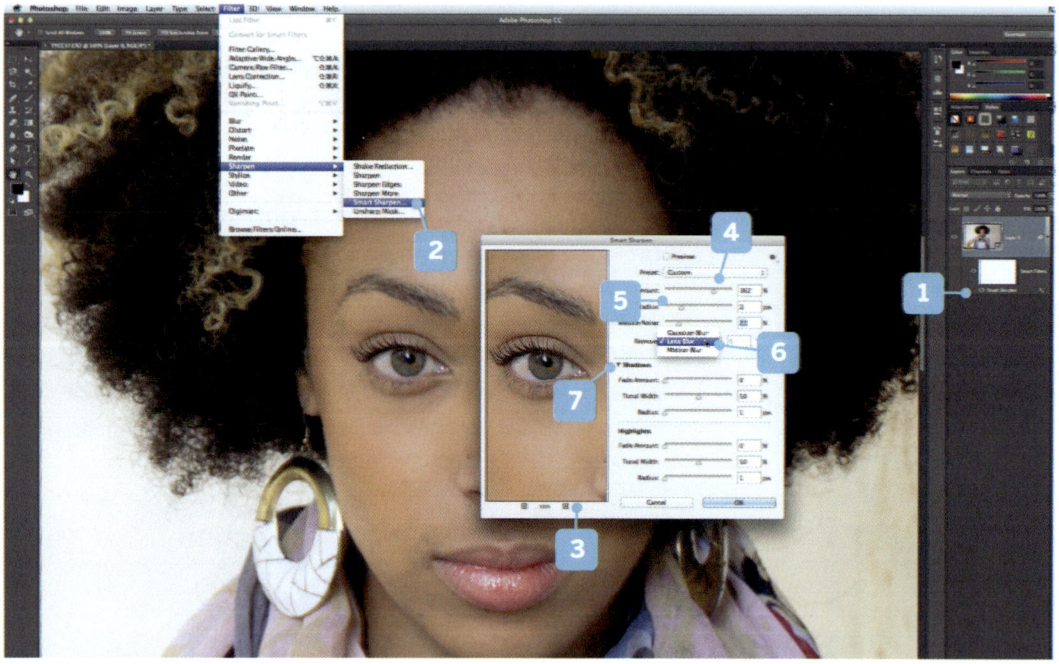

1 GET SMART

You can sharpen an image in a non-destructive way by turning the image layer into a Smart Object. You can then toggle the filter on and off.

2 SMART SHARPEN

Photoshop has many sharpening tools. The most versatile can be summoned by choosing Filter> Sharpen>Smart Sharpen.

3 GIVE IT 100%

To assess how soft or sharp an image really is, you need to look at it at 100%. By default the Smart Sharpen preview window will zoom in to this value.

4 AMOUNT

This slider increases the strength of the contrast adjustment around the edges of details in the image. This contrast boost gives fine areas, such as the eyelashes in this image, more impact and makes them look sharper.

5 RADIUS

This slider increases the spread of the Amount contrast change. A larger Radius value creates thicker darker and lighter lines that can turn into distracting halo artefacts. As a rule, stick to a maximum Radius of 2.

6 REMOVE

The most effective sharpening option in this menu is Lens Blur. The Motion Blur slider is designed to counteract camera-shake blur, but it's never been very effective. Check out the new Shake Reduction filter, opposite, however.

7 SHADOWS

Toggle open this option to selectively limit the sharpening to the shadows or highlights. This enables you to target the areas that need sharpening.

Photoshop Anatomy Shake Reduction filter

Counteract the length and direction of shake-induced motion blur

1 BLUR TRACE MARQUEE

Click the pin at the centre of the default blur trace marquee and drag it to the area that needs to look sharp. The Shake Reduction filter will then analyse the selected area to determine the length and direction of motion-blurred pixels.

2 BLUR TRACE BOUNDS

After launching the filter, Photoshop attempts to work out how long and wide the streaks of motion blur are in pixels. If you spot haloes around contrasting edges, try reducing the amount.

3 SOURCE NOISE

If your photo was captured using a high ISO such as 800 or higher, then you can set this drop-down menu to High to stop noise artefacts from being exaggerated by the shake-reduction process.

4 ARTEFACT SUPPRESSION

The shake-reduction process can add ugly artefacts such as noise, haloes and repeating edges (ghosting), especially if multiple blur trace bounds are used. This slider will reduce those artefacts.

5 SMOOTHING

This slider enables you to get a balance between smoothing out sharpening-induced noise in clear areas such as skin, while preserving details in contrasting edges.

6 ADVANCED OPTIONS

Our two Blur Trace marquees help Photoshop understand motion blur in different sections of the image. Each white blur trace icon shows the length and direction of a particular Blur Trace marquee's blur.

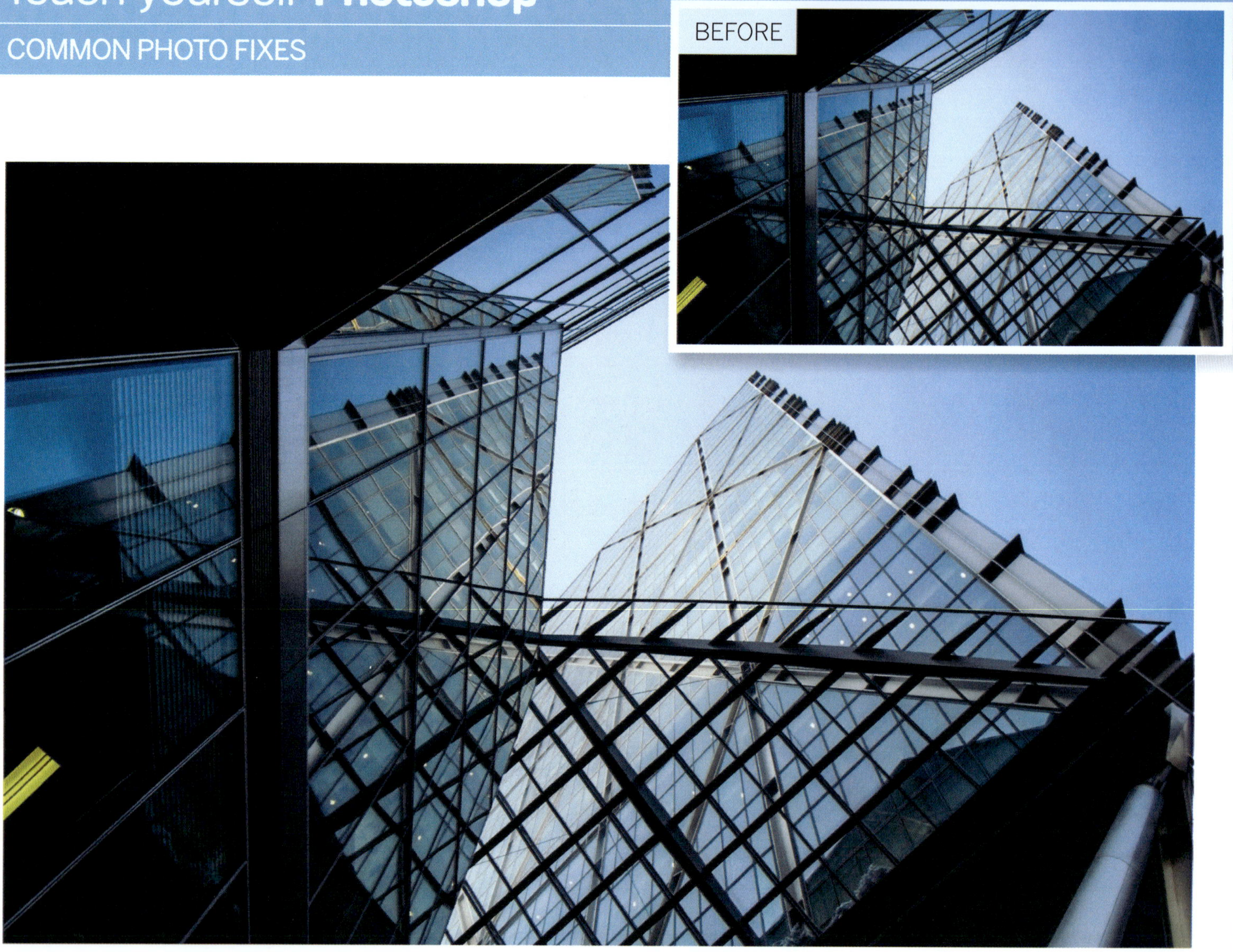

Remove noise from your photos

Smooth out undesirable image noise while preserving detail throughout the photo using the Reduce Noise filter

When shooting with a traditional film camera, you could use film with different ISO speeds to capture more detail in low-light conditions. The faster (higher) the film's ISO speed, the more sensitive it was to available light. A fast film enabled you to avoid using slow shutter speeds in low light, so you could capture detail without the need for a tripod. You could also shoot handheld in locations where a flash was prohibited, such as in a museum or church. However, fast ISO speed film added clumps of grain to your negatives. The higher the ISO speed, the grainier the images would be.

Digital cameras recreate the traditional ISO film speed effect to enable you to capture more detail in low light. As with film, higher ISO settings (such as 1600) are more sensitive to light, but they add more noise to your digital files. Digital noise is a bit like film grain, but it's sharper, uglier and more distracting. There are two types of digital noise – luminance (greyscale) and chroma (colour). Luminance noise appears throughout the tonal range of the image as tiny dots. It can be compared to grain in analogue film, so it isn't as undesirable as chroma noise, which manifests itself as multi-coloured speckles. However, you may still want to smooth out high ISO-induced luminance noise to get a more pristine digital photo.

When reducing the presence of luminance noise, you have to be careful not to blur important details. The Reduce Noise filter's sliders enable you to get a balance between removing noise while preserving detail.

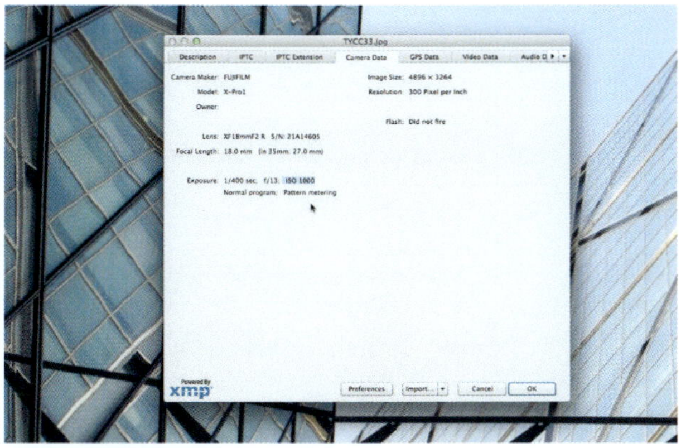

1 Analyse the noise

Open TYCC33.jpg. To see the ISO setting used to capture this image, go to File›Info and click the Camera Data tab. Here you can see that the ISO speed is 1000, so there will be noise present. Click OK. Double click the Zoom tool to display the image at 100%.

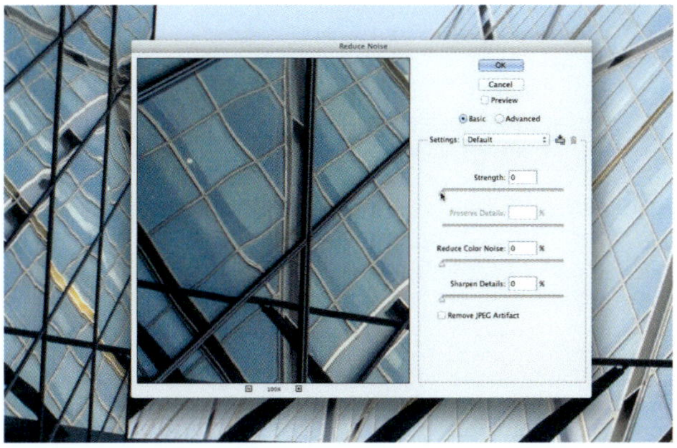

2 Open the Reduce Noise filter

Grab the Hand tool and drag to examine parts of the magnified image. Noise is especially noticeable in darker smoother areas such as the window reflections. Go to Filter›Noise›Reduce Noise. To see how the sliders work their magic, drop them to 0 to start with.

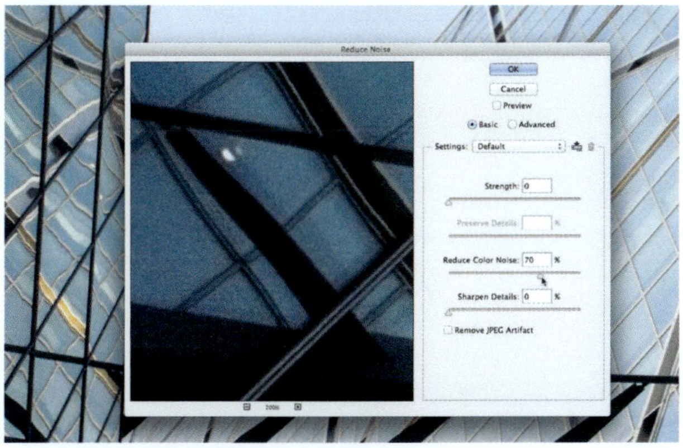

3 Reduce the colour noise

Colour noise is easy to remove because there's no risk of smoothing out important detail. Zoom in to 200% to see the noise more clearly. Drag the Reduce Color Noise slider to 70% to remove the coloured speckles. This just leaves the luminance noise for us to deal with.

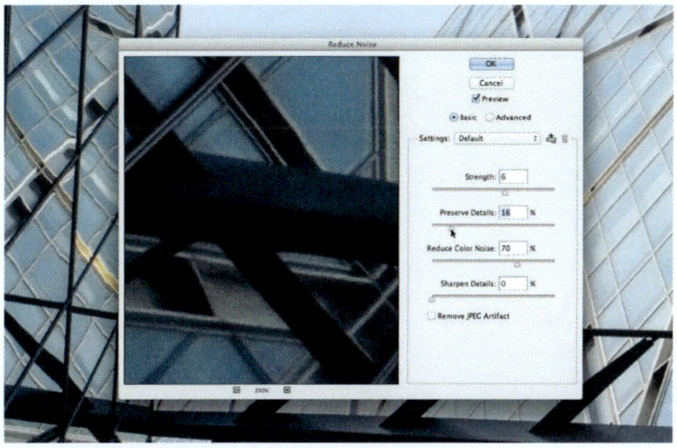

4 Blurred versus sharp

Drag the Strength slider to 6 to start smoothing out the luminance noise. This blurs the noise, but it also blurs our subject's important architectural details. Drag the Preserve Details slider until you get a balance between detail and noise. Here, a value of 16% is a good compromise.

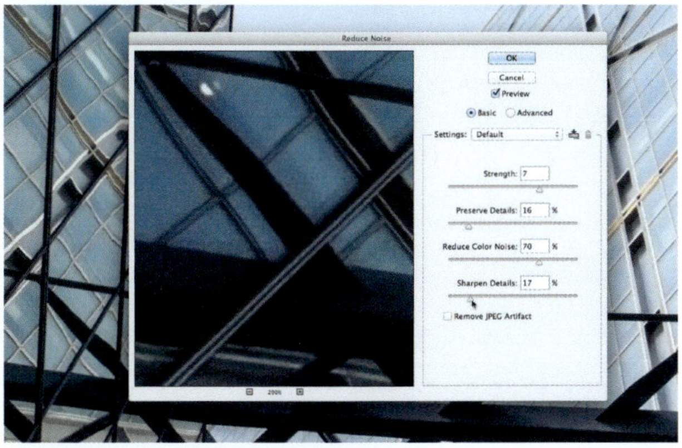

5 Before and after

The Sharpen Details slider restores features that may have blurred. Drag it to 17%. Now that you've restored detail to the image, you can increase the Strength to 7. Click the preview window to see a noisier before version. Release the mouse button to see the reduced-noise version.

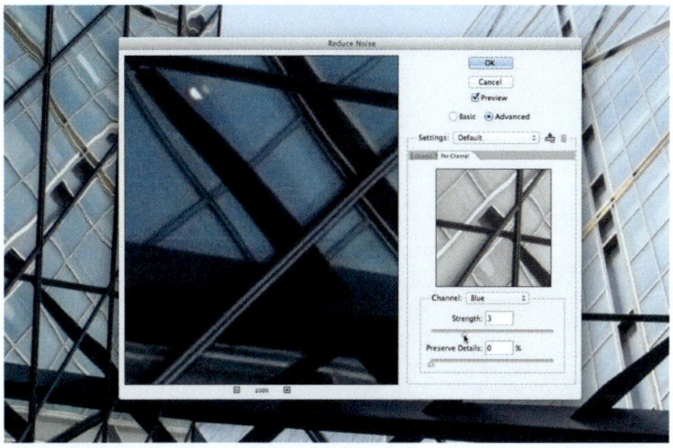

6 Advanced options

Click the Advanced button. Here you can toggle through the red, green and blue channels that make up the colour image. Traditionally, the blue channel is more prone to displaying noise, so drag Strength to 3. Click OK to remove the image noise.

Lens correction

Use the Adaptive Wide Angle filter to counteract even the most extreme unwanted effects of lens distortion

When you shoot with a wide-angle lens you may notice that the scene's horizontal and vertical lines appear curved. This is referred to as geometric distortion. The amount of lens-induced geometric distortion varies from lens to lens (and it also depends on the focal length you've used to capture the scene), but these dramatically curved lines can detract from the authenticity of a shot. Distorted lines that bulge outwards are said to be suffering from barrel distortion, while lines that curve inwards are afflicted by pincushion distortion.

Older versions of Photoshop CS enable you to tackle most types of lens distortion by using the Lens Correction filter. Geometric distortion (curved lines) can be straightened using that filter's Remove Distortion filter. Perspectival distortion – where the lines converge inwards towards the top of the frame – can also be counteracted by adjusting the Lens Correction filter's Horizontal or Vertical Perspective sliders. The Lens Correction filter is pretty effective, but it has limitations, especially when trying to counteract the extreme geometric distortion produced by wide-angle fisheye lenses.

When using the Lens Correction filter, you can speed up the correction process using Lens Profiles. These recognise the make and model of your lens by reading the metadata attached to the image, so they know how much geometric distortion there will be at any given focal length. The Lens Correction filter's profiles provide a way to automatically counteract geometric distortion such as curved horizons, but they can't deal as effectively with perspectival distortion.

The more recent Adaptive Wide Angle filter does a much better job of dealing with both geometric and perspectival distortion. It does so by providing different tools to the Lens Correction filter's slider-based solution.

Correct perspectival distortion

Use the Adaptive Wide Angle filter to straighten converging verticals

If you shoot a tall building from a low angle you risk adding perspectival distortion to the image. By tilting the camera upwards to capture the top of the building, you'll notice that the vertical walls appear to converge inwards instead of running parallel with the edges of the frame.

Photoshop's Lens Correction filter can counteract perspectival distortion in a photo like the one on the right by letting you drag the Vertical Perspective slider to the left.

This makes the top of the frame appear to lean towards the camera, straightening the converging verticals so that they run parallel with the sides of the frame. However, in this case you'll need to lose the top of the building to get the walls looking straight, which spoils the composition of the image and loses important detail.

Instead, go to Filter›Adaptive Wide Angle and use the advanced correction tools to do a better perspectival correction job.

In the Adaptive Wide Angle window, set the Correction menu to Perspective. Set the Scale slider to 86% to zoom out and see more of the edges. You're now ready to follow the walkthrough below.

Correct converging verticals

1 Draw constraints

Grab the Constraint tool. Place a point at the top left corner of the building. Place another point at the bottom left corner. A constraint line joins the two points. Draw two more vertical lines in the middle and one at the right of the building.

2 Rotate the constraints

Click the left constraint line. Drag the white circle to 90°. This straightens the building's left-hand side. Rotate the other constraint lines to make them 90°. Shift-click a vertical constraint line to set it to 90° automatically.

3 Scale transform

Click to draw constraints along any warped horizontal lines. About seven lines should be enough. Shift-click each horizontal line to make it run parallel with the bottom of the frame. You may need to Shift-click vertical lines too. Click OK.

Correct fisheye lens distortion

Straighten curved verticals and horizontals in a fisheye image

Fisheye lenses like the Sigma DG 8mm f/3.5 EX enable you to capture a much wider view of a location than you could with a conventional lens. However, by using a fisheye lens your shot's horizontal and vertical lines will be warped into curves, creating a circular shot surrounded by a black border that features parts of the lens's interior. The old Lens Correction filter has an Auto Correction tab that enables you to use Lens Profiles to counteract some of the distortion in a fisheye photo. The Auto Correction tab's Geometric Distortion option can straighten the curved pillars of this image's derelict pier, but it will still struggle to iron out the bend in the horizon and the pillars will still suffer from perspectival distortion.

Open a fisheye image and go to Filter›Adaptive Wide Angle. You'll see the camera model and lens specifications appear at the bottom left, so we know that the filter is aware of the distortion produced by the lens when set to a particular focal length.

To help produce the best results, set Correction to Fisheye. The black interior of the lens will be removed from the edges. Follow the three steps below, then crop out the edges.

Fisheye corrections

1 Polygonal constraint

Grab the Polygon Constraint tool from the filter's mini toolbar. Place four points around the corners of the left pillar. Place the last point on the first to complete the selection. The pillar's curved lines will straighten. Do the same for the other three.

2 Go vertical

Place the cursor on the left pillar's bottom left control point. Shift-click to force the polygon's tilted lines to become vertical. This will straighten the pillar in an instant. Do the same for the other three pillars. Select the Constraint tool.

3 Straighten the horizon

Draw a line that follows the curved shoreline. To help the line follow the shore, drag the middle control point upwards. Draw another line to straighten the distant horizon. Shift-click a control point to make the horizon run parallel with the frame.

Photoshop Anatomy Adaptive Wide Angle

Get to know the Adaptive Wide Angle filter's powerful tool set

1 CONSTRAINT TOOL

Use this tool to draw a line that follows a curved line in the image. Pixels close to the constraint line will then be straightened.

2 POLYGON CONSTRAINT TOOL

Use this tool when straightening complete objects like the pier support struts in this image. Click to place the last point on the first to complete the selection.

3 MOVE TOOL

Use this tool to move the image around so that you can see edge detail when you've zoomed in for finer control.

4 ROTATE

The Constraint tool has control points that enable you to bend or rotate it so that it follows the distorted lines more effectively.

5 CORRECTION

Adaptive Wide Angle knows what lens you used to capture the image, but you can still give it a hand by choosing an appropriate projection map here.

6 METADATA

To remove distortion effectively, the Adaptive Wide Angle filter needs to know the focal length and crop factor used when taking the photo.

Understanding... CHROMATIC ABERRATION

The Adaptive Wide Angle filter does a fantastic job of removing lens-induced geometric and perspective distortion, but it can't remove other lens-related artefacts like chromatic aberration. There's a cyan fringe clinging to the left of the pillar [1] and a magenta fringe running along the right-hand side [2]. These fringes are caused by the lens's inability to focus different wavelengths of light on the same part of the sensor. To remove them, you could use the filter's Chromatic Aberration sliders, but these don't always work. Instead, add a Hue/Saturation adjustment layer [3] and set the menu to Magenta [4]. You can then reduce the Saturation of that particular colour.

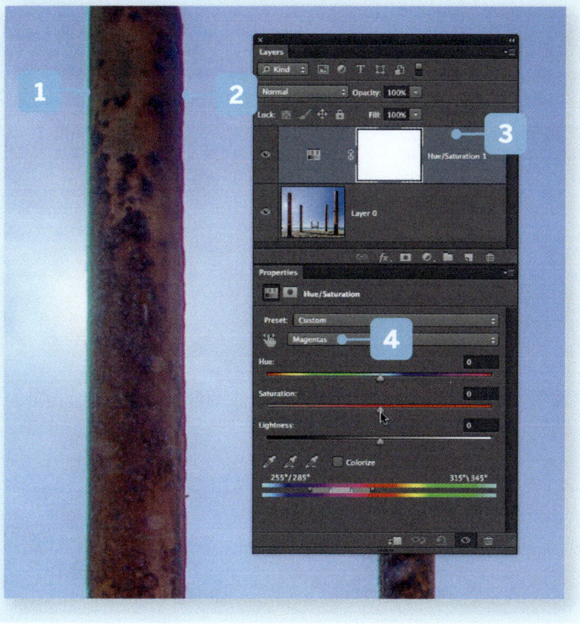

TRANSPARENT EDGES

Once you've used the Adaptive Wide Angle filter to correct distortion, you'll end up with transparent edges. To extend less complex areas such as skies and beaches into the blank space, select the transparent areas and go to Select>Modify>Expand and choose 1 pixel. Then choose Edit>Fill and use Content-Aware. This will fill the empty space with colour and texture. ■

Remove flaws from your photos

Remove unwanted objects and enhance your subject's complexion using Photoshop's image-retouching tools

If you keep clicking with the Zoom tool to the maximum magnification of 3200%, you'll see that every photograph consists of small square pixels. Photoshop enables you to change the look of a photograph by altering the properties of these tiny building blocks, such as their tone, colour, and even their positions. When it comes to retouching an image, Photoshop offers a host of tools that enable you to replace unwanted pixels with more appropriate ones. The Clone Stamp, Healing Brush and Patch tools all work in similar ways, by copying and moving pixels from one part of an image to another. In this walkthrough we'll put these related retouching tools through their paces to hide unwanted objects such as the white card and lighting rig on the right-hand side of our starting image. We'll also enhance the look of our model by removing distracting objects such as the hat's tassel, and quickly conceal spots and blemishes to create a more pleasing complexion.

The Clone Stamp, Patch, and Healing Brush tools do a similar job, but they each have their strengths and weaknesses, so we'll demonstrate how each tool can be best employed in our retouching walkthrough. This will help you to choose the right tool for a range of retouching challenges. Along the way you'll learn how to modify each tool's behaviour so that you can make it work more effectively on your own images. Some tools, such as the Spot Healing Brush tool, can be set to Content-Aware mode, so that they automatically sample appropriate pixels when retouching more complicated areas.

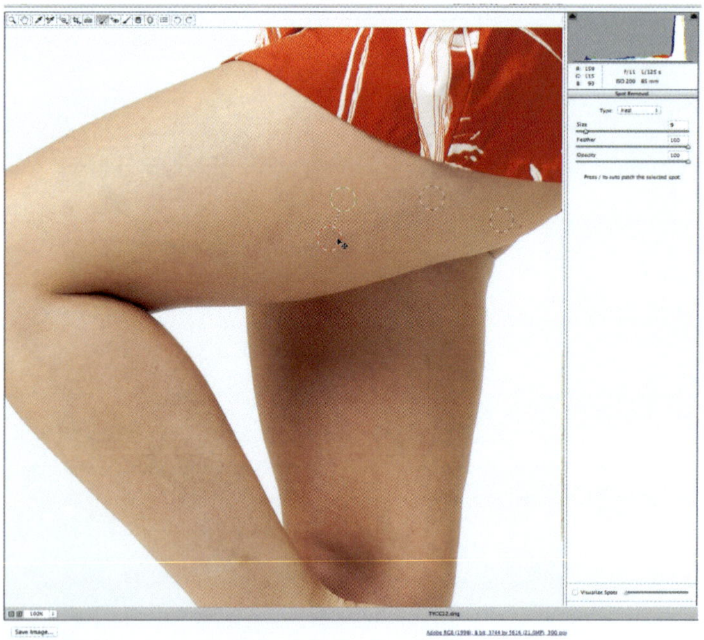

1 Remove a bruise

Open TYCC22.dng. This is a raw file so it will open in Camera Raw. Zoom in to 100%. Use the Hand tool to pan the image to the bruise on the model's thigh. Choose the Spot Removal tool. In the Spot Removal panel, set Type to Heal. This will blend transplanted skin with its new surroundings. Set Size to 9. Click the bruise to place a red overlay on it. A clear patch of adjacent skin – indicated by the green overlay – will be placed over the bruise.

2 Remove the wrinkles

The Spot Removal tool excels at hiding small blemishes such as bruises and birth marks. If you click and drag the tool you can paint along wrinkles or creases in the skin to create a smoother-looking complexion. You can fine-tune the sampled areas and the edited areas by dragging the red or green overlays around. Clear the Show Overlay box to hide the distracting overlays to see how your retouching is shaping up.

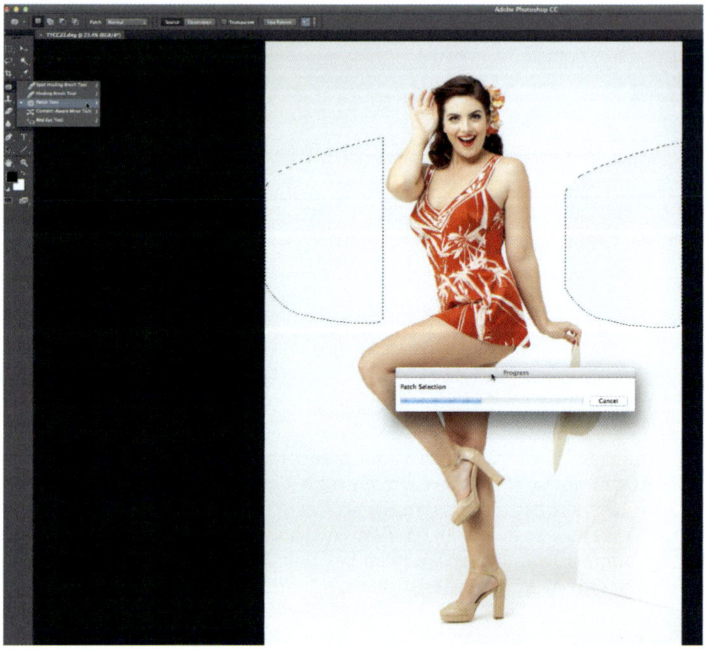

3 Open the image

The Spot Removal tool is fine for performing small retouching tasks, but to remove larger objects such as the white card backdrop and the lighting stand we'll need to call out the big guns. Click Open Image to take the image into the standard Photoshop editor. This will give you access to more retouching tools. Grab the Zoom tool and right click the image. Choose Fit On Screen from the context-sensitive pop-up menu.

4 Patch out the card

Click and hold down the mouse over the compartment that holds the Spot Healing Brush tool to see the other tools that are stored there. Select the Patch tool. In the Options bar, click the Source button. Draw a patch around the top section of the white card on the right. Click inside the patch and drag left until a clean section of white from the left-hand side of the frame fills the patch. Watch out for tonal inconsistencies.

5 Make another patch

After transplanting clean white pixels from the left-hand side of the frame into the right, the Patch tool seamlessly blends them with their new surroundings. This helps to hide the card. Draw another patch around the lower section of card and again drag it to a clean section on the left-hand side of the image. This will remove most of this white studio reflector. Zoom in to take a closer look at the remaining bits of card around the hat.

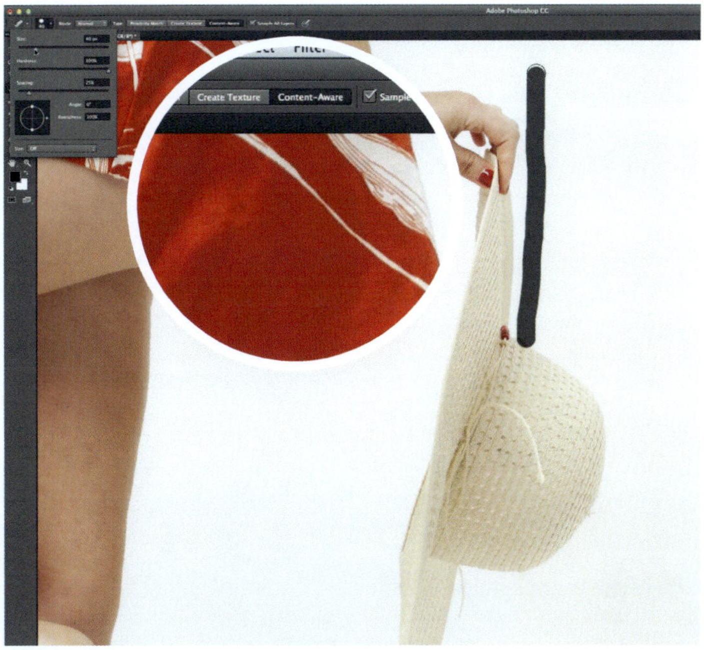

6 Use Content-Aware

Grab the Spot Healing Brush tool. If you leave this tool set to the Proximity Match option it will behave like Camera Raw's Spot Removal tool and automatically select adjacent pixels. This risks sampling and cloning bits of hat over the remaining card edge. Tick Content-Aware instead. Click the Brush Preset picker and choose a brush tip with a size of 40. Press Cmd/Ctrl+D, then paint over the remaining card edges a few times to replace it with white pixels.

7 Tidy up the loose ends

Dab the Spot Healing Brush tool over any scuffs and scratches on the studio floor to automatically replace them with neighbouring whiter pixels. Reduce the Size to 25. Paint over the stray string that overlaps the hat, and the Spot Healing Brush tool will find and replace the target pixels with a suitable hat texture. It even knows where the hat ends and the backdrop begins, so you can remove the string at the edge with a stroke.

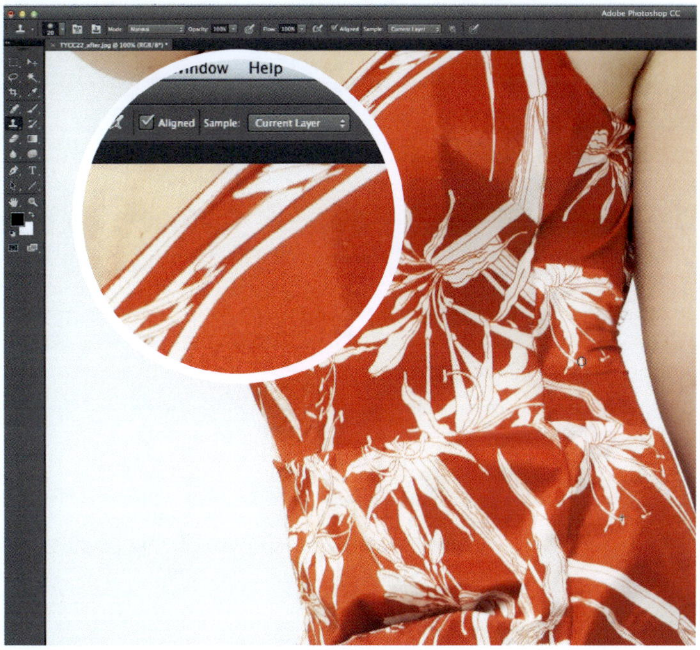

8 Clone the pattern

The Clone Stamp tool does a similar job to the Patch and Spot Healing Brush tools, but it doesn't heal the transplanted pixels. Grab the Clone Stamp tool. Choose a soft brush tip. Tick Aligned so that the sampling cross-hair maintains the same relative position to the brush tip. Set Sample to Current Layer. Alt-click to sample the pattern on the dress. Paint to clone the sampled pattern to a new location.

The healing tools

Master the Healing Brush, Spot Healing Brush, and Clone Stamp tools for speedy image tidying and flawless retouching

In this lesson, we'll look at the two healing tools: the Spot Healing Brush and the older Healing Brush. They're most commonly used to tidy up images, a task at which they excel. Whether you need to get rid of a sensor mark, hide an annoying landmark or remove imperfections on skin, the healing tools are the number one choice. Both brushes could be described as intelligent – they analyse the area you want to fix and come up with a solution of their own.

The Healing Brush works in a similar way to the Clone Stamp tool. Hold down Alt to target a source area, then use this region to paint over your imperfections. It's most effective when you target an area of similar tone and colour. For example, if you wanted to remove a pimple, hold down Alt and click a clean area next to the spot. Then paint over it and watch it disappear. The tool differs from the Clone Stamp tool in that it will automatically recognise the area you want to remove, and in most cases, match the tones and colours for a seamless fix.

The Spot Healing Brush was introduced in CS2 as the new and improved version of the Healing Brush. Unlike its older brother, there's no need to hold down Alt and define a source – you simply paint over the problem area and the tool performs a neat trick. This is one aid guaranteed to impress any non-Photoshop user who happens to be looking over your shoulder. A couple of clicks is all it takes to look like a retouching pro.

The Healing Brush gives greater control, but because the Spot Healing Brush doesn't require you to define a source, it's probably the more useful of the two. There is also a great feature called Content-Aware. This makes your fixes far more intelligent, as you'll see...

Perfect portraits with healing tools

Eradicate skin problems, tone down bags under the eyes and de-wrinkle your subjects

The healing tools are most effective when you use them to remove marks or blemishes from clean areas. This makes them ideal for working over skin to get rid of pimples, tone down any unattractive lines and give your subjects a bit of polish.

In fact, the tools perform so well that the temptation is often to go too far when retouching a face. Luckily, when you overdo it, you have the option to tone down your healing strokes, as long as you create a new, empty layer above your image layer, then check Sample All Layers in the Options bar. Once you've made your corrections, lower the opacity of the layer to make the effect more subtle.

The Spot Healing Brush feeds on nearby pixels to perform its miraculous fixes, so it's important that they're smooth, clean and low contrast. Try removing a stray strand of hair against a neutral background and the tool will do a grand job. But then try healing a grey strand in the thick of someone's hair. More often than not you'll get blotchy results.

With experience, you'll soon learn to recognise the areas where the tool will perform well, and also which ones to avoid.

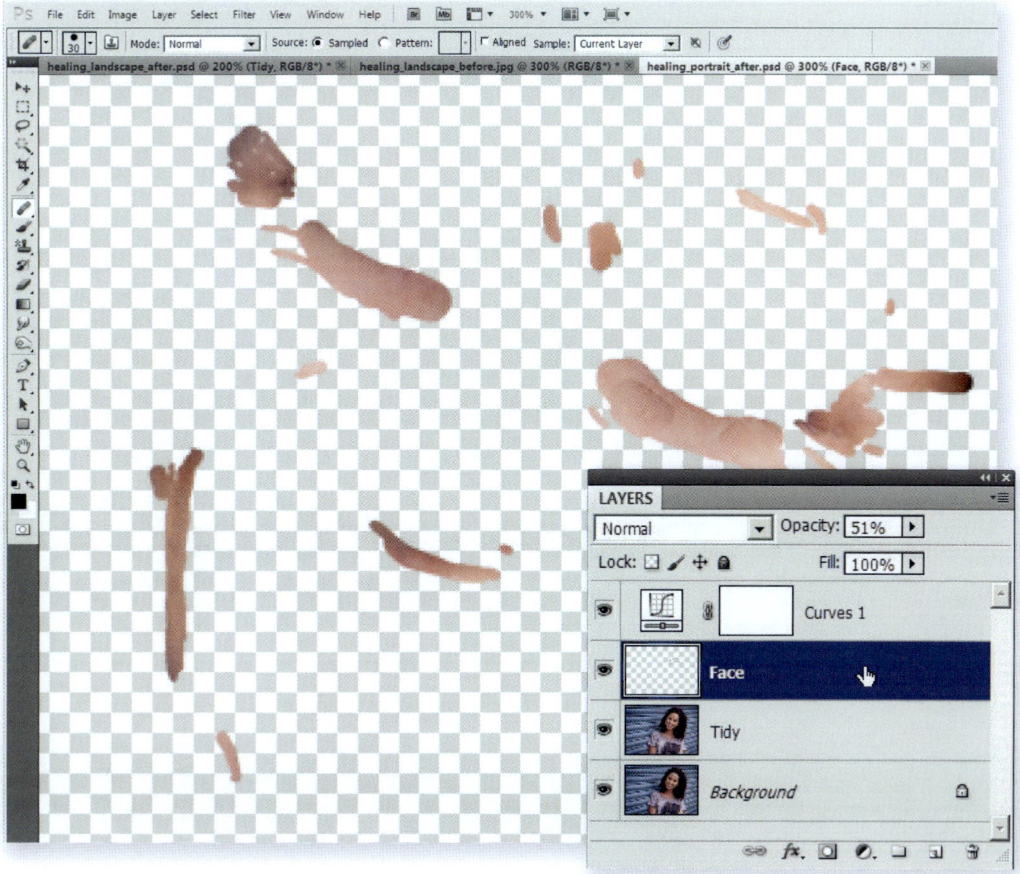

Remove blemishes

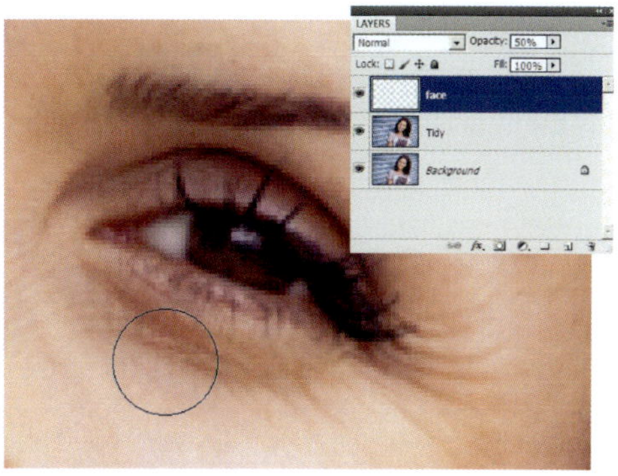

1 Duplicate background

Open a portrait and press Cmd/Ctrl+J to duplicate your Background layer. Rename it 'Tidy'. Select the Spot Healing Brush and dab over areas needing a fix. Use the square bracket keys to resize your brush as you work.

2 Start healing

Switch to the Healing Brush to work on edge areas that need more control. Hold down Alt and define a source similar to the area you'd like to fix, then paint over it. Then go to the Layers Panel and click Create new layer to get a new layer.

3 Sample all layers

Switch to the Spot Healing Brush, then go to the Options bar and check Sample All Layers. Zoom in and paint around any blemishes you want to remove. Afterwards, reduce the opacity of your new layer to 50% to fade the effect.

Get clever with Content-Aware

Tidy-up jobs are quicker and more effective with the Content-Aware healing feature

Spot Healing has been vastly improved with the new Content-Aware feature. This is now the default healing mode in the Options bar, as opposed to Proximity Match or Create Texture.

In previous Photoshop versions, the Spot Healing Brush worked brilliantly for fixing imperfections in smooth areas, but if you attempted to correct something near an edge you soon saw its limitations. With Content-Aware selected, the tool now performs with far greater intelligence. If you try healing a large area, the brush may take a few seconds to come up with a solution. This is because it's analysing data around your entire image, not just the part you're painting over.

The corrections are usually excellent, but even if they're not perfect, they give a good starting point from which you can zoom in with the Clone Stamp or Patch tools to fine-tune. Experiment with the tool by removing people or big objects from images. The results are difficult to predict but are often surprisingly effective.

Content-Aware healing is brilliant at removing distracting elements. We've used it here to erase a car, telegraph poles and wires. They needed nothing more than a few strokes to remove.

Tidying up a scene

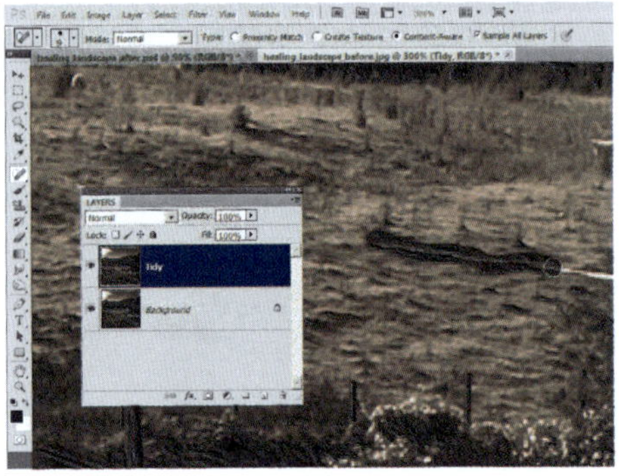

1 Copy the landscape

Open a landscape containing elements you want to remove. Press Cmd/Ctrl+J to duplicate your Background layer. Rename this 'Tidy'. Use the Spot Healing Brush to paint over the distracting elements, resizing the brush with [and] as you go.

2 Zoom in

When you've erased the smaller distractions, zoom in on a big one, such as this car. Paint over the entire area with the Spot Healing Brush, then decrease the size of your brush to dab over areas where the initial heal has failed to work.

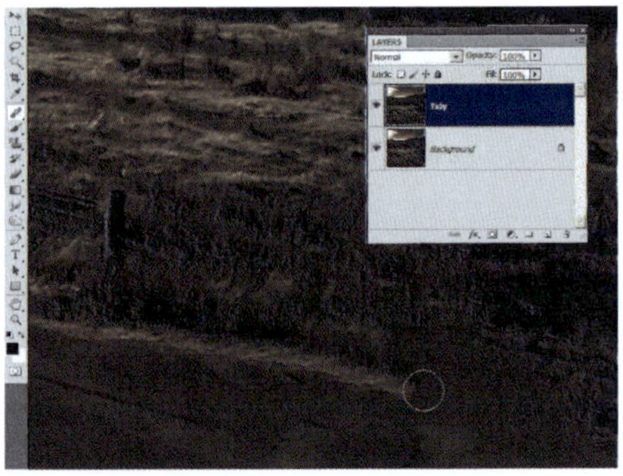

3 Bring back detail

Switch to the Healing Brush. Hold down Alt and target a joining area – where grass meets road in this image. Dab along the road edge to bring back detail. If necessary, use the Clone Stamp and Patch tools to fine-tune the region.

Photoshop Anatomy Healing tools

These tools are fully customisable and there are plenty of options to experiment with

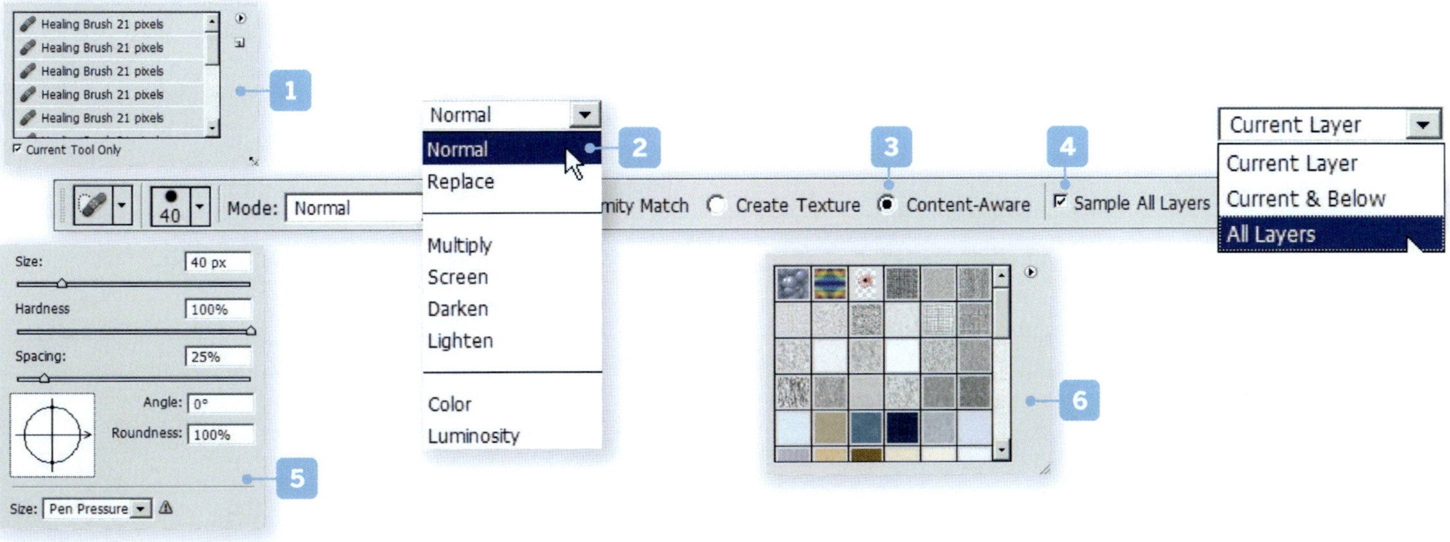

1 SETTING DEFAULTS

Use the Tool Preset Picker to save the characteristics of the healing tools, such as a certain size brush, opacity or Blend mode.

2 CHANGE THE LOOK

Use the Effect Mode drop-down menu to choose different blends for your Spot Healing Brush tool. This alters the pixels that show through when you paint.

3 TYPE OPTIONS

Proximity Match is the older mode that used to be the Spot Healing Brush's default setting. In CS5, it's changed to the superior Content-Aware feature.

4 TEST IT OUT

Sample from a combined source of All Layers or your Current Layer. Current & Below is useful when you want to carry out editable healing on a new blank layer.

5 CUSTOMISE THE BRUSH

Move the slider to alter the size, hardness and spacing of your brush. In most cases, a soft-edged tool works best.

6 SELECT PATTERNS

Choose Pattern to sample pixels from a pattern. Load in different patterns by clicking the play icon in the top right-hand corner.

Understanding... THE CLONE SOURCE PANEL

The Clone Source Panel allows you to change the characteristics of the Healing Brush tool and the Clone Stamp tools.

The five stamps placed along the top of the panel [1] allow you to set up to five different sample sources. This means that you can quickly select one of the five and there's no need to resample a source by clicking Alt within your image. You can also choose whether or not to view an overlay of your sample source within your brush tip by checking the box next to Show Overlay [2]. Change the Blend mode of your healing tool to paint with different colour transparency effects [3].

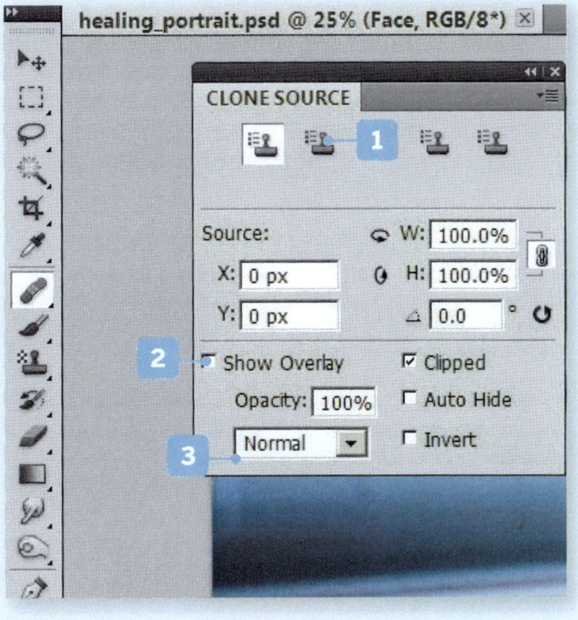

THREE TOOLS FOR SUPERB RESULTS

The two healing tools are powerful enough to give you superb results, but they occasionally slip up around areas of detail. When this happens, just hit S to switch to the Clone Stamp tool, then hold Alt to define a source. Used together, the three tools constitute a formidable retouching team. The Clone Stamp tool might not be as clever as the healing ones, but it does make it far easier to predict what your strokes will do. On portraits, the Clone Stamp tool works best when set at a low opacity of about 20%. This allows you to build up your brush strokes and vary your target source for

Content-Aware

Clone, move, patch and heal an image the smart way using the intelligent Content-Aware tools

In this Tool School, we'll explore ways to make tools perform more effectively, thanks to the Content-Aware option. This intelligent feature can dramatically speed up your editing. When you paint with the Spot Healing Brush over an unwanted pimple on a model's cheek, the tool will automatically sample adjacent skin pixels, place them over the pimple and seamlessly blend the join between cloned pixels and their neighbours. However, if the pimple is too close to a facial feature such as an eyebrow, the brush may inadvertently sample some hair and place it over the pimple. This forces you to undo the edit and switch to its cousin the Healing Brush, so that you can manually Alt-click to choose a patch of clear skin to place over the pimple.

Alternatively, by activating the Spot Healing Brush's Content-Aware option it will analyse the pimple in context with its surroundings, enabling the tool to take a suitable skin sample rather than an inappropriate eyebrow to place over the pimple.

The Content-Aware option enables tools such as the Spot Healing Brush to become a bit more intelligent, so that they can perform more effectively. However, even with this IQ boost they still have their limitations. The Content-Aware Spot Healing Brush will usually do a decent job of replacing a horizontal power cable that crosses a building's vertical lines with appropriate pixels, but if the cable overlaps a more complex shape, then the sampled and relocated pixels will be unlikely to blend successfully with their neighbours. In these instances you'll still need the Healing Brush or Clone Stamp tools to manually sample more appropriate pixels.

So Content-Aware technology isn't infallible, but as you'll see, they can be very useful when retouching certain images.

Fix photos with Fill and Patch

Use Content-Aware to remove distracting background objects

Content-Aware commands such as Fill and Patch can help you conquer common photo-fixing challenges. Take a look at our shaggy dog image. The horizon is tilted at an angle and there's a black barbecue stand cluttering up the background on the right, distracting the eye from our canine subject. You could try using the Crop tool to straighten the wonky horizon, but this would involve losing the lower edge of the dog if you need to retain the shape (or aspect ratio) of the image. Bits of unwanted barbecue stand on the right would still remain in the cropped shot, so you would also need to use the time-consuming Clone Stamp tool to replace the unwanted barbecue with clear sections of wall from the other side of the door.

To remove unwanted objects more quickly you can combine the powers of the Patch tool with the Fill command, especially as both can be made to be Content-Aware. The Patch tool enables you to replace the barbecue with blank bits of wall and then blend the relocated wall pixels seamlessly with their new neighbours. You can then rotate the shot to straighten the horizon, and use the Content-Aware Fill command to quickly fill these gaps.

BEFORE

Fill and Patch

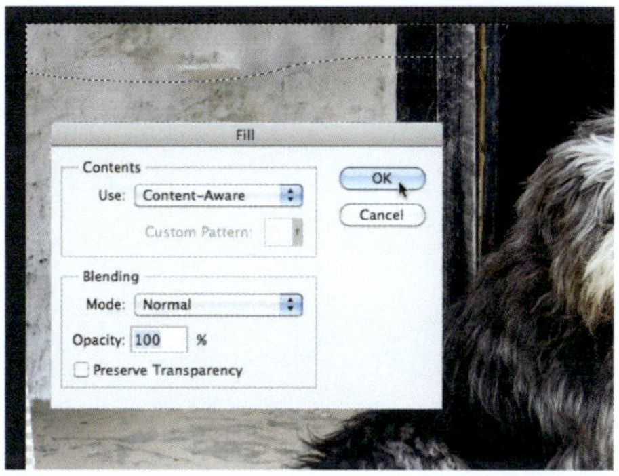

1 Draw a patch

Open an image similar to the one above. Grab the Patch tool. Set the Patch option to Content-Aware. Set Adaptation to Medium. Draw a patch around the distracting element. Drag the patch to overlap a clear section of the image.

2 Straighten the horizon

In the Layers panel, double click the locked Background layer to make it editable. Go to Edit›Transform›Rotate. Drag the corner handles to an angle of –5.00 degrees to straighten the horizon. Your own image will differ, of course.

3 Fill the gaps

Choose the Lasso tool. Draw a rough selection around a transparent corner and its adjacent pixels. Go to Edit›Fill. Set Use to Content-Aware. Click OK. This fills the selection with appropriate bits of sandstone and wooden beam.

The Content-Aware Move tool

Recompose your subjects and fill the gap that they leave with this new tool

When it comes to shooting animals (with a camera, we hasten to add!), you don't have much control over their behaviour. This can cause you to compromise when it comes to composing your photographs.

Take this photo of some sheep, for example. Ideally, we would have preferred the sheep to take a few steps to their left to fill the gap between the group and the tree. In older versions of Photoshop we could solve this problem by grabbing the Patch tool, setting it to Destination and then drawing round the two sheep on the far left.

We could then drag them closer to the tree to relocate them. We'd then need to use the Clone Stamp tool to replace the original two sheep with an empty section of ground and sky.

Thanks to the new Content-Aware Move tool in CS6 and CC you can work more quickly. In the walkthrough below you'll discover how to select the sheep, drag them into a new position and then watch the gap that they leave become filled with appropriate pixels. You'll also learn how to tweak the Move tool's Adaptation options so that the gap left by the relocated objects is filled with content that blends more effectively with its surroundings.

Recompose shots with Content-Aware

1 Set up the options

Open an image similar to the one above. In the Options bar, set the Mode to Move. If you leave it on Extend then the sheep won't be replaced by an empty bit of landscape. Set the Adaptation to Very Strict so that the space left by the sheep blends.

2 Create new layer

Choose Layer›New Layer. Click OK. Tick the Sample All layers box in the Options bar. This enables the moved and filled areas to be applied to the transparent layer, leaving the original layer untouched. Draw around the elements you want to move.

3 Drag and drop

Drag the elements to the new location. They should blend with their new surroundings, and the gap they leave should be filled with appropriate detail. You may need to draw and move a few times for the tool to work.

Photoshop Anatomy Content-Aware options

Squeeze as much help as you can from Photoshop's clever Content-Aware tools

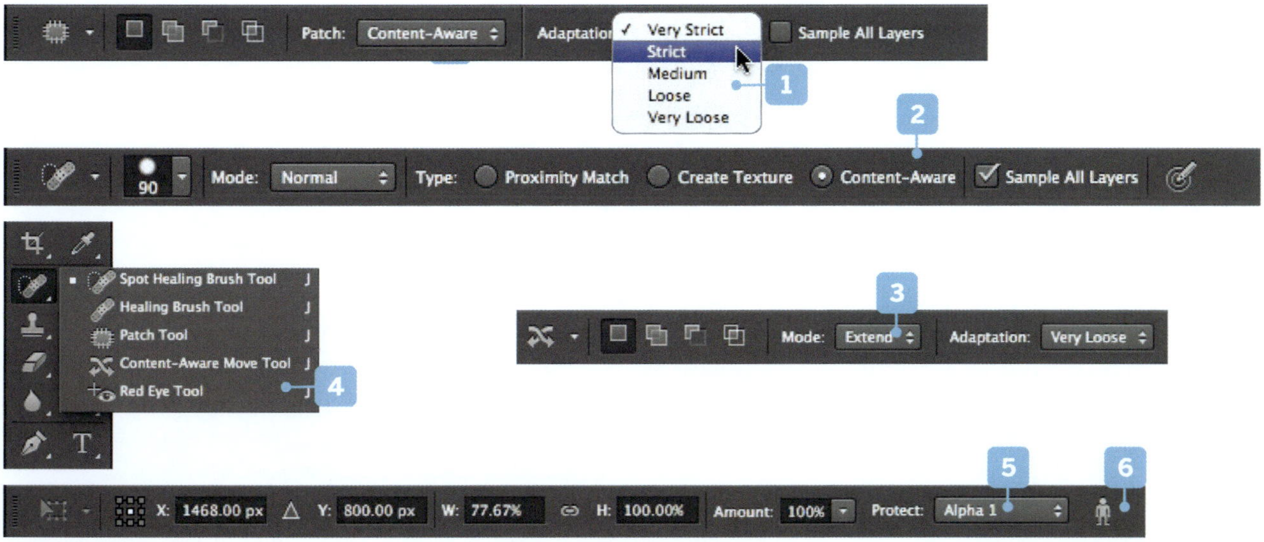

1 ADAPTATION

The Patch and the Content-Aware Move tools' Adaptation option enables you to fine-tune the way the edited pixels blend with their surroundings.

2 OPTIONS

The Spot Healing Brush can automatically sample adjacent pixels more intelligently if you enable its Content-Aware option.

3 EXTEND

The Content-Aware Move tool's Extend option enables you to select textures at the edge of the frame and drag to extend them.

4 CONTENT-AWARE

This compartment contains three Content-Aware tools – the Spot Healing Brush tool, the Patch tool and the Content-Aware Move tool.

5 PROTECTED AREAS

The Content-Aware Scale command can avoid squashing certain objects if you select them, turn them into an Alpha channel and select that channel.

6 SKIN TONES

The Content-Aware Scale command has a protect skin tones icon if your shot has any people in it. This helps to avoid squashing them too.

Understanding... CONTENT-AWARE SCALING

If you use the Edit>Transform>Scale command to scale a shot, you'll squash or stretch it. The Content-Aware Scale command can selectively squash or stretch unimportant pixels and preserve the proportions. For an example, open an image like the one on the right. Double click the Background layer's thumbnail to unlock it [1]. Go to Edit>Content Aware Scale. Drag the left control handle of the bounding box [2] to the right to transform it horizontally. The command scales the sky and grass between the tree and the cow [3] to a greater extent, while making a lesser transformation to the tree and cow [4]. This avoids squashing the animal while placing it closer to the tree.

Retouch portraits

Learn how to reshape faces and clothes, tidy and colour hair, and polish off your portraits to perfection

In this tutorial we've got a selection of professional retouching techniques for reshaping bulges in clothes, boosting skin and adding depth with the Dodge and Burn tools. Along the way we cover key skills like selections, layer masks and adjustment layers. You might not need to use every skill here on every portrait, but it's useful to have them in your retouching arsenal for when they're needed. We'll round things off with a retro colour effect using brushes. And most important, every edit in the workflow is on a separate layer, so you can keep things natural by reining in any over-the-top effects by lowering the opacity. Open retouch_before.jpg to get started. Right click the layer in the Layers panel and choose Convert to Smart Object, then go to Filter›Liquify. Zoom in to the waist, then grab the Forward Warp tool and use it to gently push the clothes into a smoother line. Next, move on to the face. Push the nose inwards slightly and tuck in the chin for a stronger jaw line. Click OK and proceed to step one.

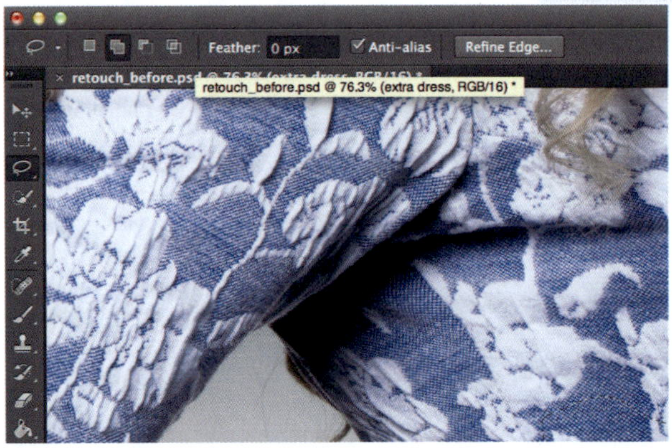

1 Copy the dress

There's a distracting fold in the clothes where the dress meets the armpit. The easiest way to remove it is to copy a similar area on top. Grab the Lasso tool from the Tools panel and make a rough selection of a nearby area of dress. Make it slightly larger than the crease we want to cover. Hit Cmd/Ctrl+J to copy the selection to a new layer.

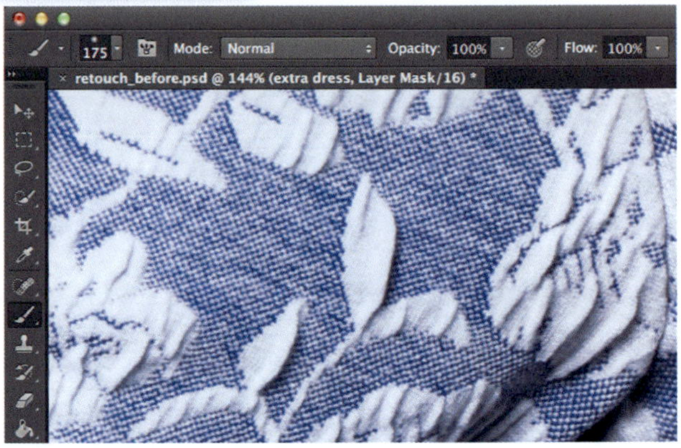

2 Hide the creases

Grab the Move tool and drag the newly copied piece of dress over the offending crease under the armpit. Try to position it so that the pattern continues unbroken. Hold down Alt and click the Add layer mask icon to hide the extra piece of dress. Grab the Brush tool, set colour to white, choose a soft-edged tip, then paint to obscure the crease.

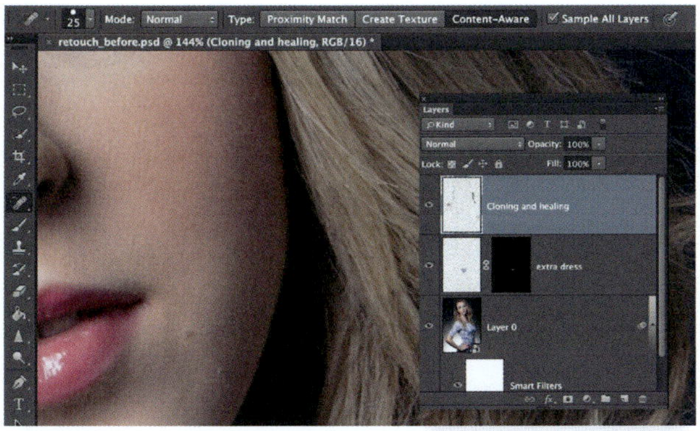

3 Clone and heal

Click the Create new layer icon in the Layers panel. Grab the Clone Stamp tool. Set Sample: All Layers in the tool options and hit 2 for 20% opacity. Smooth out any rough patches by Alt-clicking to sample clean areas nearby. To remove spots or stray hairs, grab the Spot Healing brush, check Sample All Layers, and then paint over them.

4 Add depth

Press Cmd/Ctrl+Shift+ Alt+E to merge a new layer. Set the Blend mode to Luminosity. Now we can lighten or darken tones without affecting colour. Grab the Dodge tool and set Range: Highlights, Exposure 12%, and paint to lighten the highlights on the face and arms. Switch to the Burn tool, set Range: Shadows, and paint to darken the shadows.

5 Fix her roots

To improve the darker patches of hair, create a new layer and change the Blend mode to Color. Grab the Brush tool. Alt-click over the hair to sample a colour, then paint over the dark patch. If the colour's too strong, lower the layer opacity. Hit Cmd/Ctrl+J to copy the layer, then change the Blend mode to Screen and lower the opacity to 10%.

6 Lift the eyes

Zoom in to the eyes. Create a Curves adjustment layer, then plot two points on the line to create an S-shape, boosting contrast. Hit Cmd/Ctrl+I to invert the layer mask to black, then paint with white over the iris to reveal the effect. Add a Hue/Saturation layer. Boost saturation, then Alt-drag the mask thumbnail from the Curves layer to copy it over.

7 Sharpen up

Add a Curves layer and lift the curve line. Press Cmd/Ctrl+I and paint to reveal the effect in the eye whites. Add a Curves layer, darken the image, then restrict it to the edges of the iris and pupil. Add another and boost contrast in the hair. Create a new layer. Grab the Sharpen tool. Set Strength 13% and check Sample All Layers. Paint the lashes.

8 Add some colour

Create a Solid Color adjustment layer. Change the blending mode to Soft Light, then set the colour to R: 146, G: 82, B: 165. Create a new layer and set the mode to Screen. Grab the Brush tool and paint a few large, soft spots of dark red and yellow. Lower the opacity. Add a Curves layer and plot a shallow S-curve to boost the contrast.

Dodge and Burn

Get to grips with these versatile tools to tweak the tones of your photographs with precision

In this Tool School, we look at the versatile Dodge, Burn and Sponge tools. These useful brush-based tools let you lighten (dodge) or darken (burn) shadows, midtones or highlights in specific areas, offering a quick and easy way to fine-tune exposure-related problems and reveal more detail. We'll come back to the Sponge tool in due course, because it's not a major player compared with the Dodge and Burn tools.

The Dodge and Burn tools take their names from traditional darkroom techniques. Negatives were developed by shining light from an enlarger onto a piece of light-sensitive paper. If you placed a small object between the light and the paper during the exposure, you could cast a shadow on a specific part of the print. Since the shaded (dodged) area received less light than the rest of the shot, it would remain lighter. To darken (burn) detail in a different part of the print, you needed to protect – or mask – the rest of the photo paper with a piece of card. The longer exposure time would darken the unmasked region.

Cameras use multiple points to assess, or meter, the scene's lighting. If you shoot a person against a bright sky, the camera may set the exposure to capture detail in the brighter areas, so the (darker) person will be under-exposed. Alternatively, the camera may expose a landscape to capture detail in the terrain, over-exposing the brighter highlights and blowing out sky detail. You may find that atmospheric conditions cause distant features such as mist-diffused mountains to become washed out. The Dodge and Burn tools let you target and tweak problematic areas to reveal more tonal detail, without adjusting the exposure of the scene as a whole. The Dodge and Burn tools share a toolbox compartment with the Sponge tool. Here's how to use them...

Combining Dodge and Burn with layers

Use layer blends to help you employ these powerful tools in a non-destructive way

Like many Photoshop tools, the Dodge, Burn and Sponge tools are brush-based. This means you can use the Brush Preset Picker to soften their edges, more effectively blending edited areas with their neighbouring pixels.

You can also change the size of each tool's tip to make it act upon a larger region, or fine-tune a smaller section, with precision. You can also use the Options bar in order to customise the way the Dodge and Burn tools behave.

If you want to use the Dodge tool to lighten an area's midtones without over-exposing its highlights – like on the wall in our monochrome landscape, for example – then go to the Options bar and set the Range in the drop-down menu to Shadows. This will force the Dodge tool to lighten the darkest shadow pixels, but leave the lighter midtones and highlights untouched.

When you use the Dodge and Burn tools, you permanently change the contents of the image.

In the step-by-step tutorial below, we show you how to dodge and burn a landscape image on a separate layer, which will give you the freedom to experiment without permanently lightening or darkening the tones on the original shot.

Dodge and burn non-destructively

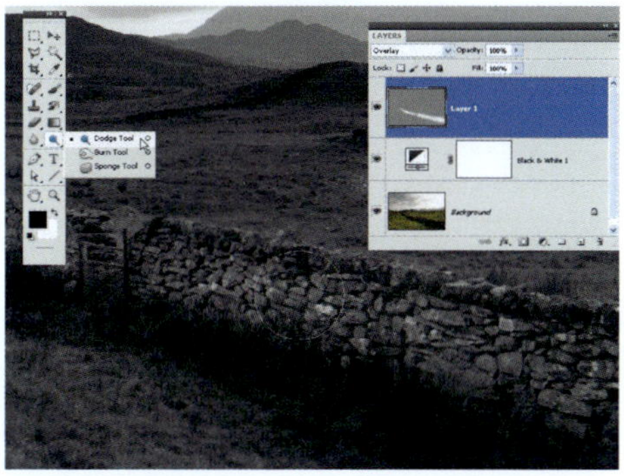

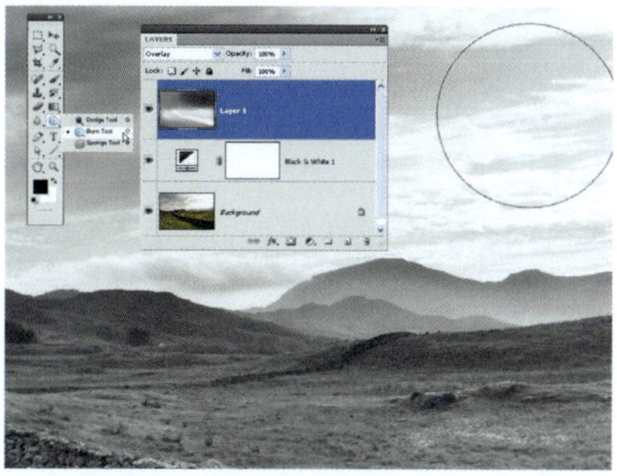

1 Fill with grey

Open a landscape image with exposure problems. Choose Layer›New Adjustment Layer›Black & White. Click the Create new layer icon. Choose Edit›Fill. Use 50% Gray, and click OK. Now set the grey layer's Blend mode to Overlay.

2 Lighten the landscape

Select the Dodge tool. Set Size to 300, Range to Midtones and Exposure to 25%. Click the Overlay layer, then paint over the landscape to lighten its midtones. The low Exposure setting lets us dodge the landscape in finer increments.

3 Darken the sky

Select the Burn tool. Set Size to 700, Range to Highlights and Exposure to 30%. Paint over the sky to reveal some of the over-exposed highlight detail. Switch between the Dodge and Burn tools to lighten or darken particular features.

Retouch a portrait

Use the Dodge and Sponge tools to correct flaws and create brighter eyes

As well as enabling you to bring out the shapes and textures in a monochrome landscape, the Dodge and Burn tools can help you enhance a portrait. In this step-by-step guide we'll show you how to draw attention to the subject's eyes by dodging their whites to make them brighter. You'll also learn how to create a more attractive smile by lightening the subject's teeth.

When dodging bright highlights, you risk creating blown-out – or clipped – areas that feature no detail. You can also create unsightly shifts in colour and exaggerate colours you don't want to see, such as red blood vessels in the subject's eyes. The Protect Tones box in the Options bar is designed to help reduce clipping, but if you dodge directly onto the image layer then clipping and exaggerated colours can still occur.

In our step-by-step guide we'll show you how to limit the Dodge tool so that it lightens tones, but leaves colours untouched. To do this, you need to dodge onto a copy of the original layer. By setting the duplicate layer's Blend mode to Luminosity, you'll only see changes in brightness, and the colours will be left unchanged.

Brighter eyes

1 Duplicate the layer

Open one of your portraits. In the Layers panel, drag the Background layer onto the Create a new layer icon to duplicate it, then set the Background Copy layer's Blend mode to Luminosity using the drop-down menu at the top of the Layers panel.

2 Lighten the highlights

Grab the Dodge tool and choose a soft round brush with a Size of 100. Set Range to Highlights and Exposure to 11%. Click the Background Copy to target that layer. Paint a few strokes over the eyes to lighten them.

3 Whiten the teeth

Drop Exposure to 5% and paint to lighten the teeth. Then choose Layer>Flatten Image. Grab the Sponge tool and set Mode to Desaturate and Flow to 40. Set the brush size to 125 and paint over the teeth to remove the stains.

Photoshop Anatomy Dodge, Burn & Sponge

Tweak tones with more precision by modifying the behaviour of these brush-based tools

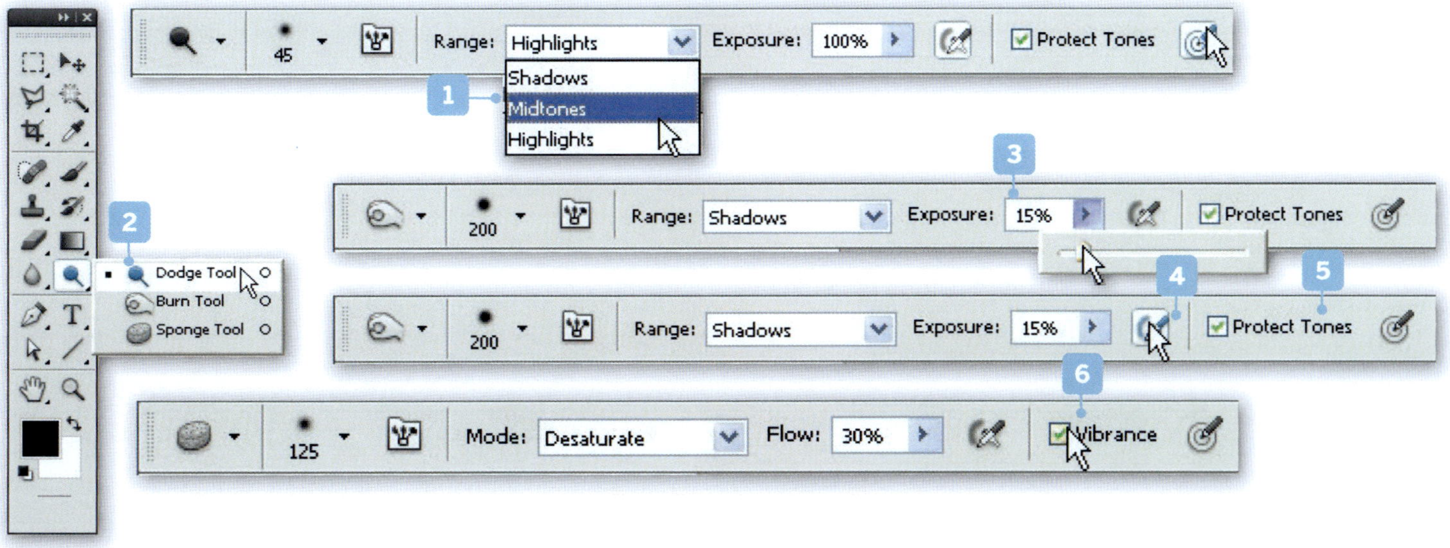

1 RANGE

You can get the Dodge and Burn tools to work with specific tones by choosing Shadow, Midtones or Highlights from the Range drop-down menu.

2 TOOL COMPARTMENT

The Dodge, Burn and Sponge tools are a tone-tweaking team, so they share the same compartment in the Tools Panel. Press Shift+O to cycle between them.

3 EXPOSURE

By using a low Exposure setting, you can dodge or burn in smaller increments. This helps you avoid going over the top with your tone tweaking.

4 AIRBRUSH MODE

This mode enables you to use a pressure-sensitive stylus to vary the exposure when dodging and burning. It works with the tablet's pressure settings.

5 PROTECT TONES

Keep this box ticked to help minimise the amount of clipping and hue changing produced by the Dodge and Burn tools.

6 VIBRANCE

This is a Sponge tool option. It stops the tool from over-saturating colours that are already vibrant; it will only alter weaker colours.

Understanding... THE BRUSH PRESET PICKER

You can increase the size of the Dodge, Burn or Sponge tools [1] to cover wide areas like a sky quickly, or tweak smaller areas like teeth with precision. To help the edited pixels blend more effectively with their neighbours, drag the Hardness slider [2] to the left. This creates a brush that produces a more gradual soft-edged adjustment. If you click this icon [3] you can preview the edited brush tip's shape in the Brushes Panel, and check how soft or hard its edge is. If you want to preserve and reuse a particular combination of Size and Hardness, click the New Preset icon [4]. You can then give your brush a name (such as 'Tooth Brush'). You'll find the saved tip by scrolling to the bottom of the Brush Preset picker.

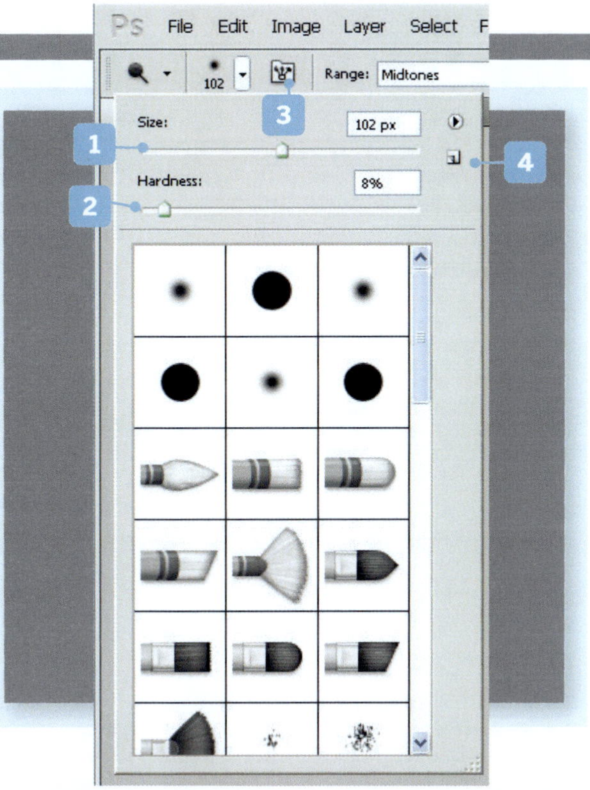

APPLYING GLOBAL TONE CHANGES

Before you begin to use the non-destructive dodging and burning technique demonstrated in our step-by-step guide here, use Layer>New Adjustment Layer>Levels to tweak the overall range of tones in the image. A healthy monochrome print needs a strong contrast between the darkest shadows and the brightest highlights, or it will look too grey and flat. In the Levels command window, drag the black input levels slider right to the edge of the histogram graph to darken the blackest shadows. Drag the white input levels slider left to the other edge of the graph. This will help the landscape's lighter details stand out even further, and increase the contrast of the image as a whole. ■

Dodge and Burn tools in action

Discover how to draw the eye around an image, using two of the most useful tools in Photoshop's creative arsenal

1 Lift the subject

Press Cmd/Ctrl+J to duplicate the background. Grab the Dodge tool from the Tools panel. In the tool options at the top, set Range to Midtones, Exposure 10%. Paint over areas of the image to gradually lighten them, using the] and [keys to change the brush size.

2 Darken distractions

Switch to the Burn tool. Set Range to Midtones for general darkening, or Shadows to push the darker areas more. Keep Exposure below 20%. Darken parts of the image you want to de-emphasise, such as distractions. If you find you need to dodge again, hold down Alt to switch back.

Photoshop Anatomy Dodge and Burn

Discover the menus and options to help you control these powerful tools

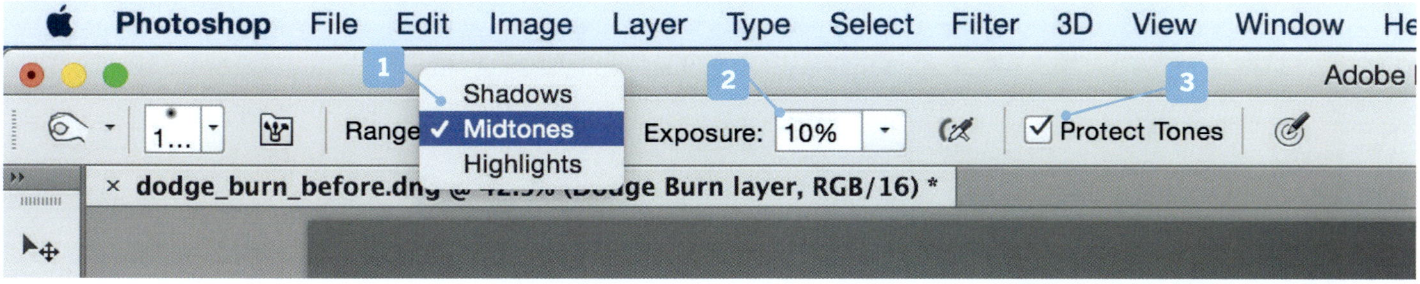

1 RANGE

Both the Dodge and Burn tools enable you to target either the Shadows, Midtones or Highlights. For general lightening or darkening, use Midtones. As a rule, don't Dodge on Shadows or Burn on Highlights. However, if you want to add contrast to an area, first Dodge on Highlights, then Burn on Shadows.

2 EXPOSURE

The Exposure slider controls the strength of the darkening or lightening effect each tool produces. It goes all the way to 100%, but it's usually best to keep it below 20% and build up the effect gradually. Use the number keys on your keyboard to quickly set a value: 1 for 10%, 2 for 20% and so on.

3 PROTECT TONES

With the Protect Tones option turned on, the tools won't clip tones to pure white or black, which is useful when burning on shadows or dodging on highlights. At times it can be useful to switch this off – perhaps if you need to lighten a white backdrop to make it perfectly clean.

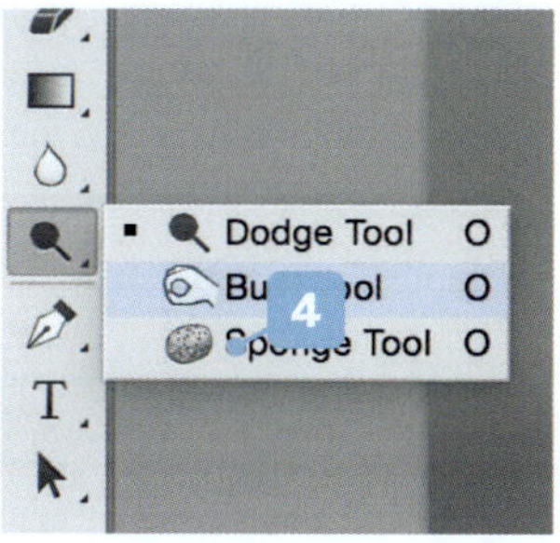

4 SPONGE

Alongside the Dodge and Burn tools in the Tools panel sits the Sponge tool. It enables you to selectively add or take out colour saturation – ideal for boosting a blue sky or toning down yellow teeth. With the Vibrance option ticked, the tool affects under-saturated colours while preserving stronger shades.

5 GREY LAYER

Fill a layer with 50% grey and set its blending mode to Overlay for non-destructive editing. To add the layer, Alt-click the New layer icon in the Layers panel, set the blending mode to Overlay and tick the Fill box. Now use Dodge and Burn with Range set to Midtones, or simply paint in white and black. To see which areas are affected, Alt-click the layer's eye icon to hide the other layers.

Understanding...
WHERE TO DODGE AND BURN

Our eyes are drawn to the lightest parts of an image first, so if you need to draw attention to your subject, lighten it [1] and emphasise any leading lines that head towards it, then darken down any distractions. Darkening down corners [2] can also help your composition by drawing the eye in towards the centre of the image and away from the edges of the frame. Objects such as the rocks here [3] and the sunlit edges of the ruin [4] will benefit from dodging the highlights to really make them stand out. And you can boost subtle colours in a sky [5] using the Sponge tool set to Saturate. Subtlety is key: always use a separate layer so that you have the option to tone down the effect afterwards by lowering the layer opacity.

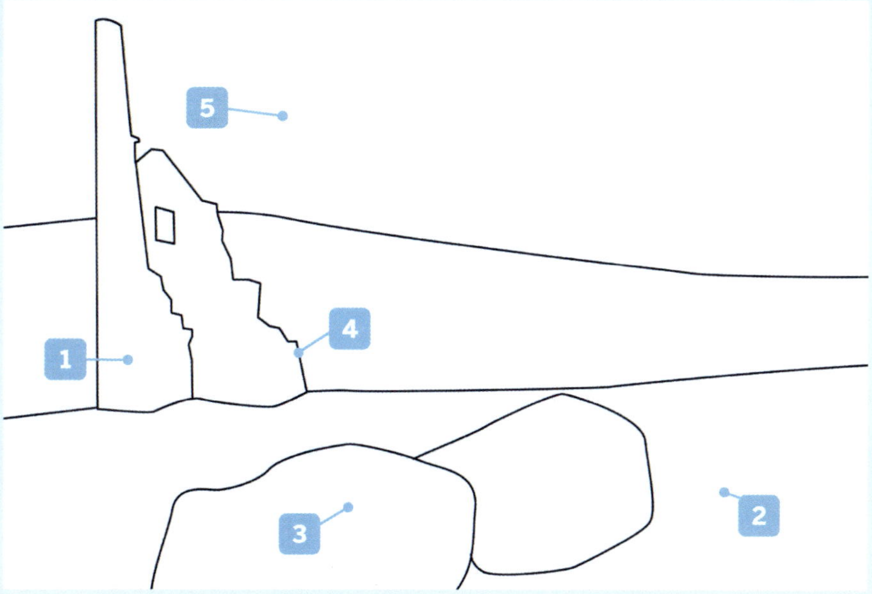

Camera Raw 9.6 - Nikon D700
Filmstrip
TYCC76.dng
TYCC77.dng
TYCC78.dng
TYCC79.dng
TYCC80.dng
R:
G:
B:

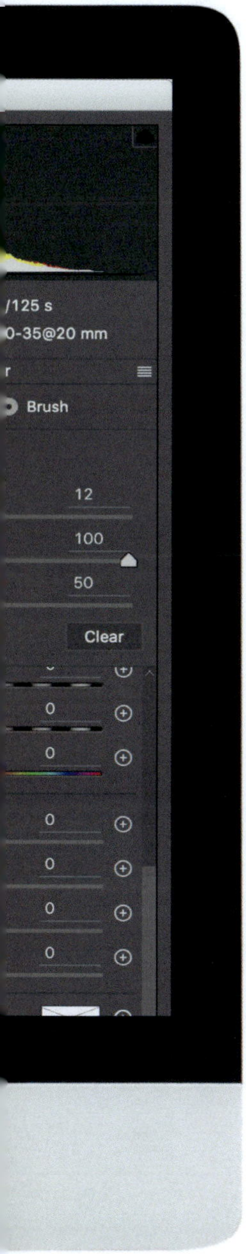

Creative effects

Discover the techniques you need to use to transform your photos with Photoshop's creative processing tools

Make a panorama

Discover how to stitch frames together with Photomerge

You can use layers and masks to combine details from different photographs to make a composite image, but these techniques can be very time consuming. Photoshop's Photomerge command, however, enables you to automate the processes of importing multiple images into a single document and blending them into a large, seamless panorama.

A photograph of a landscape can be disappointing when compared with our memory of the scene, because our peripheral vision tends to give us a wider field of view than a camera lens. You could try shooting with a wide-angle lens, but this can darken the corners of the image, and make the vertical lines at the edges of the frame curve. By panning the camera to shoot multiple images of the scene, you can capture a wider field of view with less vignetting and geometric distortion, and also produce a much larger print, especially if you shoot in portrait orientation.

You can then stitch these separate images together using the Photomerge command to create a stunning wide-angle composite that reveals more of the location than your lens could capture in a single shot. Photomerge automatically creates a wider canvas, positions the images so that the edge details overlap, and blends their edges together using masks. It also corrects vignetting and distortion, to help the images blend together.

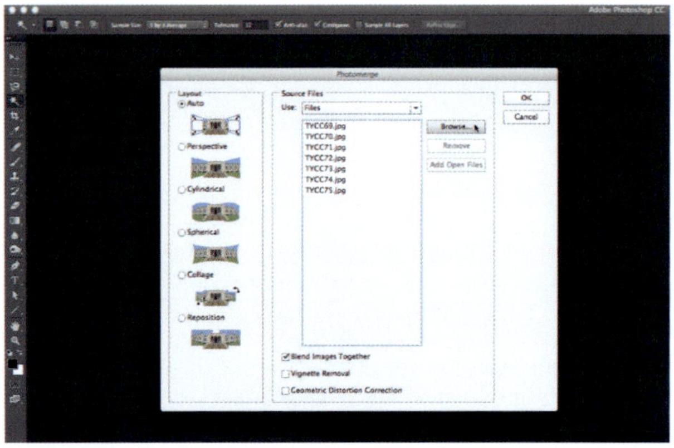

1 Select the images

Browse to the panorama source images in Bridge, Shift-click to select them and choose Tools›Photoshop› Photomerge. Alternatively, in Photoshop choose File› Automate›Photomerge. Click Browse and navigate to select TYCC69.jpg to TYCC75.jpg.

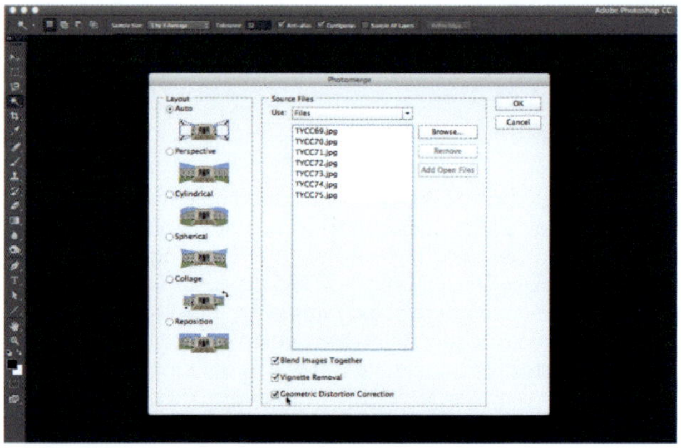

2 Choose your options

Choose the Auto Layout option. This enables Photomerge to move the images so that they overlap, and distort them if necessary to get them to align. Tick Blend Images Together to create masks. Tick Vignette Removal so that areas such as the sky will be more even.

3 Create a panorama

Click OK. Photomerge creates a wider canvas, adds the images as layers and moves them into position. You may notice transparent areas around the edges of the repositioned and distorted images. You could crop the edges, but that would create a much smaller panorama.

4 Fill the edges

Go to Layer›Flatten Image. The transparent edges will turn white. Grab the Magic Wand and select the white pixels. Choose Select›Modify›Expand. Choose a value of 4 pixels. Click OK. Go to Edit›Fill›Content-Aware. Press Cmd/Ctrl+D to deselect the marquee. The white patches vanish.

Merge panoramas with Camera Raw

Camera Raw now has some of the merging capabilities of Photoshop, and it's especially good at making panoramas

There's an increasing amount of crossover in editing tools between Camera Raw and Photoshop itself, and the panorama merging tools are a perfect example. It's now possible to create seamless panoramic images straight from Camera Raw without having to open Photoshop at all.

There are advantages to doing it this way, partly because it is faster and partly because you get some interesting and highly-effective merging tools.

Using Camera Raw is especially efficient if you shot your original images in the raw format, because there's little point in converting them and opening them in Photoshop to merge them when you can do it as a single process from Camera Raw. It also outputs a 'raw' panorama in Adobe's DNG format, so you can still apply all the usual raw processing decisions – exposure, white balance, distortion correction, curves and so on – even after the panorama has been created.

Inevitably, panoramas end up with rough edges because of the way the individual images have to be perspective-corrected, but Camera Raw has two options for dealing with this. Its Auto-Crop option crops right up to the edge of the image area, saving you from some precise and tedious manual cropping, while the new Boundary Warp option distorts (warps) the image to fill the full panorama area.

1 Open the source files

Use our TYCC99 start files if you want to follow our tutorial exactly – they are numbered 1-7. You should open them directly from Camera Raw by first selecting all seven files, then right-clicking any one of them and choosing Open in Camera Raw from the menu.

2 Merge to Panorama...

When you open more than one image in Camera Raw they're displayed as a vertical filmstrip on the left side of the window. In the top corner you'll see a drop-down menu icon, and from here you need to choose Select All and then the Merge to Panorama menu option.

3 Panorama Merge Preview

After a few moments spent merging the images, Camera Raw will open the Panorama Merge window, where you choose the 'Projection' settings and Crop and Warp settings. By default, the 'Spherical' projection is used and untidy edges are cropped off. It looks good already!

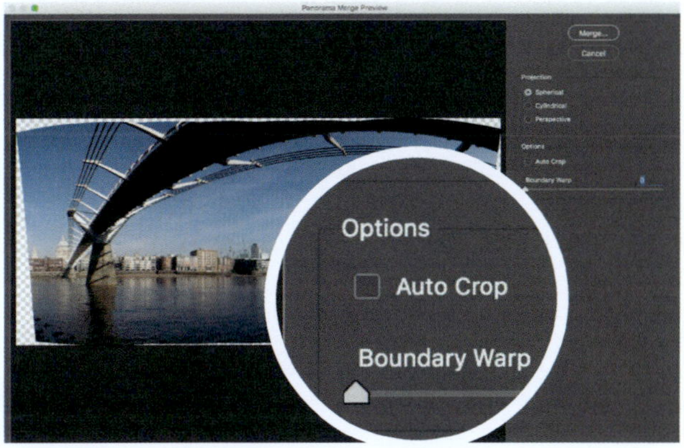

4 Projections explained

You'll see the effect of the different Projections more clearly if you deselect the Auto Crop box. Spherical projections combine the images on the inside surface of a virtual sphere, cylindrical projections use a virtual cylinder, while the Perspective option simulates a super-wide lens.

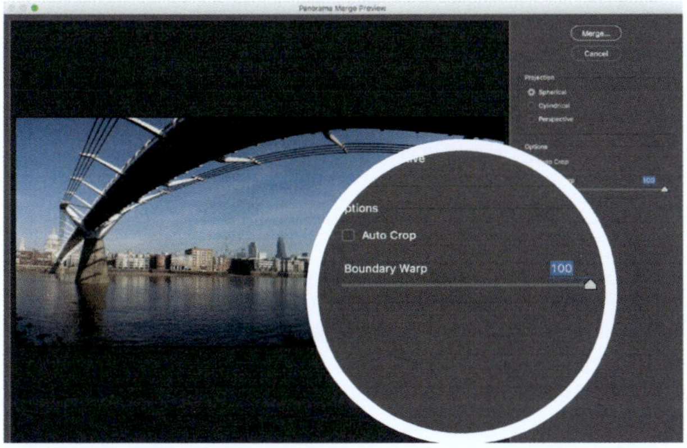

5 Boundary Warp explained

The Auto Crop option inevitably crops off some parts of the panorama, and if you don't want that, the alternative is the new Boundary Warp tool. This 'warps' the full panoramic image to push it right to the edges of the frame – the downside is that it does introduce some distortion.

6 Back in Camera Raw

When you're happy, click the Merge button in the top right corner. When the merge process is finished, a new merged DNG file appears in the Camera Raw filmstrip (even if you started with JPEGs). You can now open this in Photoshop or simply save it out as a new file.

Merge HDR shots with Camera Raw

Who needs HDR plug-ins? The HDR Merge feature now in Camera Raw produces very natural, controllable results

Photoshop has its own HDR tools, and for those who find these rather complex, there are plenty of third-party HDR plug-ins on the market. The difficulty with all of these, though, is that they introduce new jargon and processes to learn and, even when you've mastered these, it's not always easy to create natural-looking results and avoid that oversaturated HDR 'look'.

So the arrival of the HDR Merge feature in Adobe Camera Raw is really welcome. It doesn't just save time, it produces refreshingly natural-looking HDR images with little effort.

Like other HDR tools it presents an early preview of your merged image with controls for optimising the results. Camera Raw can automatically align images (useful if you weren't using a tripod) and automatically adjust the exposure (Auto Tone). It also has Deghosting options, which you may need to resolve movement between frames.

Most of our walkthrough, though, is devoted to the adjustments you can apply to your HDR image once it's been merged. You're working in the familiar Camera Raw editing environment with a flexible DNG-format image and all of the global and local adjustment tools at your disposal. The ones you'll find most useful for HDR are the Dehaze tool, Exposure, Highlight, Shadow and Clarity sliders, and Graduated Filter – between them, they can work wonders.

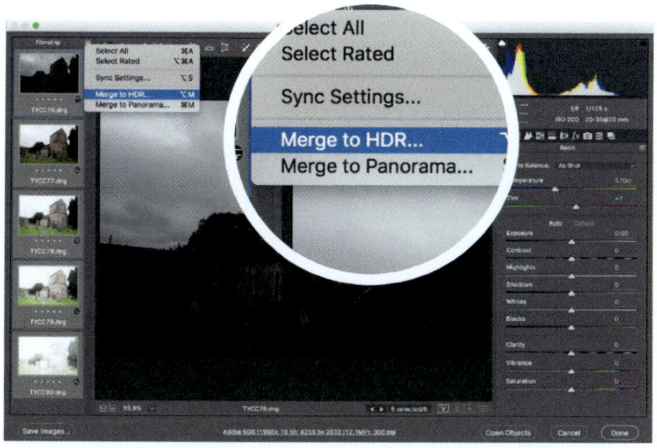

1 Open the source files TYCC76-80

Start by selecting all the source images in Bridge, then right-click any one of them and choose Open in Camera Raw from the menu. They'll be displayed in the filmstrip panel down the left side of the Camera Raw window – use the menu to Select All and then Merge to HDR...

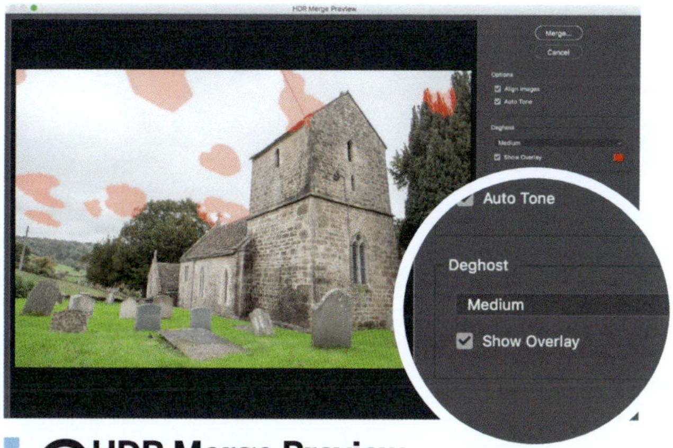

2 HDR Merge Preview

Camera Raw will merge the images and show a composite preview image in this window. You can leave the Align Images and Auto Tone boxes checked. The Deghost option is there if you have movement between frames. If you turn it on, you'll see 'ghosted' areas show in the picture.

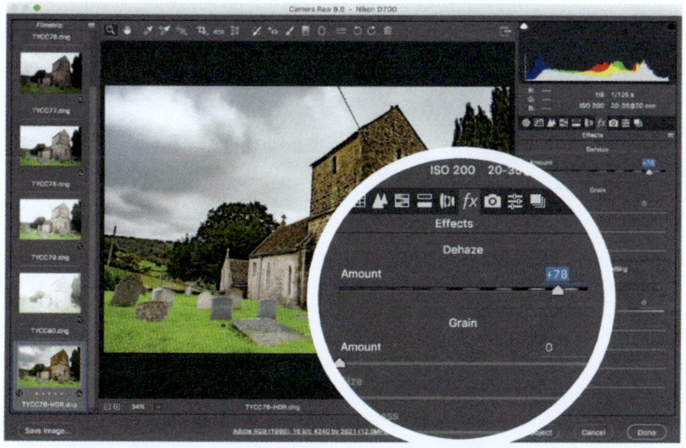

3 Use Dehaze to boost flat skies

Camera Raw will merge the separate shots into a single DNG file, ready for editing, and this is where you can really enhance the results. For example, although it's not specifically designed for skies, the Dehaze tool (Effects panel) gives our flat-looking sky a more dramatic, stormy look.

4 Exploit Highlights and Shadows

The advantage of using Camera Raw for HDR merging is that you use its regular adjustment tools to improve your picture rather than having to master bespoke and often complex HDR tools. Here, we've juggled the Exposure, Highlights and Shadows sliders to get the maximum tonal range.

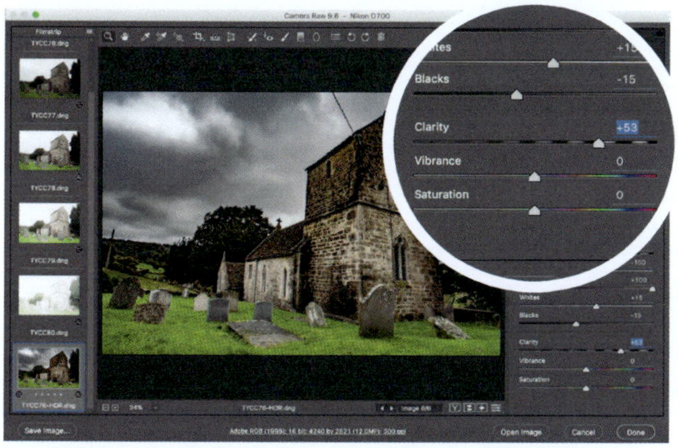

5 Clarity can cure low contrast

Sometimes you can compress a wide brightness range in an HDR shot so much that it loses contrast and looks 'flat'. If so, try giving the Clarity slider a hefty boost. This increases the localised contrast in the picture, making objects and outlines stand out much more clearly.

6 Use Graduated Filters on skies

If the sky is still a little too bright, use the Graduated Filter tool to darken it down – the DNG file almost certainly has highlight detail in reserve that you can bring out. We've finished off with the filter's Brush tool to erase the effect on the church tower where it juts up into the sky.

How to use the HDR Toning tools

Photoshop's HDR Toning adjustments can give an HDR 'look' to single images, but they can also be tricky to use

High dynamic range (HDR) images are usually created by blending a series of different exposures of the same scene. Photoshop's HDR Toning command, on the Image › Adjustments menu, however, is designed to offer HDR style effects and adjustments for single images.

In order to balance highlight and shadow detail in this way you'll need a photo with a full range of tones. It helps to start from a raw file, since this will typically offer a little more dynamic range than a JPEG. In this instance, though, our sample photo (TYCC84.jpg) does have a full range of tones and should benefit from the HDR toning treatment. The detail in the sky is fine, but the bridge and the buildings are too dark to be able to see their details clearly.

We're not using all the HDR Toning tools, so here's a quick guide to the others – and as always with HDR tools, you can expect some differences in the jargon and operation.

The Gamma and Exposure sliders in the Tone and Detail section work like brightness and contrast adjustments. Increasing the exposure will quickly clip highlight details, though, so take care. Moving the Gamma slider to the left increases contrast, moving it to the right reduces it. Lastly, the Toning Curve adjustments in the bottom section work more or less like Photoshop's regular Curves tools.

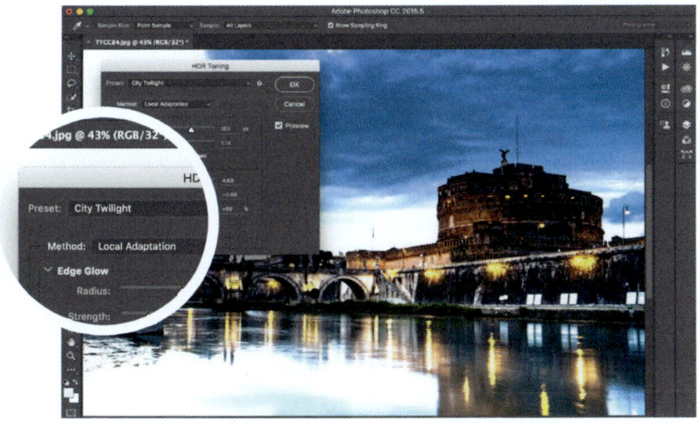

1 Try the preset effects

You don't have to get embroiled in the HDR Toning settings if you don't want to because there's a Presets menu at the top of the dialog. The effects are pretty harsh and unsubtle, though, including this City Twilight effect, which has really burned out the details in the sky and water.

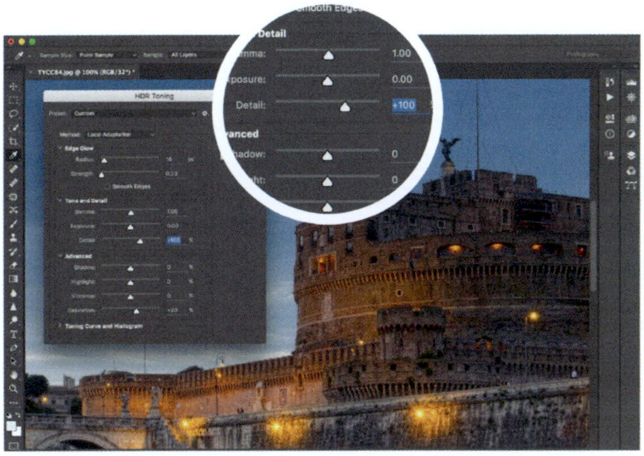

2 Now start from the defaults

If you want to create a more natural-looking result, you're better off starting from the Default settings option at the top of the Preset menu. Note that we have increased the Detail value to 100% in the Tone and Detail section – this will make the Edge Glow effects stronger…

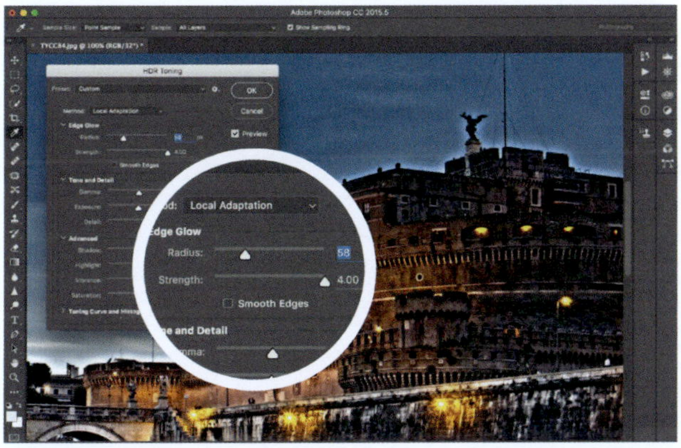

3 Glow strength

You'll notice that the default settings produce unnaturally flat detail, and the Edge Glow section is where you fix that. It works a lot like the Unsharp Mask filter – it exaggerates details but can create obvious edge 'halos' with high strength settings and low-medium radius values.

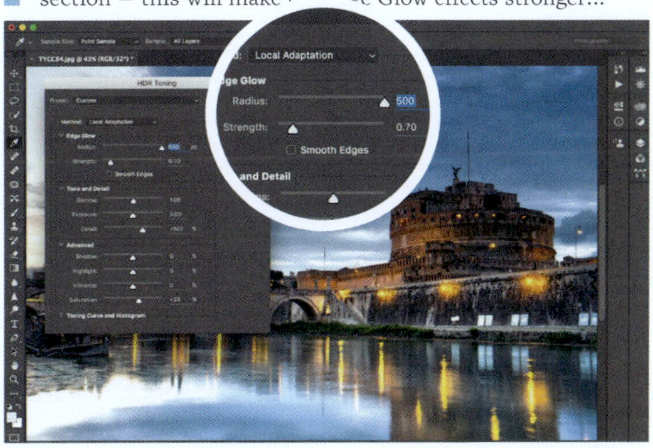

4 Glow radius

You can get a much more natural look by combining a high radius value with a low strength setting. This 'spreads' the glow effect so that it's less prominent and still gives the HDR image the localised contrast boost it needs to look realistic. It's a delicate balancing act that needs practice.

5 Recovering highlights

These adjustments have pushed the brighter parts of the sky into overexposure, but we can correct that by moving the Highlights slider to the left in the Advanced section. This tends to show up any chromatic aberration in the picture, though –note the edges of the buildings, far left.

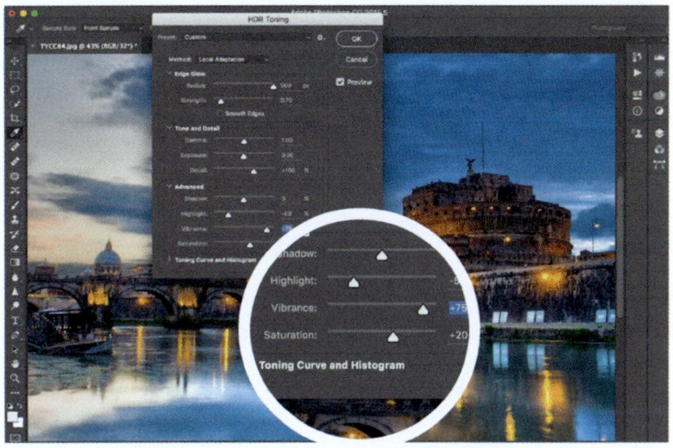

6 Saturation and vibrance

If your picture still needs a bit of a boost, try increasing the saturation and vibrance sliders in the Advanced section. The saturation slider increases the strength of all colours equally, but the vibrance slider can give better results by boosting the weaker colours more.

Make a motoring toy montage

Discover how to create fun, eye-catching composite images by shooting and combining people and toys

This tutorial is a combination of two fun techniques – forced perspective and Photoshop montage. With a little in-camera visual trickery, we can make a foot-long car look life-sized, then drop in the driver and even add a few motion effects.

Pulling off an effect like this requires some Photoshop know-how, but it's not all about Photoshop. Capturing the images properly is much more important than knowing how to paint a layer mask. The key is to shoot all the elements under similar lighting conditions and from the same angle, using a tripod for consistency. That way, when it comes to combining them, the play of light and shade is consistent across every element in the scene, making it easier to hide the joins between the images.

1 Get set up

To shoot a forced perspective scene like this, you need to match the foreground and background, and play with the angles until it looks right. To make the toy look life-size we rigged up a platform. It helps if the platform can be moved up or down, so a tripod and clamp are ideal. We covered the platform in sandpaper, and scattered stones and dirt on it.

2 Use manual mode

We set the camera on a tripod, then tweaked the camera, car and platform until the perspective matched the road. We used a 24-105mm lens wide open, making sure the camera was low enough for the car to appear life-size. Consistency across the shots is crucial, so use manual mode and fire off a few test shots to work out the exposure.

3 Shoot a stack

When you shoot objects that are close to the lens, the depth of field is very limited, and it's hard to get the entire subject sharp. Switch to manual focus and shoot a series of images, making incremental adjustments with the focus ring until you've recorded sharpness across the subject. Combining the sharp areas in Photoshop is a simple job.

4 Shoot everything else

When shooting for a composite, try to piece the scene together in your head. It's better to shoot more than you need than to overlook a crucial element. For example, we needed the empty scene to include the verges obscured by the platform. It's always useful to get a shot of the empty scene to use as a base for the other elements.

5 Shoot the model

The most important thing with composites is to shoot the elements in the same lighting and with a similar camera angle. This makes it easier to bring it all together, and helps to trick the eye. So we positioned the boy in roughly the same place, and gave him a ring to hold so that his hands would be easier to match up with the steering wheel.

6 Sweat the small stuff

Attention to detail helps to bring the elements together. We styled the model's hair to make it look windswept, and draped a black coat over the back of the chair to match the tones of the black seat in the toy car. Chance details can be helpful too. During the shoot a classic car passed us on the track, which made for a point of interest.

7 Open in Photoshop

Shift-click between car_comp1 and 4 in Bridge to highlight them. Go to Tools›Photoshop›Load Files into Photoshop Layers. Shift-click between the top and bottom layers in the Layers panel to highlight them, then go to Edit›Auto-Align Layers. Set Auto and click OK. Next, highlight the top three layers, then go to Edit›Auto-Blend Layers.

8 Select the car

Check Seamless Colors and click OK. Hit Cmd/Ctrl+E to merge the top three layers. Grab the Quick Selection tool. Begin painting over the car to select it. The tool will snap on to the edges of shapes. If it goes wrong, hold down Alt and paint to subtract from the selection. Select the entire car (be sure to subtract the gaps between the wheel spokes).

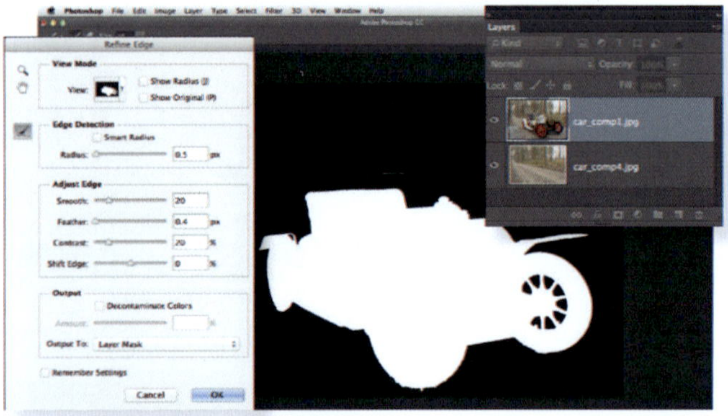

9 Improve the edges

When you're happy with the selection go to Select›Refine Edge. Press F to cycle through views, then use the sliders to improve the edges of the selection. Set Radius 0.5, Smooth 20, Feather 0.4, Contrast 20. Choose Output to: Layer Mask and click OK. Go to the Layers panel and highlight the layer mask thumbnail on the top layer.

10 Blend the ground

Grab the Brush tool. With masks, painting black hides the layer and white reveals. So press D to set the colour to white and choose a large, soft-edged circular brush tip, then paint to reveal the platform around the car, creating a seamless blend between the layers. Press X to switch to black if you need to hide any parts of the layer.

11 Select the driver

Open car_comp5.jpg, grab the Quick Selection tool and use it to select the boy. Click the Refine Edge button at the top. Check Smart Radius and set Radius to 1.2, then paint over the hair to improve the selection. Set Feather 0.3, Shift Edge -13 and Output to: New Layer with Layer Mask. Click OK and select the Move tool.

12 Select the wheel

Drag the boy up to the tab of the other image, then down in to copy the layer over. Click the eye icon to hide the boy layer, then highlight the car layer. We need to select parts of the car that we intend to be in front of the driver, to slot the driver in behind. So grab the Quick Selection tool and select the steering wheel and front section.

13 Position the boy

Go to Refine Edge and set Smooth 20, Output to: New Layer with Layer Mask. Reveal the hidden layers. Rename the layers 'boy', 'wheel' and 'car', then drag the boy layer below the wheel. Right click it and choose Convert to Smart Object. Press Cmd/Ctrl+T. Use the box to resize the layer (holding Shift) and move the driver into position.

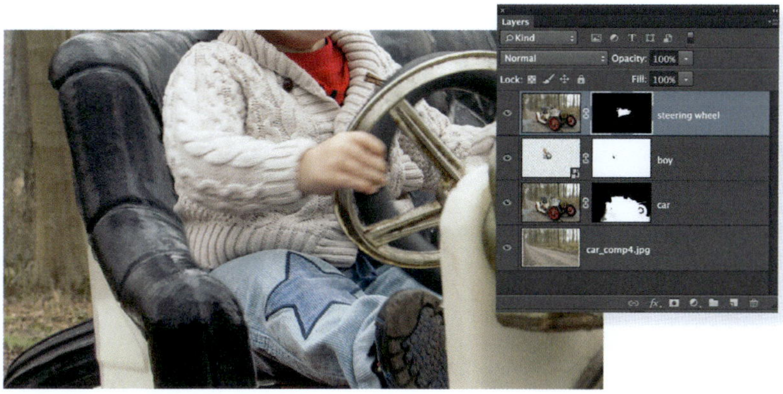

14 Mask the wheel

Press Enter to apply. Click the Add layer mask icon in the Layers panel, then grab the Brush tool and paint black over the left arm of the driver's seat to hide the boy's leg, so that he looks nestled in. Highlight the mask thumbnail on the wheel layer and paint black to hide the part of the steering wheel over the hand. Highlight the boy layer.

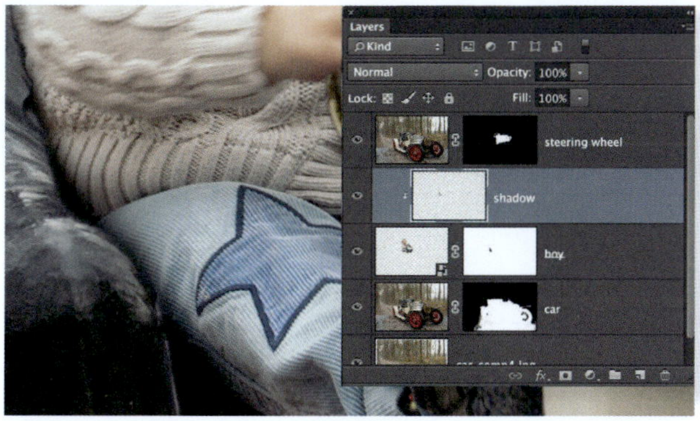

15 Paint a shadow

Click the Create new layer icon in the Layers panel. Hold down Alt and click the line between the newly created layer and the boy layer below to clip the layer. Next, grab the Brush tool, set the colour to black and hit 4 for 40% opacity, then paint along the edge where the body meets the seat to add a subtle shadow. Highlight the top layer.

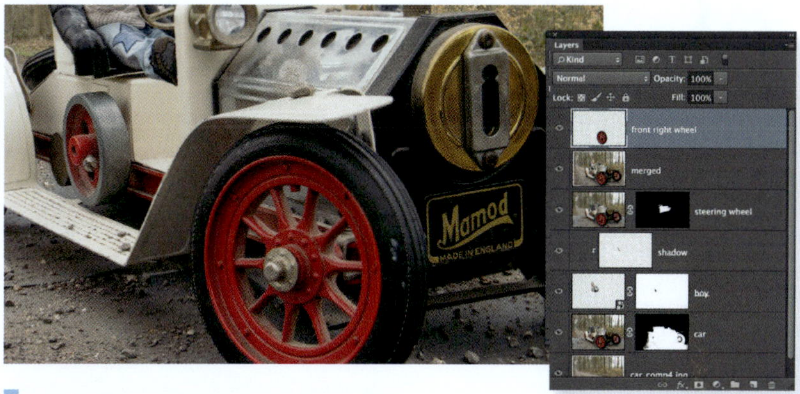

16 Select the wheel

Press Cmd/Ctrl+Shift+Alt+E to merge a copy of all the layers. Grab the Elliptical Marquee tool from the Tools panel and draw a selection over the front right wheel (use Select›Transform Selection to fine-tune it). Hit Cmd/Ctrl+J to copy the wheel to a new layer, then hold Cmd/Ctrl and click the layer thumbnail.

17 Blur the wheels

Go to Filter›Blur›Radial Blur. Set Amount 8, Blur Method Spin, Quality Best, and move the centre of the blur to match the wheel, then click OK. Next, repeat the process to add blur to the front left wheel. This time you'll need to add a layer mask and paint with black to hide the blur over the car and between the spokes. Open car_comp6.

18 Add the other car

Use the Lasso tool to select the top-left corner, then drag it in and position it with the Move tool. Create a new layer, then grab the Clone Stamp tool. Set Sample: All Layers and Alt-click to sample part of the boy's cardigan, then clone out the black ring. Clone any messy areas around the car. Crop the transparent edges with the Crop tool.

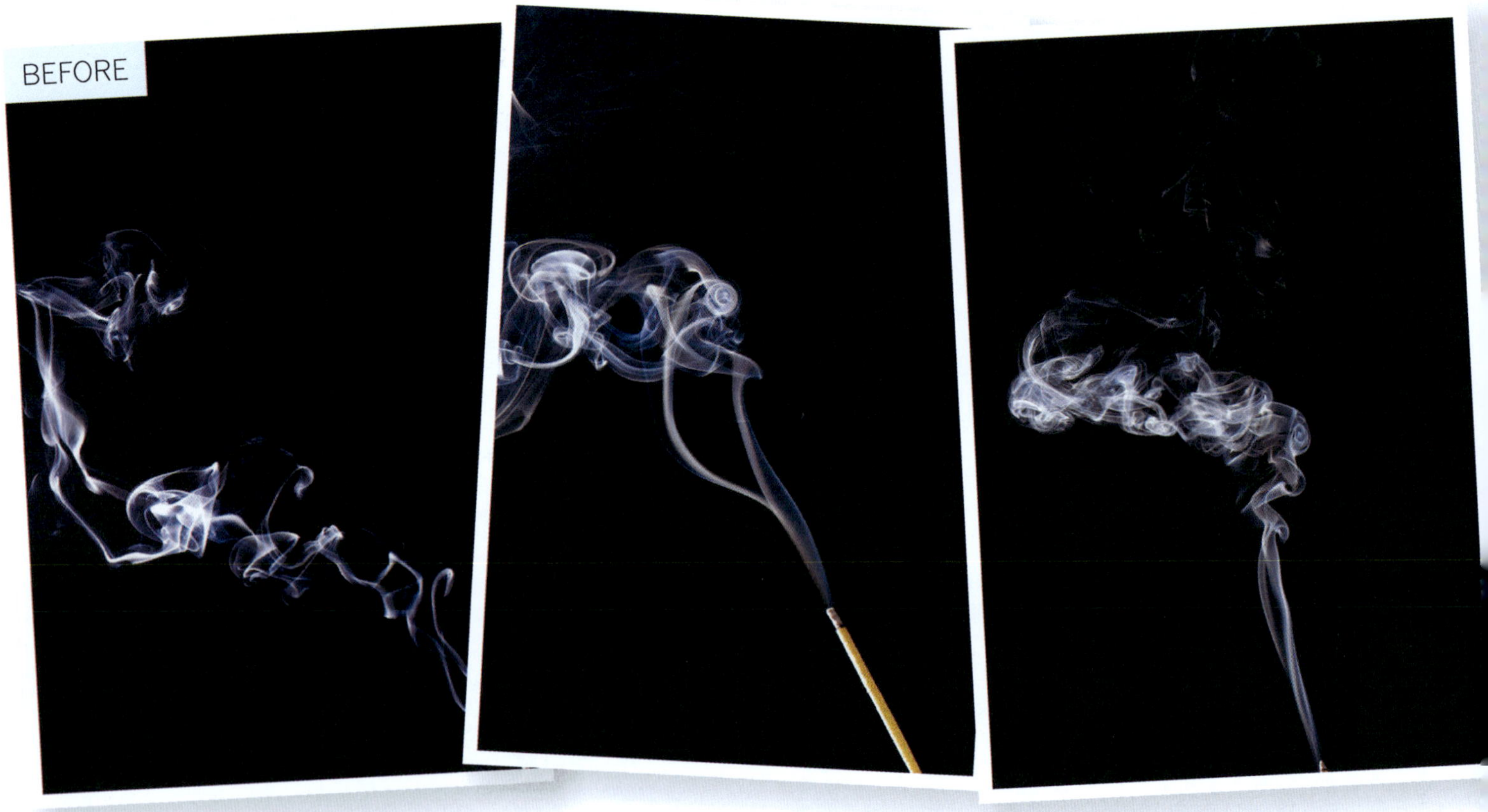

Make a smoking dancer

Craft intricate shapes out of incense smoke trails using simple blending mode and Transform controls

Smoke trails create beautiful organic shapes that are perfect for a Photoshop project. We've supplied a few smoke images, but you might want to make your own. It looks best when shot in front of a dark backdrop and lit from behind. The contrast with the background makes the smoke stand out, and the backlighting gives it a beautiful glow. The easiest way to achieve this is to light an incense stick from behind. Once done, you can turn the flowing smoke into any form you like – such as our dancer here – using simple blending mode and Transform controls. This is easier than it looks, and the results can be stunning.

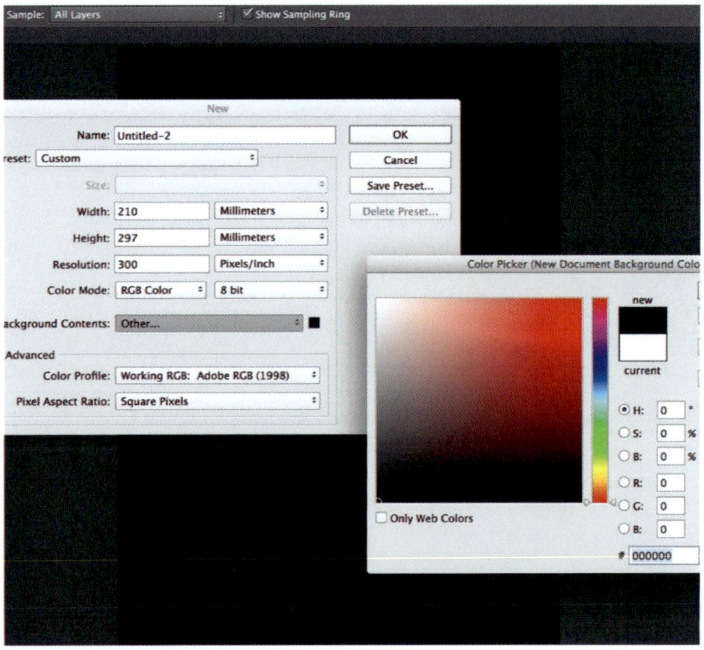

1 Make a new document

Go to File›New and use the Preset drop-down menu and Size drop-down menu to choose a size for your image (we went for A4 size). Go to the Background Contents option, set the colour to black, and click OK. Next grab the Move tool from the Tools panel. Go to the options bar at the top and check Show Transform Controls and Auto-Select Layer.

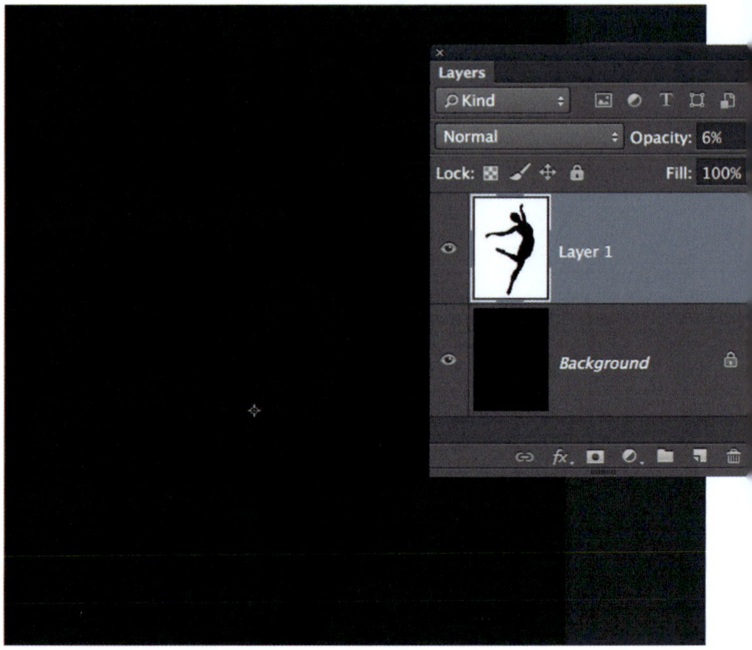

2 Add the dancer

Open dancer.jpg (or if you prefer, any shape of your own) and select the Move tool. Click the image and drag it up to the tab of your new black image, then down into the image window to copy the image over. Position it centrally, then go to the Layers panel (Window›Layers) and lower the layer opacity until the dancer is only just visible.

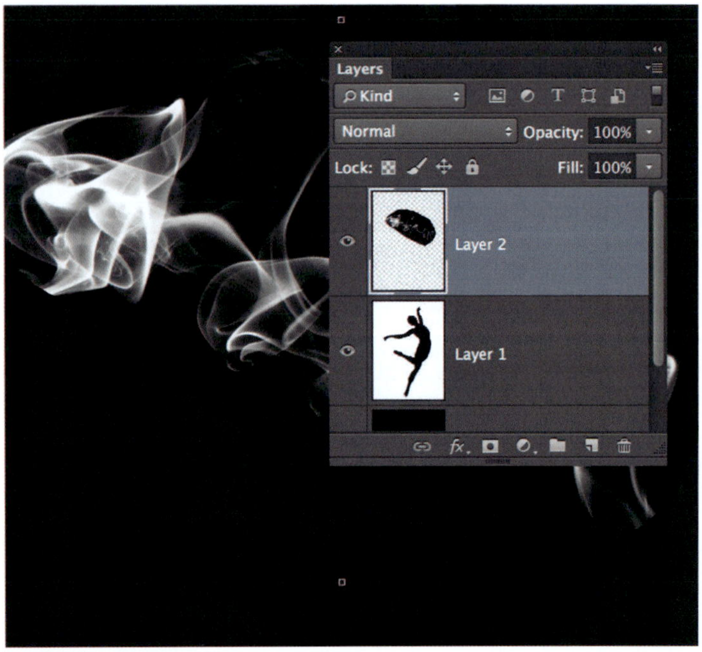

3 Select the smoke

Open Smoke08.jpg, then grab the Lasso tool from the Tools panel. Look for areas of the smoke that will match the shape you want to make. Here there's a part that looks like a head, so drag around it to make a rough selection. Grab the Move tool again and drag the selected area up to the tab of the main image, then down in to copy it over.

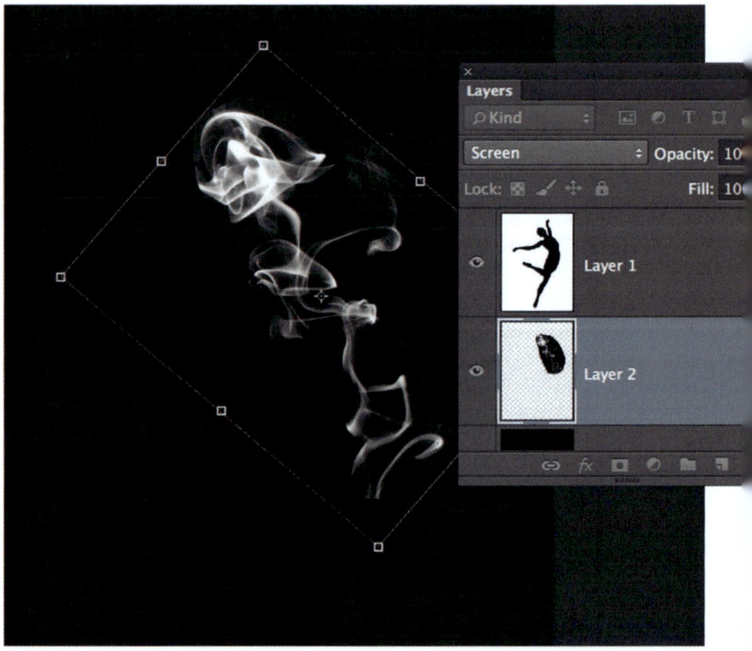

4 Blend and position

Go to the Layers panel, drag the newly added smoke layer below the dancer layer, then click the blending mode drop-down menu at the top of the Layers panel and choose Screen. Next, click the bounding box that surrounds the smoke layer to transform it. Rotate the layer to fit the shape of the dancer, using the other layer as a visual guide.

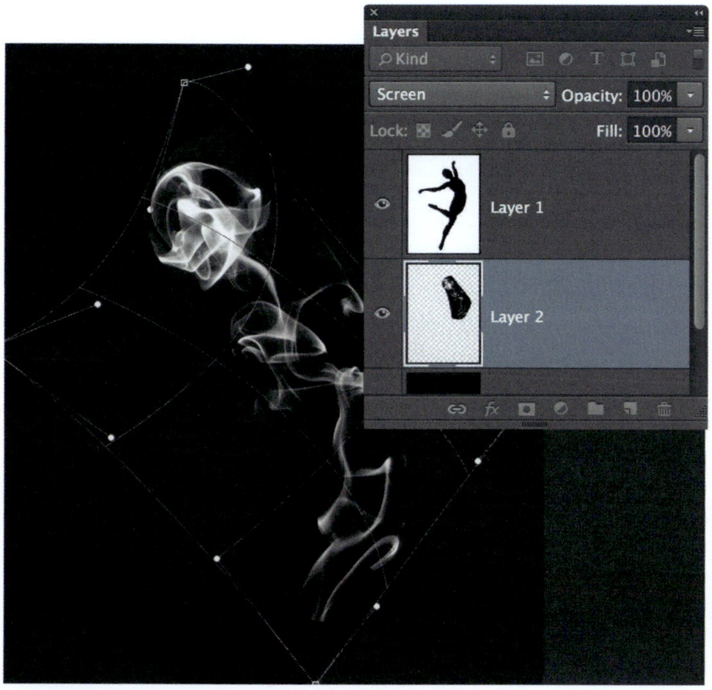

5 Warp the shape

While transforming a layer, you can right click to choose different transform options. Choose Warp, then drag different parts of the grid to warp the layer so that the smoke follows the shape of the body. Press Enter to apply. Open the other smoke images and examine them for parts of the smoke that will roughly match the body, arms and limbs.

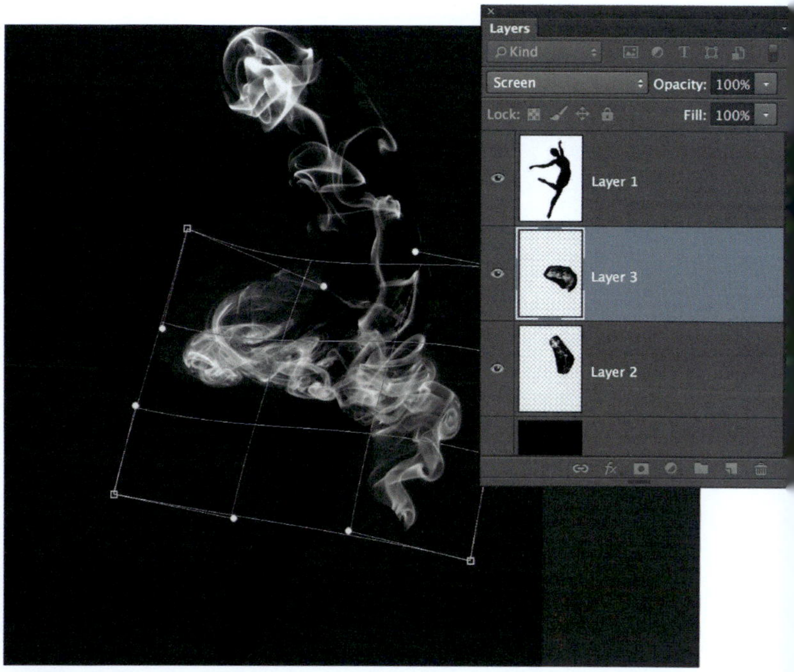

6 Make a dress

The shape of smoke03 looks kind of like a frilly dress, so use the Lasso tool to make a rough selection around the area. Once again, use the Move tool to drag it into the main image, then set the blending mode to Screen and use the Transform controls to reposition, rotate and reshape it. Press Enter to apply the transformation.

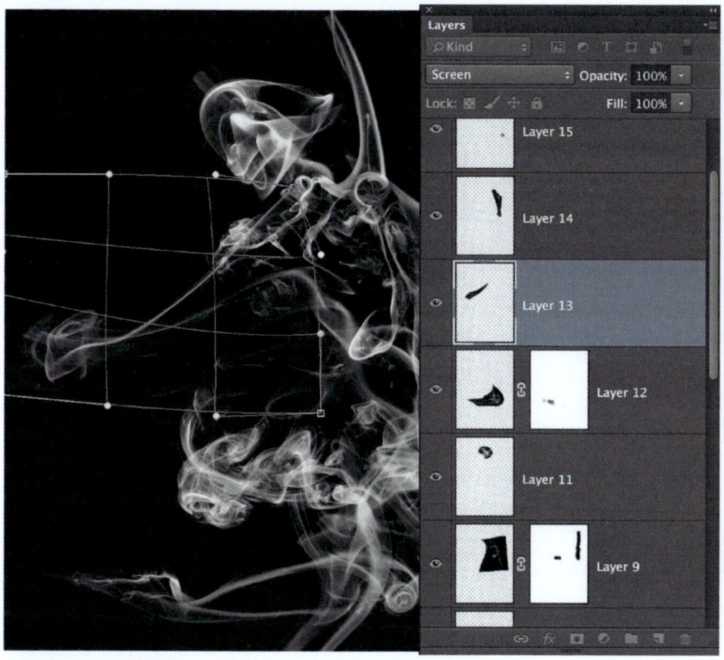

7 Build it up

Copy in more smoke layers, using the Screen blending mode to combine them, and the Warp Transform command to reshape them. If you need to hide any parts of a layer, click the Add layer mask icon in the Layers panel and paint with black directly on the mask to hide the smoke in areas that you don't want it to appear in your final montage.

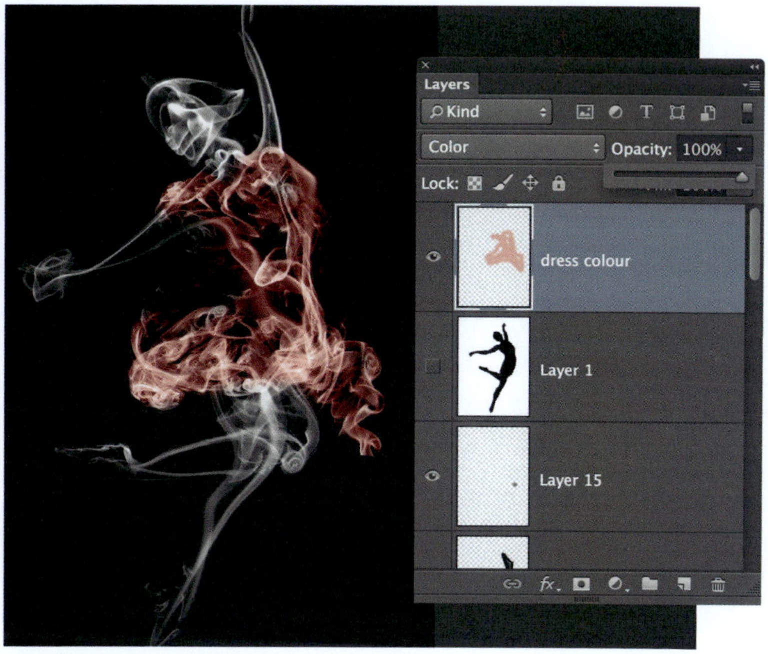

8 Add colour

When you're happy with the shape of the smoke, click the Eye icon to hide the dancer layer. Next, highlight the top layer and click the Create new layer icon. Set the blending mode to Color, then grab the brush tool, click the colour picker and choose a colour. Paint over parts of the image to colour it, then lower the layer opacity until it looks right.

Create stunning spirals

Create glowing circles of light using a simple star picture, then composite it in a photo with 3D tools

This image was born out of a mistake that happened during the shoot. The idea was to light the model from behind with a speedlight, but the positioning was slightly off and the speedlight ended up in the shot, producing an unsightly bright spot. We liked the pose, so we thought, why not turn that bright spot into an asset and build a few effects around it? To do so, we've used an image of some stars, downloaded for free from the NASA website. The spiral effect may look complicated, but with a simple shortcut, it only takes a few seconds to create.

The first stage is to render a lens flare in Photoshop. Open glow_before from the downloads. Click the Create new layer icon in the Layers panel, then press D to set the foreground colour to black, and Alt+Backspace to fill the layer. Change the blending mode to Screen, then right click the layer and choose Convert to Smart Object. Go to Filter›Render›Lens Flare. Choose 50-300mm. Follow the walkthrough overleaf to continue...

1 Add more flares

Tweak the position and click OK. You can double click the Smart Filter on the layer to re-enter the lens flare settings if necessary. Next, press Cmd/Ctrl+J to duplicate the flare layer. Double click the Smart Filter, choose a different flare type and brightness, adjust the position, then click OK. Repeat the process to add more flares across the image.

2 Add the stars

Shift-click between the top and bottom flare layers to highlight them all, then press Cmd/Ctrl+G to group them. Go to the NASA website and download a high-res image of some stars (we found ours here: **http://tiny.cc/fh62ux**). Open the image, then press Cmd/Ctrl+A to select all, Cmd/Ctrl+C to copy, then go to the main image and press Cmd/Ctrl+V to paste the stars in.

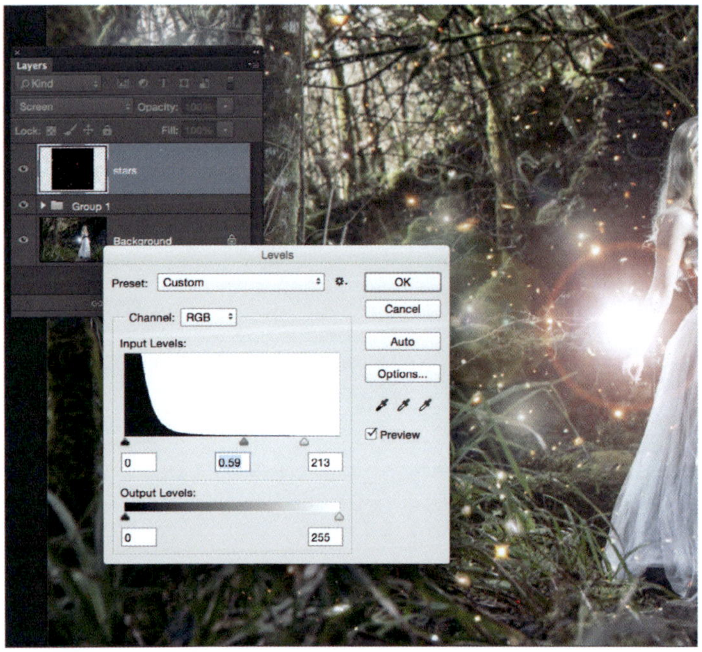

3 Blend with Screen

Press Cmd/Ctrl+T to transform the layer, then hold down Shift while dragging the corner to enlarge it. Press Enter to apply. Go to the Layers panel and change the blending mode of the stars layer to Screen. Press Cmd/Ctrl+L for Levels, then drag the midpoint to the right slightly and the white point inwards to add contrast and get rid of some of the background noise.

4 Copy, rotate and shrink

Press Cmd/Ctrl+J to copy the stars layer, then press Cmd/Ctrl+T to enter Transform mode. Hold down Shift+Alt and drag one of the corner points inwards to make the box slightly smaller from the centre point, then drag outside the corner point to rotate the layer slightly. Press Enter to apply the transformation. Now comes the clever bit...

5 Create the spiral with step & repeat

Press Cmd/Ctrl+Shift+ Alt+T. This duplicates the layer and repeats the last transformation command all in one go, creating the beginning of a spiral pattern. Press the shortcut many more times to repeat until you have lots of copies of the layer that gradually get smaller and smaller, resulting in a spiralling pattern of stars.

6 Merge the layers and make a mesh

Shift-click between the top and bottom star layer to highlight them all, then press Cmd/Ctrl+E to merge them all into a single combined layer. Go to 3D›New Mesh from Layer›Postcard. Go to the 3D panel (Window›3D) then highlight the new merged layer. Use the axis controls to rotate and reposition the spiral as shown in the screengrab.

7 Add the depth of field effect

We can add depth-of-field effects to 3D shapes. Highlight Current View in the 3D panel, then go to the Properties panel. Set Depth to about 1.3, then use the Distance slider to adjust the point of focus to keep the centre of the spiral sharp. When you're happy with the blur, right click the 3D layer in the Layers panel and choose Rasterize 3D. Click the Add layer mask icon.

8 Mask and tone

Grab the Brush tool and paint with black to hide the spiral over parts of the body to make it look like it's behind the figure. Finally, add a Hue/Saturation adjustment layer, set the blending mode to Soft Light. Check Colorize and set Hue 37, Saturation 15. Finally, copy in the stars image again, set the blending mode to Screen and position a few more small stars in the background.

Save for Web (100%)
Tip: Use File > Export > Export As... or right click on a layer for a faster way to export assets
Learn More
Original
Optimized
2-Up
4-Up
Preset:
JPEG
High
Prog
Opti
Emb
Conv
Preview:
Metadata
Color T
W: 2000
H: 3000

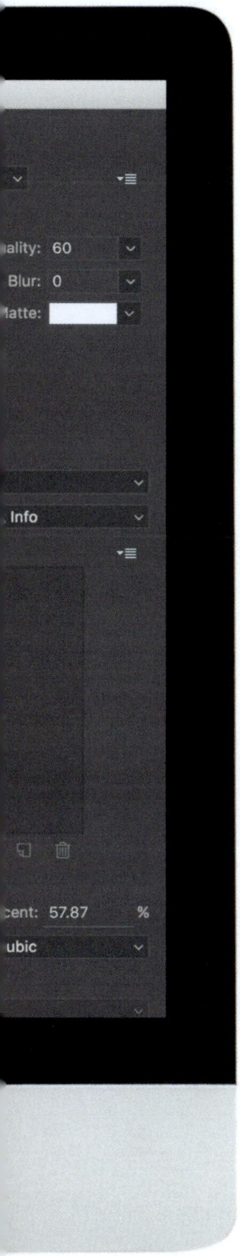

Advanced features

Discover how to enhance your creative projects with paint effects, custom text captions, 3D models and more

Automated Actions

Streamline your image-editing workflow by turning repetitive tasks into automated Photoshop Actions

In this Tool School we examine ways to trim down the time it takes to perform typical but laborious photo-fixing tasks, so that you can spend more time shooting and less time editing. Some of the most common problems you'll encounter as a photographer are with exposure. Your shots could be under-exposed and lack contrast, as well as being desaturated, for example.

Automated commands such as Auto Tone, Auto Contrast and Auto Color can improve images quickly and easily, but they are likely to introduce unwanted effects such as colour casts that can make a warm shot look too cool. Actions enable us to automate our photo fixes more effectively.

The term 'Action' is pretty self-explanatory. You can perform a series of step-by-step photo-fixing operations such as adjusting Levels or resizing a canvas, and Photoshop will record each step in the editing process as an Action. You can then open a new image and play back the recorded Action to edit the image using the same techniques.

Imagine you've returned from a shoot and are perusing your pictures in Photoshop. Photos that looked correctly exposed on your camera can look dull and flat on your computer's correctly calibrated display. This means that you'll have to tweak the colours and tones of every shot to make them look their best. Thanks to Photoshop's Actions panel, this doesn't have to be a repetitive task. If you've used the same camera settings to capture every shot then you can use the same Action to fix them all.

In this Tool School we'll show you how to record your tonal adjustments as you fix an image, turn them into Actions, and apply them to the rest of the photos in the series. You can even apply an Action to an entire folder of shots as an automated operation.

Lights, camera, Action

Create an Action that will crop and resize an image to a specific resolution

When shooting a model in a studio you may end up with a collection of photos that contain more background space than you'd prefer. By cropping the shot in Photoshop you can lose boring bits of background and make the model look more prominent in the frame.

You may also want to resize your cropped studio shots so that they have typical print dimensions such as 5x7 inches at 200 dots per inch.

Cropping and resizing a series of similar images would be tedious and time-consuming, but by recording the edits as an Action you only need to perform them once. You can then apply the Action to crop and resize similar images in your series with a click. Open a portrait from a series you've shot that has a bit too much space on one side. Go to Window›Actions. Click the Create New Set icon at the bottom of the panel. Name the set 'Photo Fixes'. Now click the Create new Action icon. Name the Action 'Crop and Resize (5x7)'. Make sure it goes in the Photo Fixes set. You can also assign a colour label. Click Record and follow the guide below...

Record an Action

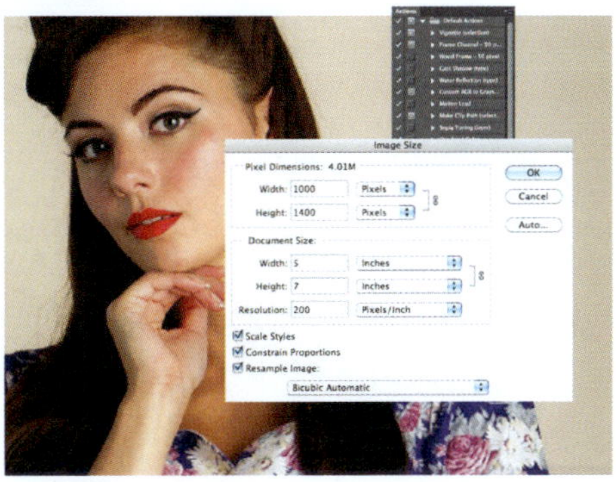

1 Set the crop size

Grab the Crop tool from the Tools panel. In the Options bar menu, choose Size and Resolution. Set Source to Custom. Set Width to 5 Inches. Set Height to 7 Inches. Set Resolution to 200 Pixels/Inch. Click OK to set your crop settings.

2 Stop the recording

Drag the corner handles to tighten the crop overlay around the subject. Hit Enter to lose some of the backdrop. Hit the Stop icon in the Actions panel to stop recording the edits. You now have a cropped photo measuring 5x7 inches.

3 Apply the Action

You can now open similarly composed shots in the series. Click your crop and resize Action. Hit the Play Selection button. The images will be automatically cropped and resized to the desired composition and resolution.

Create a more complex Action

Add extra instructions to your Actions so they do more

Now we'll create a more complex photo-fixing Action that improves contrast, cools down the warm colour temperature of our studio shots and adds a vignette to the edges.

The vignette-creating section of the Action involves drawing an elliptical marquee to select the edges that you want to darken. You can get the Action to duplicate the marquee shape that you drew when recording the Action, or you can tell it to stop in mid-flow so that you can draw a new marquee to suit the composition of each image. Start by opening the first in the series. Create a new Action called Colour, Contrast and Vignette and save it in the Photo Fixes Set. Click Record. For this image we created a new Levels adjustment layer and set the white highlights slider to 231 and the grey midtones slider to 1.15 to boost the contrast. We created a new Photo Filter adjustment layer, set it to Cooling Filter (82), and reduced the Density to 19. We clicked the Background layer and pressed Cmd/Ctrl+J to duplicate it, then set the Blend mode to Multiply. Follow the three-step walkthrough below to add some instructions to an Action so that you can customise its vignette by manually drawing a marquee.

Complex Actions

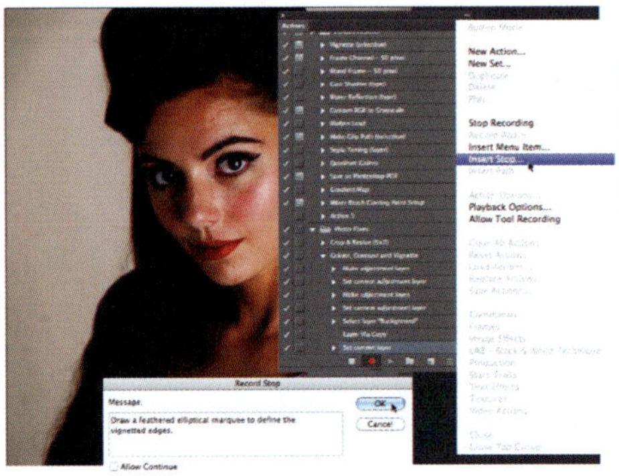

1 Insert a stop

After recording tweaks to colour and tone (see above), click the little fly-out icon at the top right of the Actions panel and choose Insert Stop. A command window will now appear. Type the message 'Draw a feathered elliptical marquee'. Click OK.

2 Finish the recording

Don't draw a vignette at this stage. You can do so when playing back the Action to edit various portraits. Click the Add layer mask icon to add a mask to the Background copy layer. Press Cmd/Ctrl+I to invert the mask. Press the Stop button.

3 Test the Action

Choose File›Revert to test the Action. Click the Action and hit the Play icon. Click Stop when the message you created in the previous step appears. Draw a feathered circle with the Elliptical Marquee tool, then click the Play button again to continue.

Photoshop Anatomy Action options

Get even more from Actions with our in-depth look at this useful tool's extra attributes

1 CREATE DROPLET

Choose File>Automate>Create Droplet. You can then turn any Action into a droplet. Drag a photo onto the droplet to open the image and apply the Action to it.

2 ALLOW TOOL RECORDING

This tick-able option in the Action panel's fly-out menu enables you to include the strokes of tools such as the Burn tool in your Action.

3 NEW ACTION

When you create a new Action you can choose which Set to keep it in, assign a keyboard shortcut to it and colour code it.

4 PHOTO FIXES

Click the triangle next to a folder icon to list the Actions contained in that set. Click it again to close the set.

5 DIALOG ON/OFF

Click here to toggle any dialog boxes you've set to appear (to define the attributes of a process, for example) in the Action on or off.

6 ACTION EDITS

Toggle each step inside an Action to discover which adjustments or commands will be applied to your image with that particular Action.

7 STOP

You can make the automated Action stop at any stage so that you can perform a manual edit such as drawing a marquee.

8 COMMANDS

If you click the Action Panel's fly-out icon you can load in new sets of Actions such as Commands. This is full of Actions that perform typical commands.

9 KEYBOARD SHORTCUTS

Many Actions in a set can be triggered by keyboard shortcuts. In the Commands set you can clear the history states and clipboard by pressing Shift+F3.

10 TRANSPORT BUTTONS

Here you'll find the Actions panel's Stop, Record and Play controls. You would use these to insert a manual action with the automated ones.

11 CREATE NEW SET

Click this folder icon to create a new set of Actions. Like Layer Groups and layers, you'll find this feature most useful when the number of Actions grows.

12 BUTTON MODE

After colour coding an Action, you can choose Button Mode from the Action panel's fly-out menu. You can then click a coloured button to trigger the Action.

Create and apply Actions

Record adjustments you frequently make to your photos, then quickly apply them to other images with one click

Many of the problems you'll encounter as a photographer will be exposure- or colour-related. Some images will lack contrast, some will be desaturated, and so on. Photoshop attempts to provide you with quick ways to tweak colour and tone thanks to its Auto Tone, Auto Contrast and Auto Color menu options. However, while these automated commands can give a washed-out image stronger contrasting shadows and highlights, they are also likely to introduce unwanted colour casts that can make a warm image look too cool, for example. Actions enable you to automate your common photo fixes more effectively.

While performing a series of photo-fixing operations such as adjusting contrast or boosting colour strength, Photoshop can record each step in the editing process as an Action. You can then open a new image and use the pre-recorded Action to edit the image using the same colour and tone-tweaking settings.

In the following tutorial we'll show you how to create an action that records some basic photo-fixing techniques. Although you need to click a record button to capture your image adjustments as an Action, you don't need to feel under any time pressure. The Action only records the adjustments you make, not the pauses between them.

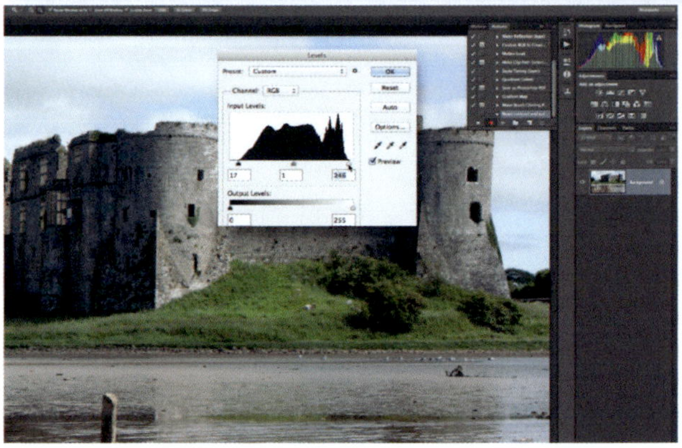

1 Create a new Action

Open TYCC65.jpg. The image is a little drab and lacks contrast. Go to Window›Workspace›Photography. This will reveal the Actions panel icon. Click to expand it. Click the Create new action icon. In the New Action panel, Name the action 'Boost contrast and colour'.

2 Boost the contrast

You can assign a function key to trigger the action. Click Record. Go to Image›Adjustments›Levels. Drag the black input level slider to 17 to darken the shadows. Drag the white highlight input level slider left to 246 to lighten the highlights.

3 Adjust the Vibrance

Like many photos, this image has under-exposed midtones, so drag the grey slider left to 1.11 to lighten them a little. The image now has stronger contrast. Click OK. The Levels adjustment you made will now be recorded in the Actions panel. Go to Image›Adjustments›Vibrance.

4 Stop recording

Boost the Vibrance slider to +56 for stronger greens and blues. Click OK. A Vibrance step will appear in your Action. Click the Stop icon. You can now open a similar image, click the 'Boost contrast and colour' Action, then click the Play icon to instantly enhance the photo.

Explore Photoshop's creative brush tips

Enhance your creative projects with natural-looking brush strokes that mimic real-world brushes, pencils, charcoal and other natural media

Many of Photoshop's tools are brush-based. By changing the size, softness and opacity of a brush-based tool, you can fine-tune the way it alters the pixels in a photograph. If you attach a stylus to your PC then you can use changes in pressure to create lighter or darker strokes and work with even more precision.

You can also use brushes to mimic natural media. Select the Brush tool, then click the Brush Preset picker and scroll down to find more creative shapes such as Chalk, which produces a grainy texture. You'll also find creative brush tips such as Leaves, which scatters random leaf shapes. By clicking the Brush panel icon you can modify the way a preset shape behaves, such as making the leaves scatter in less dense clumps.

To make Photoshop's brush tips behave more like their real-world counterparts, the Brush panel and Brush Preset picker offer a range of bristle-brush tips. These deform as you paint, and leave bristle-like strokes on the image. By combining a bristle-brush tip with a tool such as the Mixer brush, you can turn a photo into a painting, as you'll see in the tutorial on the following pages. But first, we'll demonstrate how the Brush panel changes a bristle-brush tip's attributes, so you can produce realistic-looking strokes.

Photoshop Anatomy The Brush panel

Change the way bristle-brush tips behave by editing their attributes

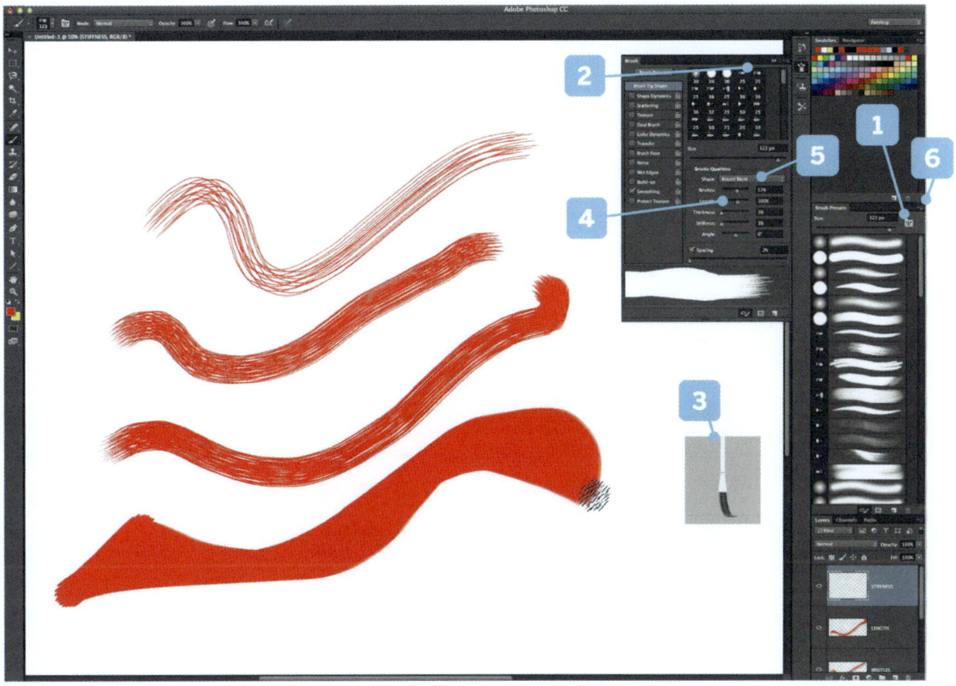

1 BRUSH PANEL

When using the Painting workspace you can summon the Brush panel by clicking this icon. Alternatively, you can click the same icon in the Options bar when you use any brush-based tool.

2 BRISTLE BRUSH

The four strokes in our annotation were drawn using the same Round Blunt bristle-brush tip. We modified the tip's attributes in the Brush panel to create this diverse range of strokes.

3 LIVE TIP PREVIEW

Click the eye and brush icon at the bottom of the Brush panel to summon this handy tool. As you modify the bristles, the preview will change to show the new length and thickness. The preview will also deform as you paint so you can see how loose or stiff it is.

4 BRISTLE QUALITIES

Drag the sliders in this section to change the style of stroke produced by the currently active bristle brush. To create the stroke at the bottom of the screen, we reduced the Stiffness of the bristles.

5 CHANGE TIPS

Instead of clicking the bristle-brush tip icons in the Brush Preset picker or the Brush panel, use this drop-down menu to change the shape of the brush tip.

6 MORE TIPS

Click the Brush Preset picker's fly-out icon to load in new sets of bristle-brush tips that mimic a wide range of natural media. The sets include Wet Media brushes, which are great for watercolour projects.

Understanding... ERODIBLE BRUSH TIPS

As well as bristle brushes, which deform as you paint, you can mimic media such as charcoal sticks courtesy of erodible tips. These tips are indicated by a pencil icon [1]. Erodible tips wear out as you draw, creating more realistic and organic-looking strokes [2]. To make a tip wear out more quickly, increase the value of the Softness slider [3]. The stroke will get thicker as the tip erodes (and the Live Tip Preview will show the tip becoming more blunt). For a sharper tip click the sharpener button here [4]. There's a range of erodible tips, such as Erodible Round and Erodible Square. Choose the one that suits your needs.

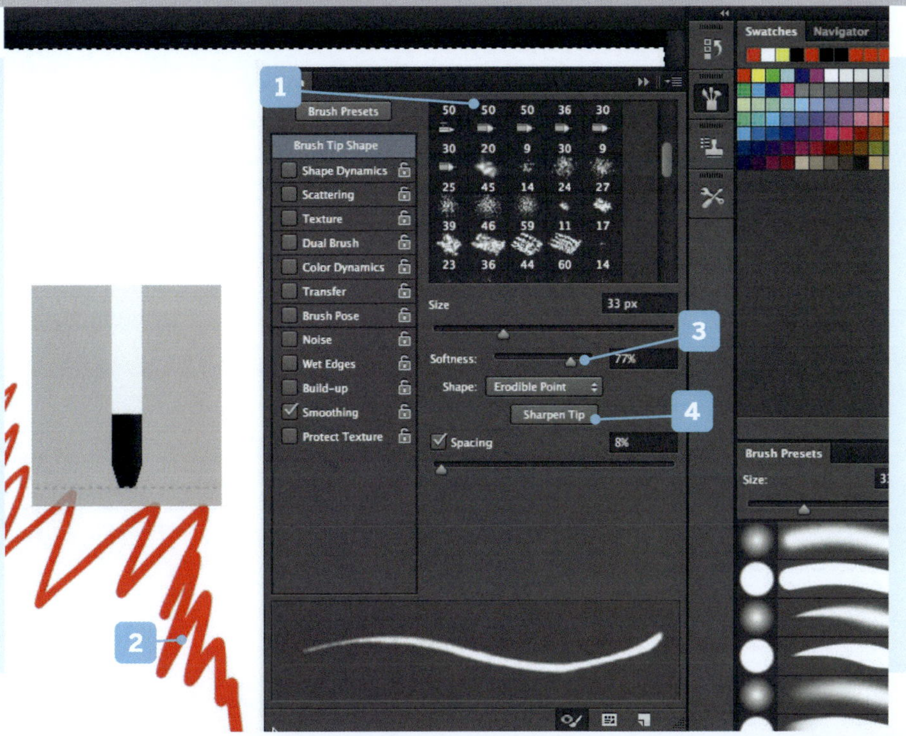

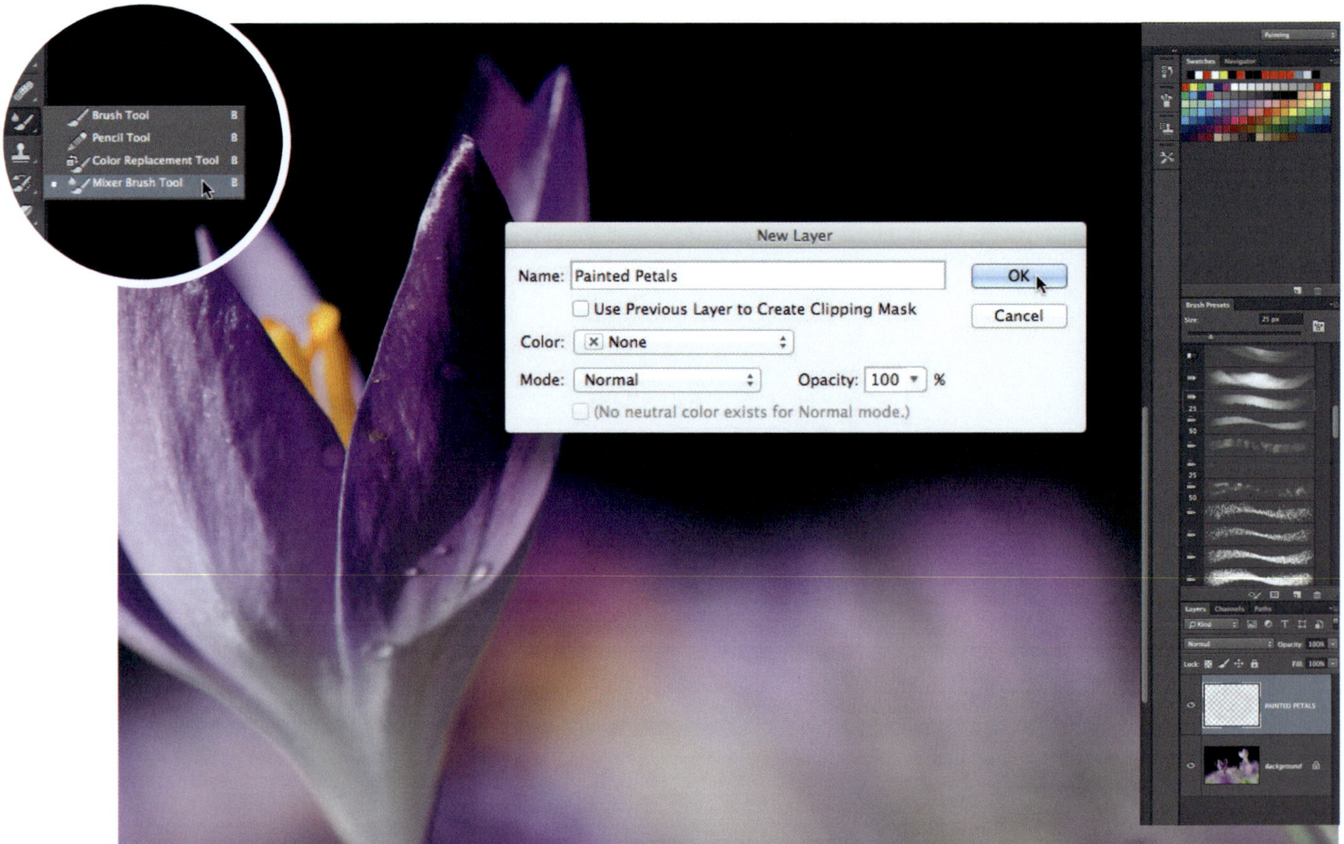

1 Choose the Mixer brush

Open TYCC08.jpg. Go to Window›Workspace›Painting. Go to Layer›New›Layer. Name the layer Painted Petals. Hold the mouse button down over the Brush tool's compartment in the Tools panel and choose the Mixer brush. Choose the Round Watercolor erodible tip from the Presets.

2 Paint and smear

Set the size to 90 pixels. In the Options bar, choose Very Wet, Heavy Mix. Tick Sample All Layers. Click the transparent Painted Petals layer. Paint strokes that follow the flower's curves. The Mixer brush samples colours from the image below and turns them into wet smears of paint.

3 Check your progress

Click the Background layer's eye icon to hide it. The Mixer brush's paint-like strokes create a simplified version of the petals, while preserving their colour and tone. Make the Background layer visible once more and continue using lots of short strokes to paint in the rest of the petals.

4 Add realistic mistakes

When you mix paint in the real world, colours often pollute other colours, especially if you don't clean your brush regularly. To add authentic mixes of different colours, untick the Clean the brush icon in the Options bar. Now paint on the yellow stamen and then paint on the purple plant.

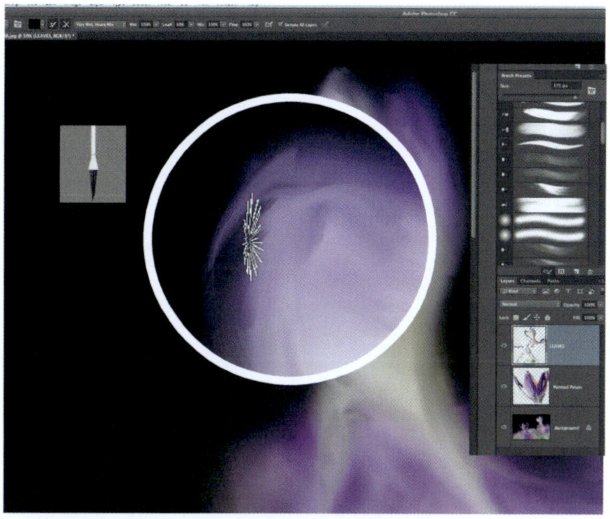

5 Impressionistic effects

Create a new transparent layer. From the Brush Presets picker, choose the Flat Point Medium Stiff bristle-brush tip. Set the size to 50. Paint over the leaves to render them as rough-and-ready paint strokes. Create a new transparent layer and go to Edit›Fill.

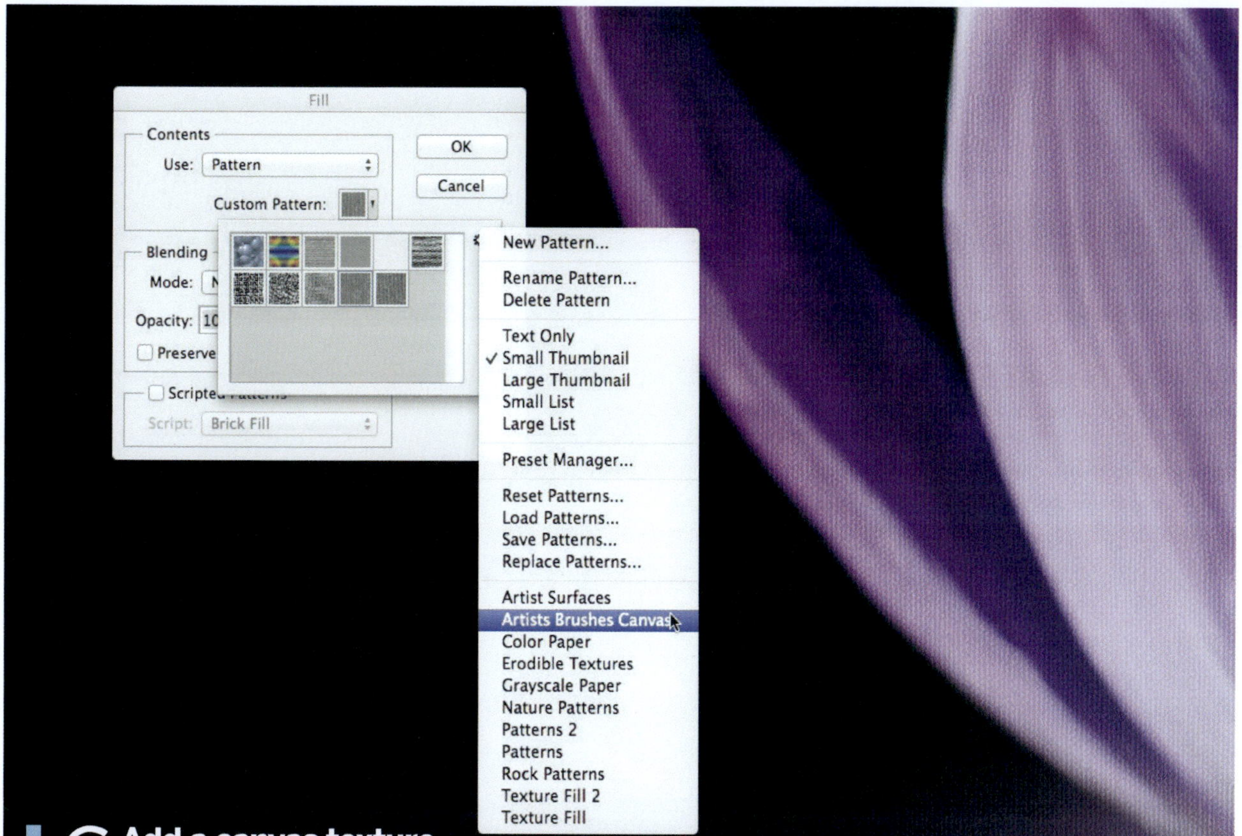

6 Add a canvas texture

Set the Contents menu to Pattern. Click the Custom Pattern window. Click the gear icon in the thumbnail window and choose Artists Brushes Canvas. Click Append. Choose Yankee Canvas. Click OK. Set the pattern layer's Blend mode to Overlay and reduce its opacity to 13%.

Create elaborate titles and captions

Add customisable text to enrich your creative projects using Photoshop's powerful typography tools

The Horizontal Type tool and its Tool panel compartment cousins enable you to enrich your creative projects in many ways, such as providing posters or book covers with eye-catching typography, or turning text into a key component of an illustration by inserting a photo into the fonts.

At first glance, the Type tool works in a similar way to word-processing packages. As you move the mouse onto a Photoshop document a text cursor will appear. Click to place the cursor on a particular spot and start typing on your keyboard to add text to the document as a new layer. You can treat this text layer like any other Photoshop layer, and use the Move tool to fine-tune the position of the text in the design.

As with word-processing packages, you can change text in Photoshop in a variety of ways. Double click to select a word, or drag to select a few letters. Like shapes produced by the Pen or Custom Shape tools, text is created mathematically as vector shapes, so you can increase the size without making the edges fuzzy. You can distort text too using the Create warped text option, and edit the size, font or spelling of the warped text if need be. However, to apply other filters and commands you'll need to convert it to a raster layer.

Photoshop Anatomy The Type tools

Get to know the key features of Photoshop's Type tools

1 TOOL COMPARTMENT

The Horizontal and Vertical Type tools functions as their names suggest. Hold down Shift and tap T to cycle through the four versions of the Type tool in this compartment.

2 MARVELLOUS MASKS

The mask versions of the Horizontal and Vertical Type tools create text-shaped selection marquees as you type. You can then paste a copied photo into the layer to add texture to your typography.

3 FONT FAMILY

Click here to open the drop-down font family menu and then scroll through the dozens of options to find a font to suit your needs. If the text layer is highlighted, use the up or down arrow keys to change the fonts.

4 ALIGNMENT

If you press Enter while typing, you make a new line. If you have a few lines of text selected, click these options to align the text to the left, centre or right.

5 CHARACTER PANEL

When using the Typography workspace, you can get easier access to the powerful text-tweaking Character panel, with its ability to change properties such as the text height, width and the gaps between the letters.

6 LAYER STYLES

You can make 2D text look like solid 3D shapes by adding a Bevel and Emboss Layer Style to the layer. This helped our design's text look like it was carved from marble.

7 CREATE WARPED TEXT

This option provides quick ways to warp your text in creative ways. We used the Wave option to help the text follow the contours of the buildings in the background image. Warped text remains editable.

Understanding... THE CHARACTER PANEL

Choose a font for your text by clicking here [1]. You can modify many fonts to turn them bold or italic here [2]. Increase the value in this field [3] to change the selected text's vertical scale. By adjusting the baseline shift [4] you can raise the text up or down. By adjusting the leading [5] you can narrow the gap between lines of text (or make them overlap). Adjust Tracking [6] to widen the gaps between the letters. Increase Horizontal scale [7] so that shorter words on one line will stretch and match the width of longer words on another. Click these icons [8] to turn lower case characters into capitals or underline text, for example.

1 Type some text

Open TYCC84.jpg. Go to Window›Workspace› Typography. Choose the Horizontal Type mask tool from the Tools panel. In the Options bar, click the font family menu and choose Gill Sans. Set the style to Bold. Type a Size value of 200 points. Hold down Shift and type ITALIA.

2 Warp the text

Move the cursor away from the text until it changes to an arrow. Drag the text near to the skyline. Right click and choose Warp Text. Set the Style menu to Wave. Tick the Horizontal button. Drag the Bend slider left to −34 so that the text warps to flow above the buildings. Click OK to apply.

3 Add a texture

Choose Layer›New›Layer. Label the layer 'Italia'. Click OK. Open TYCC83.jpg. Choose Select›All and then Edit›Copy. Go back to the TYCC84.jpg document and choose Edit›Paste Special›Paste Into. Drag inside the text with the Move tool to reveal the ripples from the copied image.

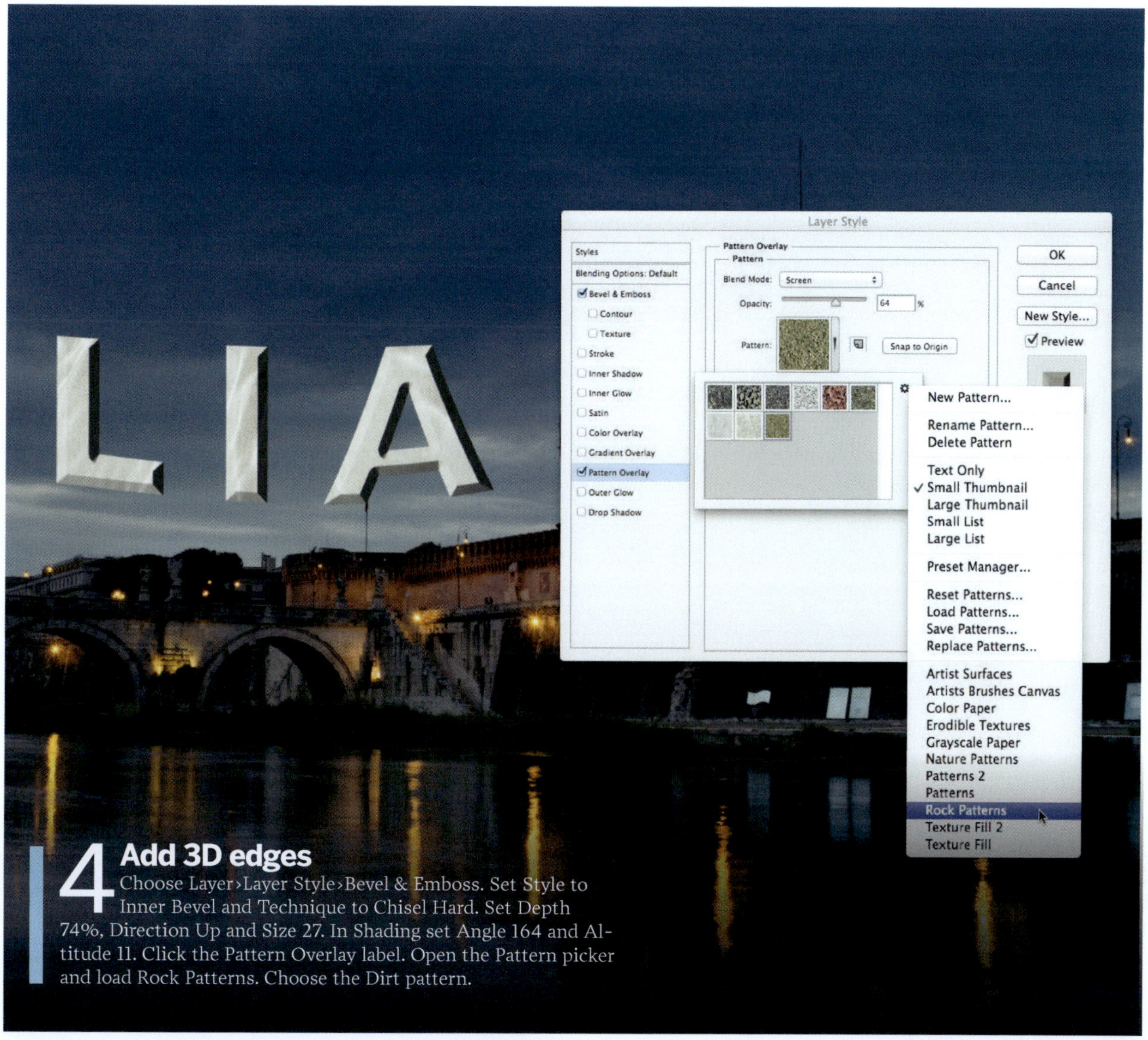

4 Add 3D edges

Choose Layer›Layer Style›Bevel & Emboss. Set Style to Inner Bevel and Technique to Chisel Hard. Set Depth 74%, Direction Up and Size 27. In Shading set Angle 164 and Altitude 11. Click the Pattern Overlay label. Open the Pattern picker and load Rock Patterns. Choose the Dirt pattern.

5 Create a reflection

Set the Blend mode to screen and opacity to 64%. Click the 'Italia' layer. Press Cmd/Ctrl+J. Click between the duplicated layer and its mask to link them. Choose Edit›Transform›Flip Vertical. Use the Move tool to drag the text to the bottom of the frame. As you drag, hold down Shift.

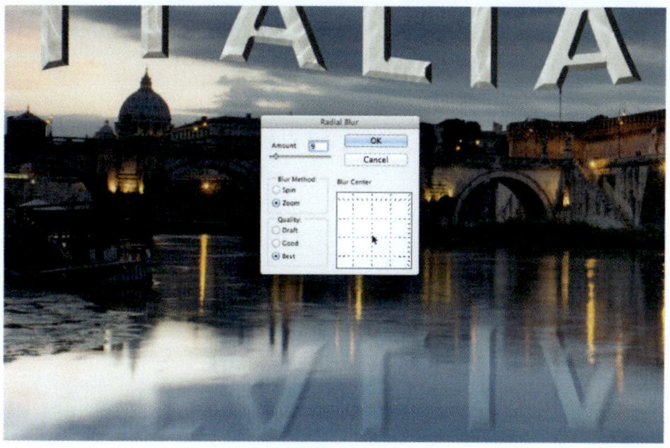

6 Add some blur

Click 'Italia copy' and choose Layer›Rasterize›Layer Style. Set the layer's Blend mode to Overlay and drop its opacity to 75%. Go to Filter›Blur›Radial Blur. Set Amount to 9, Blur Method to Zoom and Quality to Best. Drag the Blur Center to make it match the text above.

Make a 3D chess set

Learn how to make a 3D chess set from scratch and match it perfectly with another photo

If you've ever wanted to add 3D objects to a 2D photo, then this project will show you how. Here we'll take you through the process of making a politically-themed chess board. We've coloured and ordered the pieces along party lines, but you can use the same techniques to create and manipulate all kinds of 3D objects directly within Photoshop without any need for dedicated 3D software. The key here is to make a good cross-section of each piece with the Pen tool (there are ready-made paths within the starting image), then extrude and bend the shape to make a circular object. Once done, you can colour, light and position lots of similar pieces. It's a great introduction to 3D in Photoshop. We've created kings, queens and pawns to keep with the political theme, but you can make rooks, bishops and knights using the same 3D techniques.

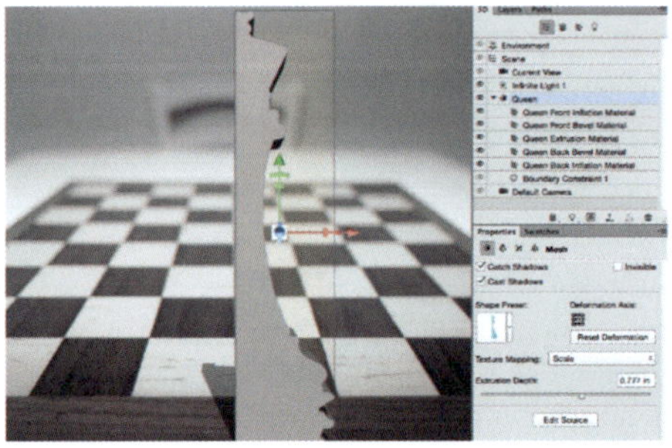

1 Make a shape

Open chess_board.psd. We'll define the cross-section of the first chess piece. Draw a path with the Pen tool to create half a cross-section of the desired shape, or use the path supplied within the document. Go to the Paths panel (Window›Paths) and highlight the Queen path. Make a new layer and name it Queen, then go to 3D›New 3D Extrusion from selected Path.

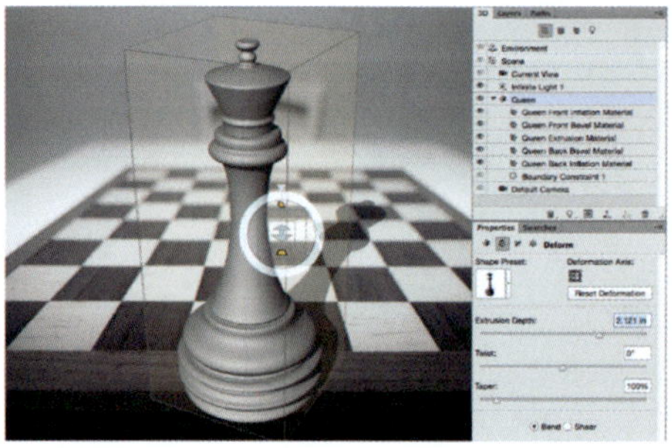

2 Rotate the extrusion

Click Current View in the 3D panel, then grab the Move tool. Click the Orbit icon in the tool options, then drag to see the 3D shape at an angle from above. Highlight the queen shape in the 3D panel, then go to the Properties panel and click the Deform icon at the top. Set Horizontal Angle to -360, then drag the Extrusion Depth slider until the shape looks right.

3 Restore perspective

Go to the Layers panel and hide the Queen layer, then highlight the background layer and go to Filter›Vanishing Point. Click to make a box shape that follows the lines of the chess board in the image. When you're happy with the alignment of the box on the board, click OK. Next, you can use the grid to match the perspective in the scene with your 3D objects.

4 Change the Current View

Highlight the Queen layer again, then go to the 3D panel and click Current View. Go to the Properties panel, then set View: Vanishing Point Grid. The view of the queen piece will alter to match the perspective of the grid. Next, grab the Move tool, click the object and drag the centre cube of the axis widget to scale it down to a suitable size.

5 Fit the piece to the scene

Go to 3D›Move Object to Ground Plane (you can then go to View›Show›3D Ground Plane to hide it), then use the Move along X or Move along Z axis arrows to drag the chess piece around the image (if necessary, rotate it around the Y axis to make it easier to position). Notice how it now matches the perspective of the chess board.

6 Colour the object

Go to the 3D panel and click Queen Extrusion Material. Click the Diffuse colour box and choose a colour, then set Shine 37%, Reflection 19%, Roughness 5%. To check the results, grab the Rectangular Marquee tool, select a small area of the shape, then do a test render by clicking the Render icon. Grab the Move tool.

7 Match the lighting

Click Infinite Light in the 3D panel. Drag the handle up so that the light comes from above. Go to the Properties panel and increase the Shadow softness to 30%. Add a second infinite light: click the Light icon in the 3D panel and choose Infinite Light, then direct it from the right, lower the intensity and increase the Softness.

8 Add the reflections

Go to the 3D panel and click Environment. Go to the Properties panel and set the Ground Plane reflections to about 20%, roughness 40%. Once again, make a rectangular selection and click the Render button in the Properties panel to check the effect, then adjust the settings if necessary. Make a new layer and name it Pawn.

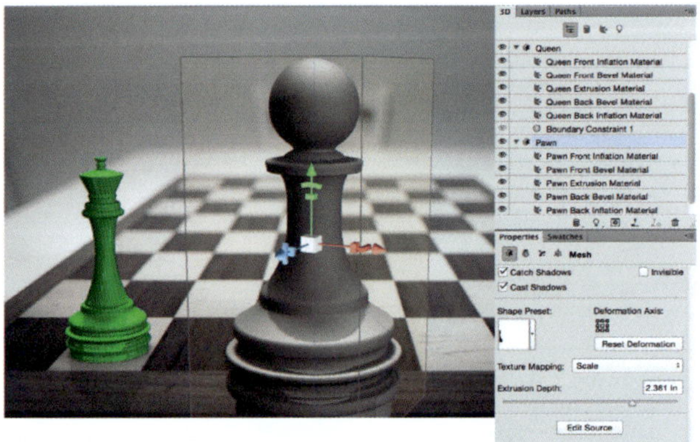

9 Make a pawn

Go to the Paths panel, click the Pawn path, then extrude it to a 3D shape. Once done, press Cmd/Ctrl+E to merge the Pawn layer with the queen. Go to the 3D panel and click Pawn, then go to the Properties panel, click Coordinates and make sure X, Y and Z rotation are all zeroed, then use the Move tool to position the piece on the board.

10 Match the material

Highlight the Queen Extrusion Material, click the material preset drop-down menu, then click the flyout menu and choose New Material. You can then highlight the Pawn Extrusion Material and apply the green preset. Next, right click Pawn in the 3D panel, choose Duplicate Shapes, then use the Move tool to reposition the copy.

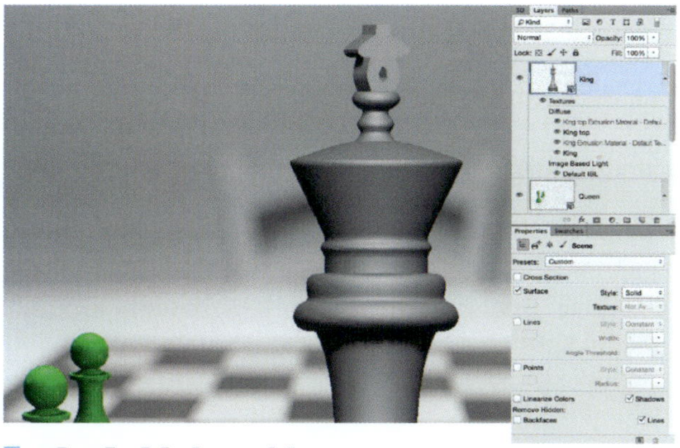

11 Make a king

Make a 3D shape for the King Body path. Make a new layer, highlight the King Path (top) path, then go to 3D›New 3D Extrusion from Path. Use the Extrusion depth without rotation, then position the shape on top of the king piece (use the coordinates to reset any rotation). Highlight all the 3D layers and press Cmd/Ctrl+E to merge the layers.

12 Add another colour

Highlight the two king shapes, right click and choose Group Objects. Click parts of the king piece to highlight the Extrusion material, then go to the Properties panel, add the green material preset and change the Diffuse colour to Red. Duplicate a few of the pawn shapes, move them behind the red piece, and change the colour.

13 Build up the set

Continue adding more pieces and colouring them in the same way. Use the Slide Object Move tool to move the pieces around the board, and make sure they all line up with the ground plane. It can be useful to store your chosen colours as swatches in the Swatches panel for easy access and to keep them consistent.

14 Distort the shapes

Once you're happy with the position and colouring, you could try distorting some of them slightly so that they look less uniform. Use the axis widget to scale along Y to stretch the sizes slightly, then make sure you go to 3D›Move to Ground Plane once you've finished to reset the positions, else the pieces won't look quite right.

15 Apply shallow focus

Finally, we can add a depth-of-field effect. Go to the 3D panel and click Current View, then set Depth of Field Distance 0.28, Depth 2.2. Click the Render button to render the scene. This may take a while. Once it's finished, press Cmd/Ctrl+Shift+Alt+E to merge a 2D layer of your scene, then save it.

Introducing the Motion workspace

Discover how Photoshop CC enables you to enhance video clips with adjustment layers, text effects and more

The latest cameras have the ability to shoot HD video clips as well as stills. To reflect the fact that you may have video clips in your collection, Photoshop now enables you to import video footage into its workspace. Unlike dedicated non-linear video editing applications such as Adobe Premiere, you wouldn't want to use Photoshop to edit a large collection of clips. However, you can use Photoshop to enhance the colours and tones of clips in the same way as you'd adjust a still image. Video is just as prone to suffer from problems with exposure and colour balance, so you can improve colour in video using a Photo Filter adjustment layer, or lighten the midtones with a Levels adjustment layer, for example. This enables you to fix video problems without needing to master complex applications such as Adobe After Effects.

Like many non-linear video-editing applications, Photoshop has a Timeline. This displays frames in a horizontal bar. You can scrub the playhead back and forth to fast forward or rewind the footage. You can also add text to your clips and use the Timeline's preset motion commands to make the text move. This enables you to produce slick title sequences that you can export and add to video projects in Adobe Premiere.

Photoshop Anatomy The Motion panel

Treat a video clip like an image layer and animate using the Timeline

1 TIMELINE

The Timeline is like the Layers panel, except it enables a layer's content (such as text) to change position or opacity over time. The Timeline in this example has text layers and a video clip running parallel.

2 MOTION

To quickly animate a layer (such as the 'Life' text layer in this example), click this fly-out icon and chose a preset motion such as Rotate & Zoom. You can manually set the angle of movements such as Pan.

3 PLAY

To preview a layer's movement and changes in opacity, click this icon. You can also preview the animation by tapping the space bar, or by dragging the playhead to the left or right.

4 KEYFRAMES

These diamond-shaped symbols indicate that keyframes have been added at two different points on the Timeline. Photoshop will automatically animate a layer's properties (such as its opacity or position).

5 GROUPS

When you create text it will appear in the Video Group folder, and will appear once the video clip has played. To make the text run parallel with the footage you need to drag its thumbnail out of the Video Group.

6 ADJUSTMENT LAYER

You can enhance your video sequences by adding adjustment layers that tweak the colours and tones. Here we've used a Hue/Saturation adjustment layer to give the greens and yellows a more autumnal hue.

7 LAYER STYLES

We've added a glow to our text courtesy of Layer Styles, and used the Timeline's automatic motion presets to make it zoom and rotate. The Overlay Blend mode mixes the text with the video.

Understanding... ANIMATABLE PROPERTIES

Click here [1] to toggle open the targeted layer's animatable properties and set keyframes. The Transform channel [2] enables you to add keyframes that make the layer's content move from A to B over a specific duration. The Opacity channel [2] records the opacity value of a layer. By changing this value you can make a layer's content fade in or out (as we have with our text layers). You can add keyframes to introduce Layer Styles [3], such as the Outer Glow on our text. You can also animate the Text Warp [4] option to make text change shape as it moves about.

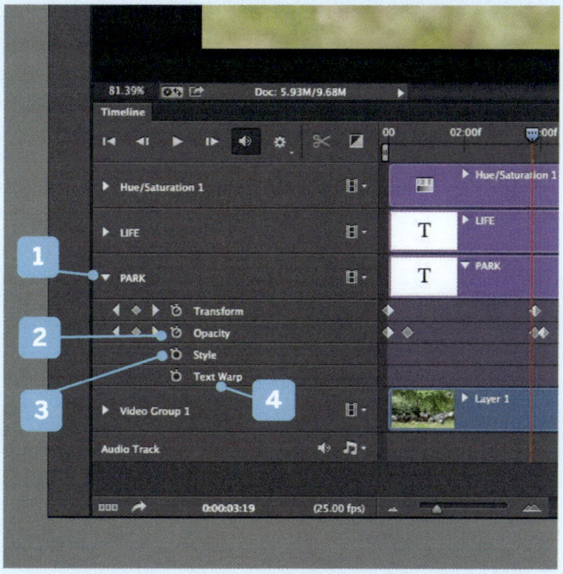

WARP FACTOR

To warp a text layer, you need to add a keyframe to record its original shape and then another to record the warped version. The Timeline will then create all the frames between the start and end keyframes to make the text warp smoothly. Scrub the playhead to frame 1 and click the stopwatch icon in the Text Warp channel to enable keyframe animation. Scrub the playhead forward a few frames and click the Create Warped Text button in the Options bar. Choose a warp effect such as Arc. Click OK. Click the diamond-shaped Add key frame icon in the Text Warp channel. The text will now warp between the two keyframes. Use this technique to record changes in Layer Styles too. ■

Enhance a video clip

Use the Motion workspace to augment video footage with animated text and tweak the colours using adjustment layers

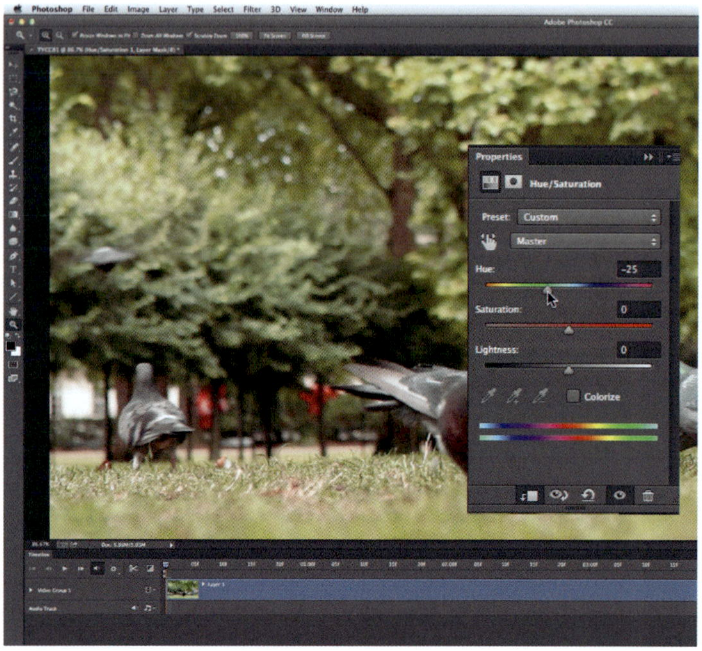

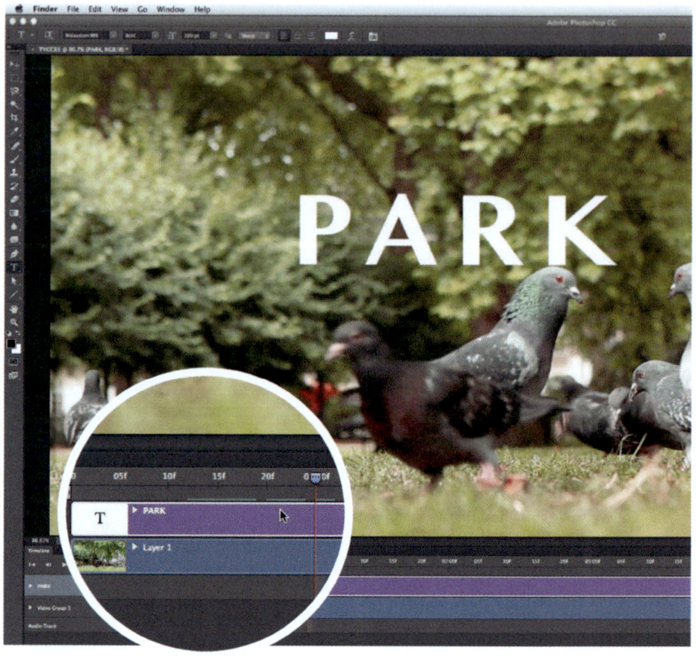

1 Add an adjustment layer

Go to Window›Workspace›Motion. The Timeline will appear. Go to File›Open and browse to our short video clip – TYCC81.mov. Click Open. The clip will appear in the Timeline as a Video Group. It will also appear in the Layers panel. Choose Layer›New Adjustment Layer›Hue/Saturation. Drag Hue to –25 to add a more autumnal hue to the scene. You can use any adjustment layers to alter the colours or tones of a video clip.

2 Add some text

Select the Horizontal Type tool. Choose a font and set the size to 300 and the style to Bold. Type 'PARK'. By default, the text will be placed after the video clip in the Timeline. Go to the Layers panel and drag the Text layer's thumbnail out of Video Group 1, so that it exists as a separate layer at the top of the stack. In the Timeline drag the text layer to run parallel with the footage.

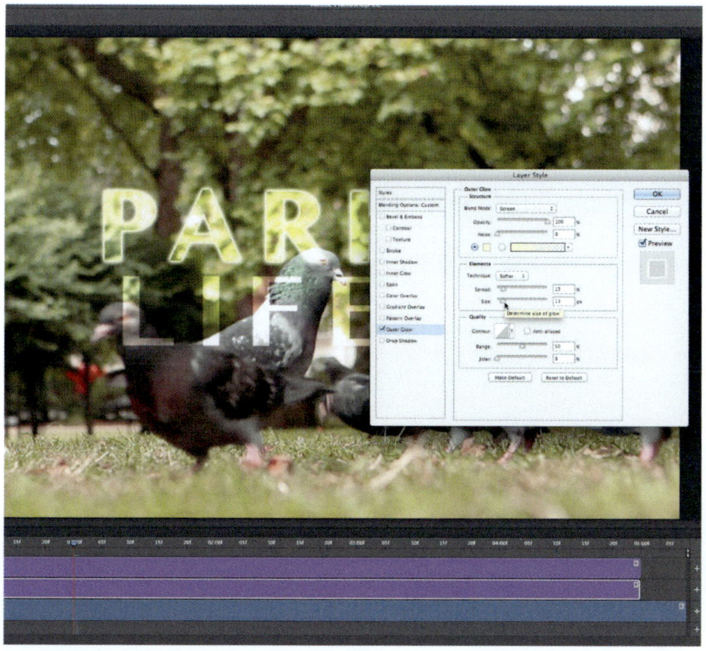

3 Add a Layer Style

Click the PARK layer and press Cmd/Ctrl+J to duplicate it. Double click the copied layer's T icon and change the text to 'LIFE'. Use the Move tool to position the text as shown above. Change the Blend mode of both text layers to Overlay. Click the Layer Styles icon and choose Outer Glow. Click the Outer Glow label and set Spread and Size to 13 pixels. Click OK. Add the same Layer Style to the LIFE text.

4 Add some movement

In the Timeline, click the Motion fly-out icon on the LIFE layer and choose Rotate & Zoom. Choose Clockwise. Set the PARK layer to rotate and zoom in a counter-clockwise direction. Toggle open the LIFE layer and swap the position of the Transform attribute's two diamond-shaped keyframe icons. This reverses the movement of the text so it starts tilted and ends up horizontal. Do the same with PARK.

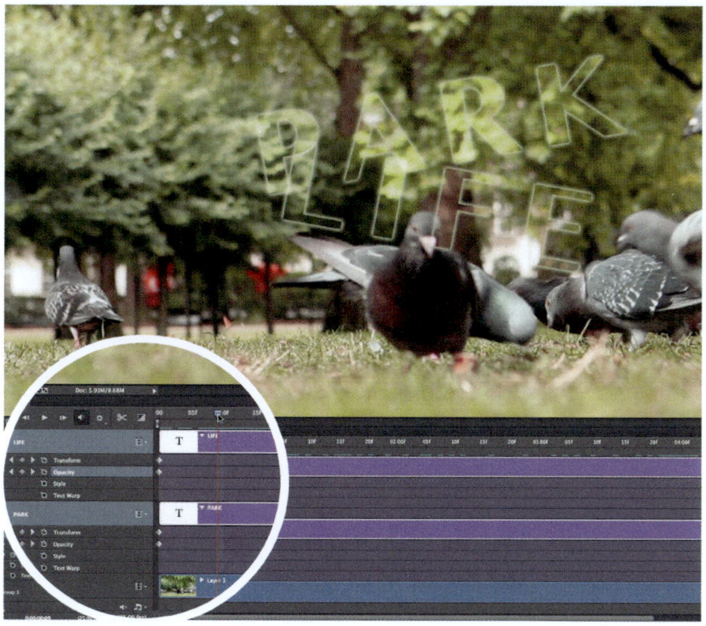

5 Fade in

Scrub the playhead to the first frame. In the Layers panel, set the opacity of the PARK and LIFE layers to 0. In the Time-line, click the Stopwatch icons in the opacity channels of both text layers to add a keyframe. Scrub the playhead to 2 seconds. Restore the opacity values to 100% in both layers. Two new opacity channel keyframes will appear automatically. Now the text will fade in. Scrub the playhead to preview the movement and fades.

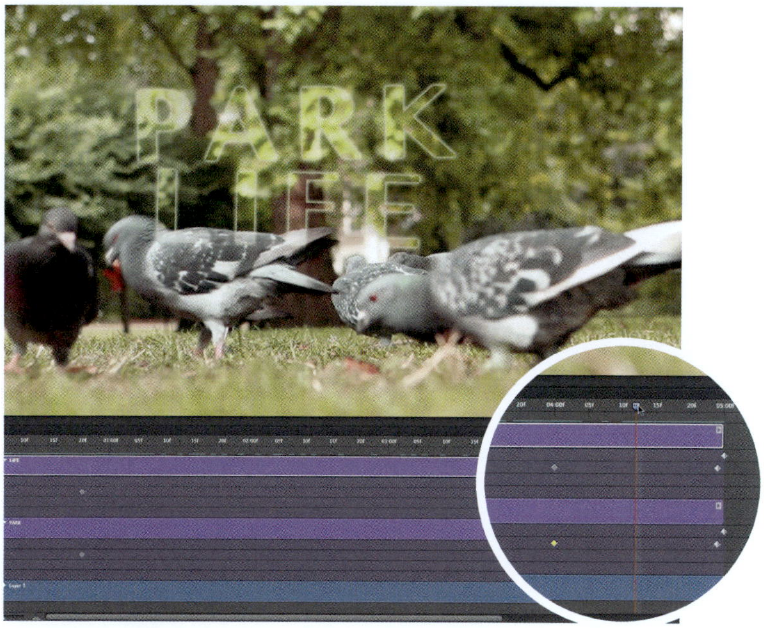

6 Fade out

Scrub the playhead right to 4 seconds along the Timeline. Click the diamond-shaped Add keyframe at playhead icon in the opacity channels of both the PARK and LIFE layers. Scrub to just before the end of the sequence, then set the opacity of both text layers in the Layers panel to 0%. New keyframes will appear automatically in the Timeline, so the text will start fading out after 4 seconds until the end of the clip.

Animation tools

Add motion to your still images and enhance HD video clips with animated, layered special effects

A standard Photoshop document has two dimensions – width and height. In this Tool School we'll show you how to add a third dimension to your Photoshop projects – time. In CS6 and CC, the old Animation panel has been rebranded as the Timeline, which makes it sound more video-friendly. Video-editing packages (such as Premiere Elements) have a timeline that enables users to swap clips around or trim their duration and refine raw footage into slick sequences. Despite the name, the Timeline isn't really up to the task of turning Photoshop into a video-editing package. It's too slow and unwieldy to deal with hours of raw footage. What it does do is enable you to split clips into chunks and add transitions.

If you're serious about editing footage in a conventional way, you'd be much better served by using dedicated non-linear software such as Premiere Elements. Photoshop's Timeline is a closer cousin to the tools in After Effects – a package that enables you to add effects to short clips.

Photoshop's Timeline can add movement to still images in a similar way to a traditional rostrum camera. A rostrum video camera is mounted on a pole and points down at a board. You mount artwork or photos onto the board and then use the rostrum camera's rig to zoom and pan around the image. By recording the camera's moves onto video you can create moving video sequences from still images. Video-editing packages often refer to rostrum-produced zooms and pans as the 'Ken Burns effect', named after a famous rostrum camera practitioner. The Timeline in Photoshop has a series of preset rostrum-style camera moves, such as Rotate & Zoom. This is a big improvement on the Animation panel featured in older versions – that tool only allowed you to pan around a layer by changing its position with the Move tool.

Add action to stills

Turn your layers into an animated DVD menu sequence

The Timeline enables you to turn a group of stills into a dramatic animated sequence to act as a background to a DVD menu screen, for example. On this page we'll look at how to prepare stills as a layered document, and then use the Timeline to add a series of animated effects. We'll show you how to use the Timeline's rostrum-style presets to add instant camera moves to a layer, so that the camera can zoom and pan towards a subject such as our wartime nurse. We'll also demonstrate how to move a layer's content by adding keyframes, so that our aircraft can fly in a precise direction. The beauty of the Timeline is that it uses keyframes and tweening. This means that you choose a start position and an end position for a layer's content, and then the Timeline automatically creates all the required frames to make the content move between the two points over a specified range of frames.

For this project we created the image on the left. To create this file we used selection tools to isolate and place the nurse, buildings and aeroplanes on separate layers. In the three steps below we'll show you how we added the movement...

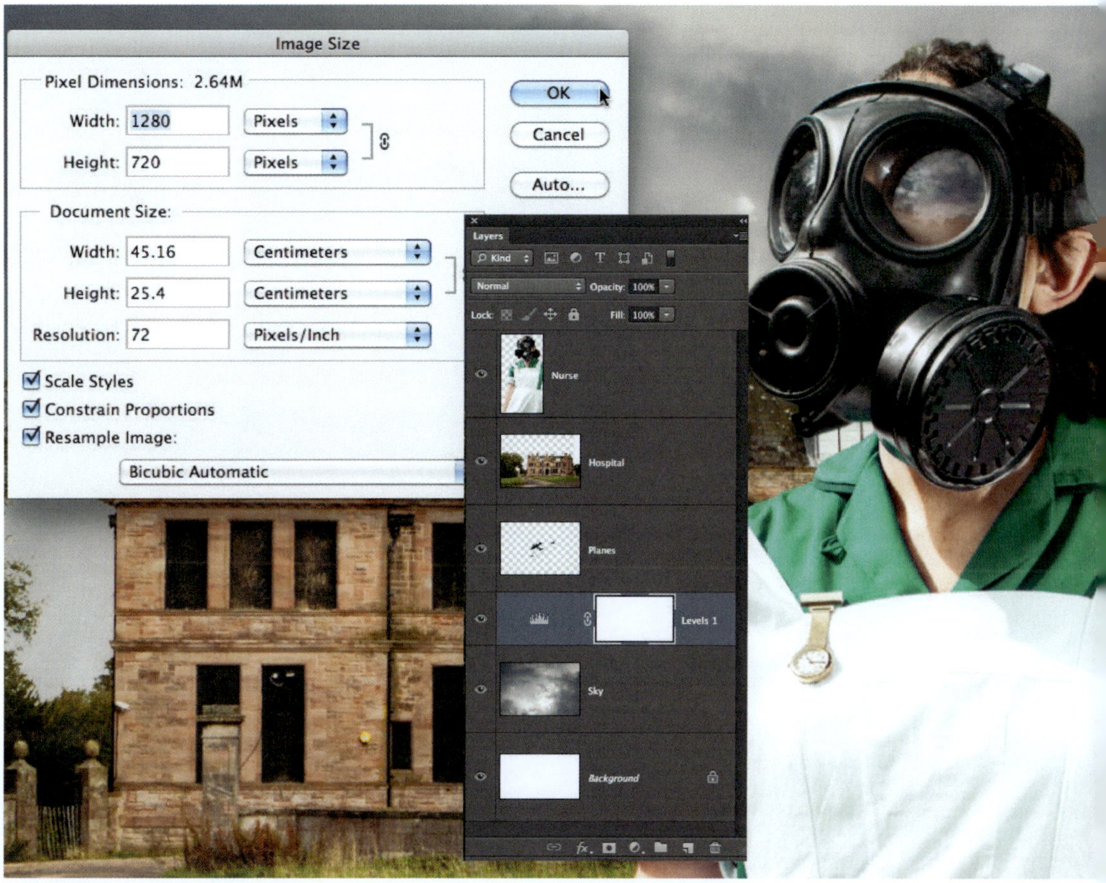

Animate a still image

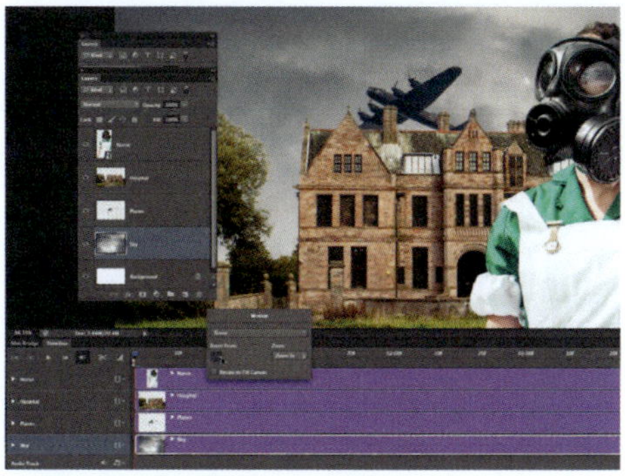

1 Create a zoom

Open an image with three elements such as above. Go to Window›Timeline. Click Create Video Timeline. Right click a layer and choose Zoom. In the Zoom From section, tick the middle reference point in the right column. Clear Resize to Fill Canvas.

2 Change the duration

Press the space bar. Add the same zoom to the next layer. Drag the end of the first layer so that it finishes at 03.00. Drag the Set End of Work Area bar to the same point. This makes the camera zoom in more quickly on the first layer.

3 Animate another layer

Drag the playhead to frame 1. Select another layer and click the Position attribute's stopwatch icon to add a keyframe. Scrub to frame 03.00 and use the Move tool to drag the third layer. A new Position keyframe will appear.

Video clip special effects

Use the Timeline to add special effects to your video clips such as sky replacements

Once you've used the Timeline's rostrum camera zooms and tweening keyframes to add motion to stills (see our three-step technique on the previous page), you can tap the space bar to preview the animation. This renders a rough preview of each frame into Photoshop's video cache, enabling you to get an idea about the project's movement and pacing. If you make any changes to a layer's animation you'll need to re-render the preview with another tap of the space bar. To see a smoother flowing, high-quality version of your animation, you'll need to render the project as a movie. Check out our Understanding Video Rendering box on the following page for more information on how to export your Timeline-produced animations.

As well as turning stills into video, you can use the Timeline and its image-editing tools to augment existing footage with a variety of special effects, such as replacing a dull sky with something more dramatic. You can also animate a Levels adjustment layer to change the video's lighting, enabling you to add flashes of lightning to your new sky, for instance...

Video sky replacement

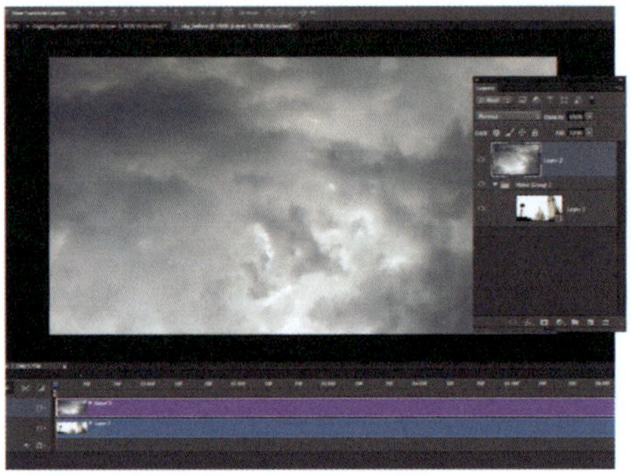

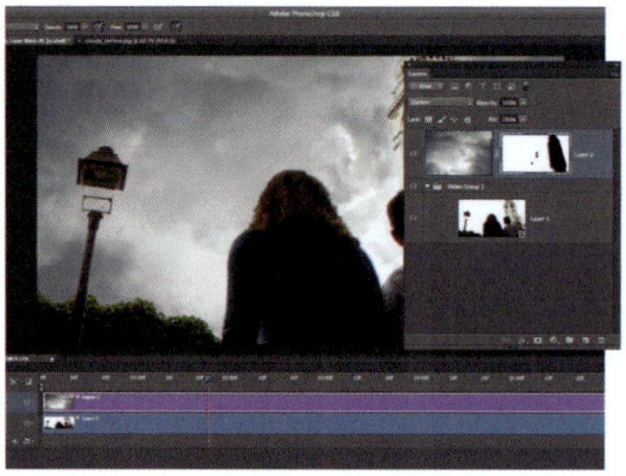

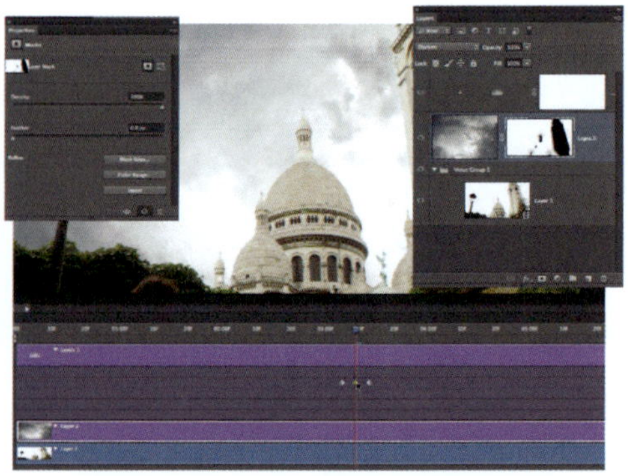

1 Organise the layers

Open a video clip containing a sky. Open a photo of some clouds. Choose Select›All and then Edit›Copy. Edit›Paste the clouds into the document. In the Layers panel and the Timeline, drag 'Layer 2' above 'Video Group 1'.

2 Blend and mask

Place the clouds over the background video. Set the cloud layer's Blend mode to Darken. This causes the clouds to replace the lighter sky on the layer below. Add a layer mask to the cloud layer and hide clouds that cover the detail in the video.

3 Add the lightning flash

Add a Levels adjustment layer. Set the white slider to 219. Set Opacity to 0%. Open the Levels layer and scrub to halfway through the video. Add a keyframe. Move the playhead again. Set Opacity to 100%. Scrub forward and then reduce opacity back to 0%.

Photoshop Anatomy Timeline options

Discover which Photoshop features can be animated using the Timeline's attributes

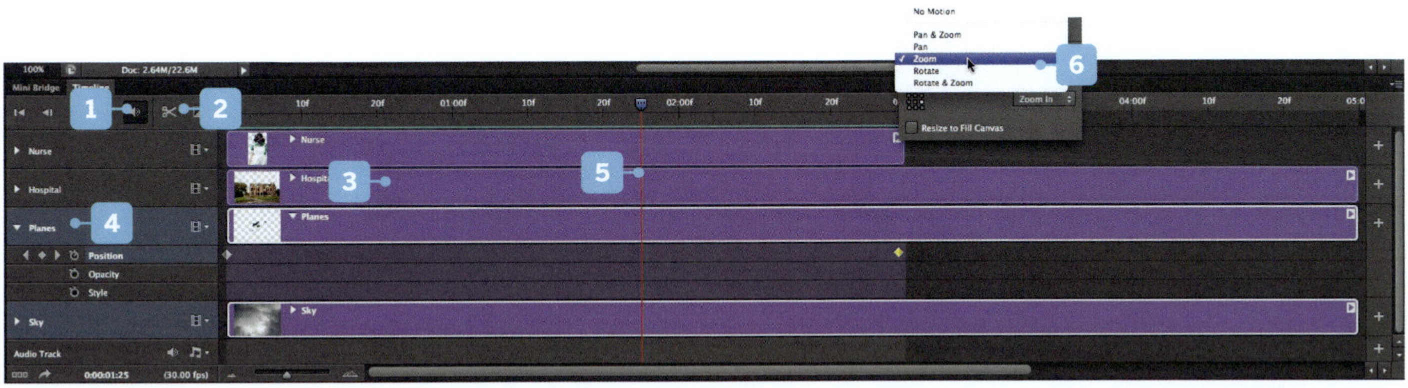

1 TIMELINE

The Timeline panel automatically opens when you import a video clip. To animate image layers, summon the Timeline via the Window menu.

2 CUTS AND TRANSITIONS

The Timeline enables you to split a clip at the playhead by clicking here. You can also use the adjacent icon to add a video transition (such as a cross fade).

3 WORK AREA

Two adjustable grey sliders enable you to define the start and end points of your animated video sequence.

4 EDITABLE ATTRIBUTES

Toggle this arrow to access the layer's editable attributes. You can animate a layer's position, opacity and any Layer Styles that have been added.

5 PLAYHEAD

Drag the playhead back and forth to preview a frame. Tap the space bar to play the video. The green bar below the playhead indicates rendered frames.

6 MOTION

Clicking this arrow opens the Motion panel. Here you can choose a preset move such as Rotate & Zoom, and apply it to a layer's content.

Understanding... VIDEO RENDERING

When you watch a preview of your animated project in Photoshop, it looks fuzzy and low-resolution. To see a high-quality version, go to File>Export> Render Video. The Render Video window will appear [1]. Choose a Format from this drop-down menu [2]. H.264 enables you to produce high-definition videos that don't use lots of disc space. The Preset drop-down [3] has a wide range of output formats, including YouTube-friendly options. Size [4] enables you to choose an aspect ratio such as HDV/HDTV 720p, enabling the clip to play as HD footage. You can render the entire work area, or choose a range of frames from here [5]. You'll probably want to use All Frames.

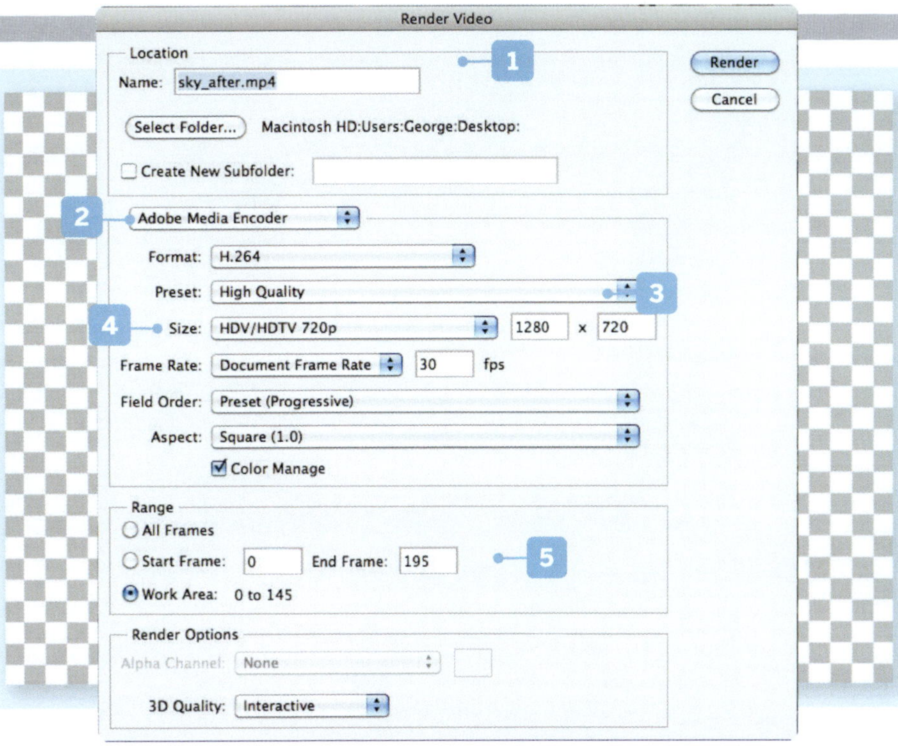

Prepare your photos for print

Produce perfect colour prints of your photographs by optimising Photoshop's colour space for printing

After processing a photo to look good onscreen, you may end up with a print that suffers from shifts in colour. The discrepancy between the screen and print colour is caused by a variety of factors. Your computer's screen produces millions of colours by mixing reds, greens and blues (RGB) together, while most domestic printers combine cyan, magenta, black and yellow (CMYK) inks to create a narrower range of colours. Colours that can't be printed are referred to as 'out-of-gamut' colours.

In this tutorial we'll demonstrate how to prepare a picture for print and avoid colour-related disappointments. By default, Photoshop uses the screen-friendly colour space called sRGB (standard RGB). You can change this colour space to a narrower, more printable one called Adobe RGB (1998) that helps you reduce the number of out-of-gamut colours. There's also a handy gamut warning that you can summon to identify unprintable colours.

We'll show you how to set up Photoshop's colour management tools so that you can convert files that have an unprintable sRGB colour space to the printer-compatible Adobe RGB (1998) colour space. We'll also demonstrate how to change Photoshop's colour mode so it's compatible with the printer's CMYK ink-mixing technique, so that your images have a vibrant, printable range of colours.

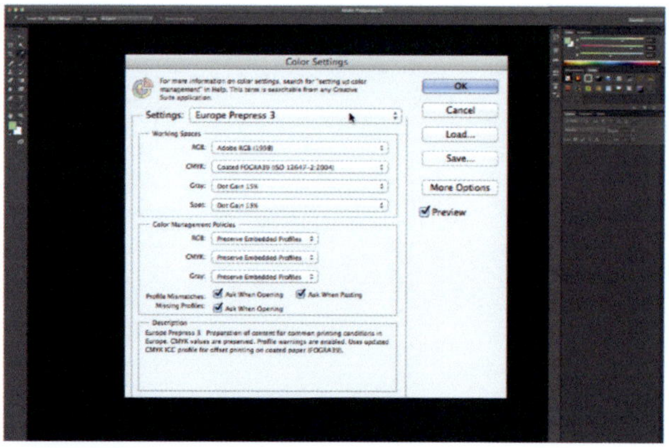

1 Manage your colours

Go to Edit›Color Settings. In the Color Settings window, choose an appropriate location-based profile such as Europe Prepress 3. This will ensure Photoshop uses a print-friendly colour space called Adobe RGB (1998) instead of the default sRGB one. Leave the Profile Mismatch boxes ticked.

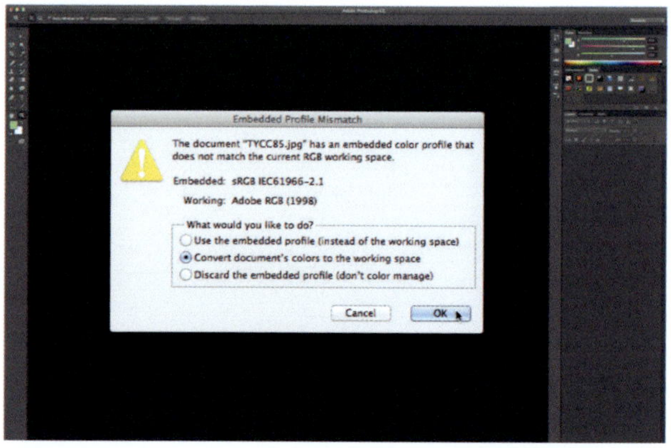

2 Convert the embedded profile

Open TYCC85.jpg. The embedded colour profile of this image describes its colours using the screen-friendly sRGB colour space. You can change the sRGB profile to a printer-compatible one by ticking the 'Convert document's colors to the working space' button. Click OK.

3 Gamut warning

To discover remaining unprintable colours, choose View›Gamut Warning. Problematic colours will appear as patches of grey. You could use a Vibrance adjustment layer to reduce the saturation of the colours. The gamut warning patches would vanish, but other colours may look a bit drab.

4 Change the mode

Go to Mode and choose CMYK Color. Click OK. This forces the colours into a print-compatible CMYK colour space. The gamut warning patches will vanish. Choose Mode›RGB Color. You can now use a Vibrance adjustment layer to boost the saturation without producing warnings.

Optimise your shots for the web

The image settings for online display are very different to the print settings, so here's how to save web-ready photos

Older versions of Photoshop came with a Save for Web dialog that brought together all the settings needed to optimise photos for online display. If you've upgraded to Photoshop CC, though, you might be wondering where this option has gone – but never fear, because it's still there and you can find it under File › Export › Save for Web (Legacy). Here's why you need it...

First, it's a really good 'safety net' that automatically applies important web settings that you might otherwise overlook. Second, it offers a super-easy way to resize photos to appropriate dimensions for web pages without having to do that manually in Photoshop first. Third, it's an image export tool which creates a brand new photo, so there's no risk of accidentally overwriting your original image with a smaller version – it also converts the original filename into a web-ready version with no spaces or other illegal characters.

Bear in mind that Photoshop is a tool for designers and illustrators too, so some of the options in the Save for Web dialog won't be relevant. For example, the GIF format is no good for photos because it has a 256-colour limit (that's what the Color Table panel is there for), and it's really designed for solid-colour illustrations. The PNG format is not very helpful either, unless you need to create cutouts with transparent backgrounds. For photographs, the JPEG format is best.

1 Choose a preset

You can save a lot of time by choosing one of the Save for Web dialog's export presets. The GIF format is useful only for logos, short animations and artwork, while the PNG format is best kept for high-quality illustrations. Choose the JPEG High preset as the best starting point for photos.

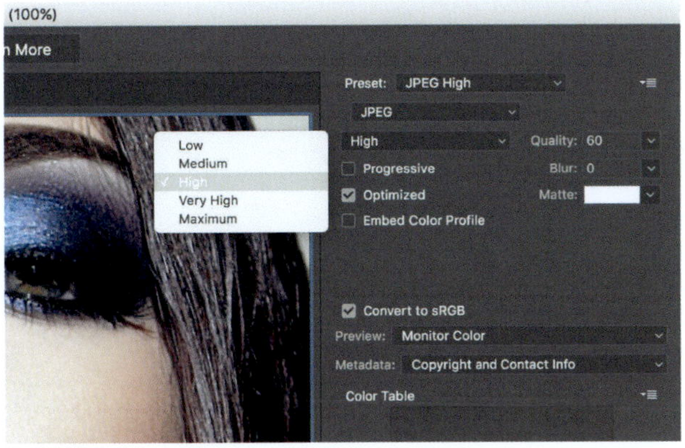

2 JPEG quality settings

The JPEG High preset actually sets a Quality value of 60, which is not exactly 'high' in quality terms but does produce decent images with small file sizes. You can change the quality setting using the drop-down menu or by dragging the Quality slider over on the right hand-side.

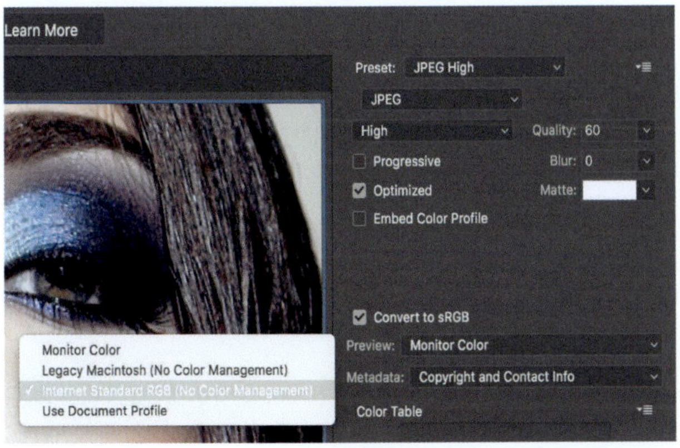

3 Convert to sRGB

This checkbox is really important. Many people shoot using the Adobe RGB colour space, but this produces flat, unsaturated images online, where images should always be sRGB. The Preview drop-down just shows you how colours will appear on different devices, it doesn't affect the output.

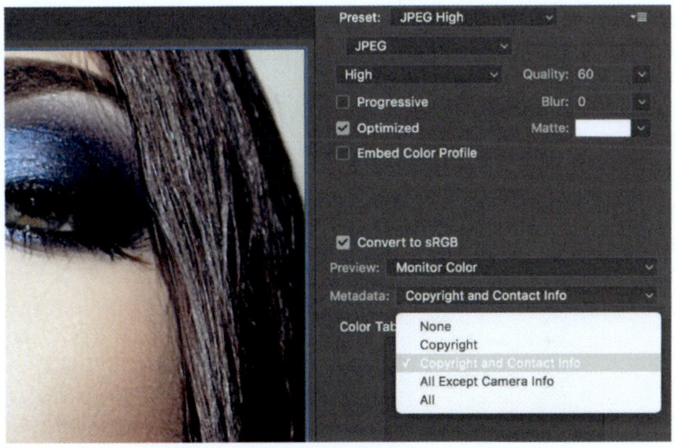

4 Copyright and Contact info

This is a useful feature which it's easy to overlook. If you add copyright and contact information to your photos' metadata, this option will preserve it in images published online. Others can see your image is protected by copyright, and can ask your permission to re-use it.

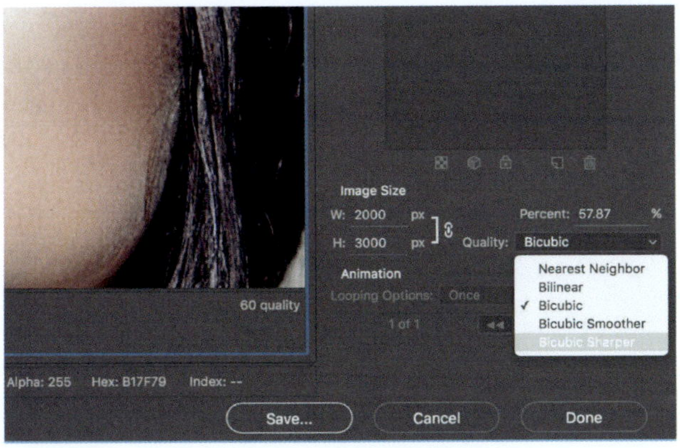

5 Image Size and Quality

You're unlikely to want to publish your photos online at their native resolution, so just type in the required width or height value in pixels, or a percentage value. The Quality drop-down controls how Photoshop resamples photos – choose Bicubic Sharper when downsizing.

6 File size and preview

One of the key points of the Save for Web process is to keep file sizes down, and you can check the file size in the bottom left corner of the window. This predicts the size of the file using the current settings and the estimated download time with different connection speeds.

Paint & Draw WATERCOLOURS
Dozens of step-by-step tutorials for beginners and seasoned pros alike
Simple Steps to Crochet
Practical Painter
CONCEPT ARTIST
Ultimate WILDLIFE EXPERIENCES
Paint Like THE Masters
Learn from the greats and find out how to re-create popular styles
Ultimate ROAD TRIPS
Paint & Draw ACRYLICS
WordPress for Beginners
CODING MADE SIMPLE
101 dream TRAVEL LOCATIONS
Find inspiration in the world's most spectacular travel locations
Create Crochet AMIGURUMI
Paint & Draw ANATOMY
Paint & Draw PASTELS
ANIMATION ARTIST
100 BEST TYPEFACES EVER

MANGA ARTIST
Quick and Easy CROCHET
PROJECTS TO BRIGHTEN UP YOUR HOME AND WARDROBE
TOYS · HOME DECOR · CLOTHING · HOLIDAYS
SKETCHBOOKS
Paint & Draw PORTRAITS
Simple Steps to Knitting
ANATOMY essentials
50 BEST LOGOS EVER
The definitive guide to the world's greatest logos

101 PLACES TO VISIT BEFORE YOU DIE
WEB DESIGN FOR BEGINNERS
QUILTING & PATCHWORK FOR BEGINNERS
Teach yourself Photoshop
NEW
FREE PRACTICAL VIDEO TUTORIALS
Fantasy Art essentials
BIG BOOK OF CROCHET STITCHES
Paint & Draw OILS

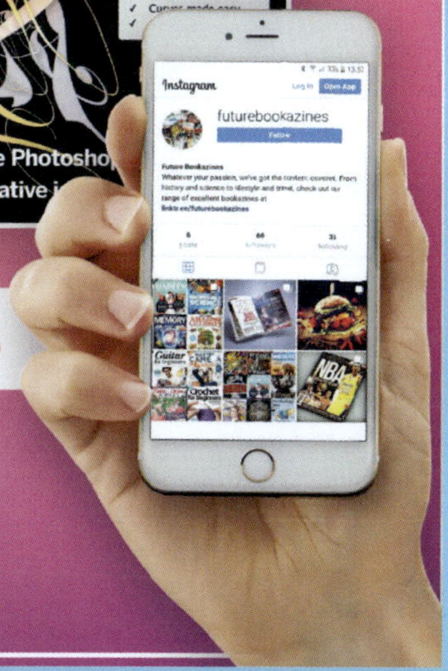

HOW TO USE FileSilo

EVERYTHING YOU NEED TO KNOW ABOUT ACCESSING YOUR NEW DIGITAL REPOSITORY

To access FileSilo, please visit **www.filesilo.co.uk/bks3664**

01 Click on the link above to access the content at any time and download it to your desktop.

02 You are now free to explore the wealth of content available on FileSilo, from great video tutorials and exclusive online guides to superb downloadable resources.

03 You can access FileSilo on any desktop, tablet or smartphone using any popular browser (such as Safari, Firefox or Google Chrome). However, we recommend you use a desktop to download content, as you may not be able to download files to your phone or tablet.

04 If you have any problems with accessing content on FileSilo take a look at the FAQs online or email **filesilohelp@futurenet.com**.

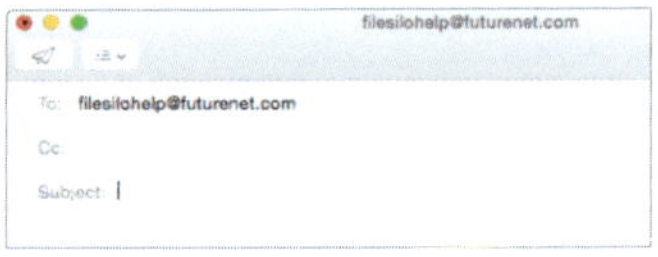

Printed in Dunstable, United Kingdom

91220091R00112